MAN AND HIS MUSIC

VOLUME FOUR

This book is published also as Part IV in a one-volume, illustrated, bound edition containing all four volumes. The cross-references to page numbers, Parts, and Plates, refer to that edition and should be disregarded here.

MAN AND HIS MUSIC

THE STORY OF MUSICAL EXPERIENCE IN THE WEST

WILFRID MELLERS

VOLUME FOUR

BARRIE & JENKINS

COMMUNICA - EUROPA

© Wilfrid Mellers 1962

First published in paperback in 1969 by
Barrie & Rockliff (Barrie Books Ltd)

Reprinted 1973, 1977 by
Barrie and Jenkins Ltd
24 Highbury Crescent, London N5 1RX

ISBN 0 214 66583 6

Made and printed in Great Britain by
J. W. Arrowsmith Ltd., Bristol 3

CONTENTS

VOLUME IV

ROMANTICISM AND THE 20TH CENTURY

PREFACE

THE point of view from which my share of this history has been written was discussed in the Preface to *The Sonata Principle*. What I said then is relevant to this volume also; all I would like to add here is a comment on the things I have left out, and on the proportionate amount of space I have given to the composers I have included.

My aim has been—to adapt a phrase from the Preface to *The Sonata Principle*—to understand the relationship between the private and public life in the work of composers living between the birth of the sonata and the first two or three decades of the twentieth century. A composer such as Rameau, whose music is full of intimations of the sonata principle, none the less belongs to the world of the classical baroque, and is therefore discussed in detail in *Late Renaissance and Baroque Music* rather than in *The Sonata Principle*. Gluck, on the other hand, whose art was also rooted in the heroic ideal, reinterprets that ideal so fundamentally that he belongs to the epoch of the sonata. In this volume I end with the work of composers who may be said to have become a part of history. I include no composer born later than the early 1880s, with the single exception of Hindemith, who became an Old Master and influential teacher at a phenomenally early age. I do not claim to have included all the minor composers who have preserved vitality enough to qualify as a part of history. But I do not think the composers I have omitted make much essential difference to the story of 'the mind of Europe'.

In dealing with the individual composers who make up the creative evolution of Europe's music I have tried to understand rather than to evaluate. An act of understanding is, however, an implicit evaluation: so, writing as a historian rather than as a critic, I have tried to make my understanding as honest, as free from the grosser personal prejudices, as I can. Looking back on the book in retrospect, I suspect that prejudice has got the better of understanding in my discussion of at least two composers: whom I had best leave unnamed. If that is so, and I was not able to do anything about it when I was writing the book,

I should clearly be no more successful at a second attempt. In any case, the composer is not at the mercy of the historian; he will always have the last word, if he has anythng to say that is worth saying.

By and large, the book seems to come as close to 'historical', rather than merely personal, judgment as I had any hopes of making it. I did not attempt to cover the ground or consciously to allot to composers or groups of composers an amount of space proportionate to their 'significance'. Reading the book over some months after it was written, I was none the less surprised to find that there does seem to be a broad relationship between the attention a composer gets and what seems to me his work's 'value'. That said, we can dispense with any degrading competition between creative minds in the aspiration to Greatness: content that all minds should be inexhaustibly interesting in so far as they *are* creative. To understand 'history' is to understand, however imperfectly, why human beings behave as they do and are what they are: noble, tragic, strong, frail, comic, and grotesque.

WILFRID MELLERS

I

CHOPIN, SCHUMANN, AND MENDELSSOHN

Sonata, we have seen, was the expression of a creative ideal. Because it involved conflict, it implied too a basic conception of order, associated with a clearly defined scheme of tonality; throughout the works of Haydn, Mozart, and Beethoven the dualism between individual passion and the accepted norm grew increasingly acute. Ultimately, the force of the personal will was to destroy the old notions of tonality and order, creating in Wagner's operas a new mythology out of subjective dream. But this colossal deification of the ego was, at the turn of the century, still far distant. The general tendency in instrumental music around 1820 was for the sonata principle to be superseded by small forms expressive of the passing whim and fancy; and this intimate approach to personal feeling was in particular associated with the development of the piano.

We have commented on some of the reasons why Schubert found the piano an ideal instrument for the poetic reveries and drama of his songs. As a solo instrument, it had the advantage that it possessed an orchestral range of sonorities while remaining under the control of the individual's hands and spirit— almost always those of the composer himself. It lent itself readily to harmonic experiment, through which—rather than through melodic growth or counterpoint—the romantic cult of personal feeling found expression (in this connexion, the fact that Wagner always composed at, whereas Berlioz could not even play, the piano is a matter of more than biographical interest). Even the virtuoso element prompted by the composer-pianist's dexterity was a form of emotional revelation. The artist who retreats into his private dream emphasizes his distinction from *hoi polloi* by an exhibition of his magical powers.

A disintegration within the sonata principle is evident as early as the sonatas of Muzio Clementi [1752–1832]. Trained in the Mozartian tradition, Clementi had a ripe command of Italian operatic lyricism, along with a feeling for tonal drama comparable with Beethoven's. The element of rhetorical drama within him was too strong for him to achieve Mozart's classical equilibrium.* On the other hand, as an Italian, he was neither (like Beethoven) willing to relinquish operatic melody in favour of a new ideal: nor (like Schubert) to evolve a more intimate, subjective lyrical style. As a result, Clementi's sonatas, while containing magnificent music, seem uncertain in aim. His late G minor Sonata admits its operatic origin in its sub-title, which projects his personal passion into the abandoned Dido. Its first theme is operatically sighful in a flowing dance rhythm, harmonized with dissonant appoggiaturas in a manner that significantly suggests Chopin (compare the first theme of the G minor Ballade). The tonal conflicts of the development are bold and grandly planned; yet they lose direction because the theme itself does not imperatively demand this kind of development. Compensatorily, Clementi tries to give the movement concentration by calling on his contrapuntal skill. As such, his counterpoint is impressive; but—unlike Mozart's counterpoint—it does not succeed in tightening up the movement's *dramatic* development. Only rarely does Clementi create a taut work like the B minor Sonata of opus 40, which, in fusing aria, recitative, and sonata, gives full vent to his operatic lyrical ardour, while achieving a Beethovenian trenchancy in tonal drama.

If in Clementi's sonatas operatic melody and instrumental drama are becoming uneasy partners, in Weber's sonatas—as we have seen—the two elements hardly attempt to come to terms: flamboyant operatic melody alternates with improvisatory harmony and virtuosity.† Dussek [1760–1812] preserves the externalities of classical convention, while allowing the wayward beauties of romantic harmony to distract attention from strenuously argued tonal conflict. In the sonatas of Hummel [1778–1837], who had studied with Mozart and with Clementi, the divorce is complete. Italian lyricism becomes elegiac, pianistic arabesque emulating the vocal decoration of opera: tonal drama becomes rhetoric. It is easy to understand why Hummel was the most fashionable composer of the salons. He does not call for the radical reorientation demanded by a Beethoven. He offers the delights of intimate feeling in the sonorous spacing of his keyboard texture and his occasional chroma-

---

* See Part III, pp. 612 et seq.   † See Part III, pp. 736 et seq.

ticisms and enharmonics: a hint of regret for the past in the valedictory, Bellini-like contours of his slow melodies: and an ebullient acceptance of the present in the improvisatory brilliance of his virtuosity which binds us, wizardlike, in its spell. At least, such was its effect on contemporary audiences. If it now seems less spellbinding than the finest work of Clementi or even of Dussek, that is because it came from a nature not insincere, but comparatively superficial. His themes and melodies are not strong enough to bear the complexity of his texture and ornamentation: so that his historical significance—in his treatment of the keyboard and in his intermittent concern with harmonic surprise unrelated to structure—is more considerable than the intrinsic value of his compositions.

This is clear enough in his influence on John Field [1782–1837]—one of the few composers of talent and personality to work in England, but in a cosmopolitan idiom—in the early years of the nineteenth century. His opus 1 consists of three piano sonatas dedicated to his master, Clementi, who had settled in London. Compared with Clementi's finely rounded themes, complex part-writing, and refined counterpoint, Field's sonatas seem impoverished, even rudimentary, in technique. Yet comparison with Clementi is perhaps hardly valid; for these sonatas are no longer within the classical tradition. The caprice of the modulations has become an end in itself. The emotional point of the first sonata lies in the 'false' recapitulation in the tonic minor, which surprisingly invests a conventional theme with melancholy. Even the insouciance of the salon-like rondo finales acquires, through the improvisatory modulations, a poignant frailty. The glitter suggests impermanence: and therefore an element of pathos beneath the frolics, similar to that in the *vers de société* of Field's contemporary, the consumptive Winthrop Praed.

One might almost say—discounting his clumsy technique—that the significant features of Field's sonatas and concertos are a contradiction of the sonata principle. It is not therefore surprising that the music by which he still lives is contained not in his sonatas, but in the short pieces for which he coined the term Nocturne. He found a hint for these pieces—in which his technique is as expert as in the opus 1 sonatas it is gauche—in the slow movements of Hummel which translated Bellinian *bel canto* into pianistic terms. But his shy temperament comes much closer than Hummel's to the intimacy of Bellini's style. The melodic line—in its smoothly arching contours and its irregular arabesques which emulate the nuance of the singing voice—is a stylization of Bellini's virginal grace: consider this exquisitely 'vocal' *sospirando* passage from the E minor Nocturne (Ex. 1):

Ex.1. Field: Nocturne in E minor

The widely arpeggiated accompaniments are both harmonically and decoratively less congested than Hummel's; for although Field was a virtuoso pianist who made his living by demonstrating pianos for Clementi's music warehouse, his nocturnes are never display pieces. Operatic lyricism becomes elegiac self-communing in these tenderly melancholic reveries, which are in simple ternary song form, or in a binary form devoid of any hint of sonata conflict: consider the etherially remote modulations in the Fourth Nocturne, in A. Here the quintessence of romanticism flowers—as it does in Bellini himself—from classical tradition. It is appropriate that Field should have been a kind of Irish Harlequin—a cross between Chatterton and Oliver Twist—who worked, dismally unhappy and undernourished, in a London music shop;* should have exiled himself in Russia after a concert tour; and should have had in later life a brilliant cosmopolitan career as a virtuoso, only to die, homeless, of 'dissipation and despair'.

Chopin [1810–1849], like Field, was a voluntary exile from his native land. Born into an affluent and cultivated family, he

---

* Spohr, in the *Autobiography*, describes Field as "a pale, melancholy youth, awkward and shy, speaking no language but his own, and in clothes which he had far outgrown".

spent his adolescence in a world of glittering gaiety and grace.
At the age of twenty he left Poland, partly to gain a deeper
knowledge of the culture of Europe, partly because political
troubles at home threatened his aristocratic world. After a
short period in Vienna, where he heard much Italian opera, he
settled in Paris in 1831. Here he became the idol of an aristocratic *élite*, and was soon the friend, not merely of musicians
such as Berlioz, Rossini, and Bellini, but also of the leading
painters and poets congregated in Paris. Only against the
background of this glamorous social and intellectual life can
we understand the loneliness of his heart.* His spiritual exile
had little connexion with his physical exile; for although he
identified his own sufferings with those of aristocratic Poland,
he was more at home in the artistic life of Paris than he would
have been anywhere else. Poland became for him a mythical
dreamland: a symbol of nostalgia not for a 'native land', but
for the human solidarity he lacked. This subjective nostalgia
he expressed entirely through the medium of the piano, for
which he created both a new idiom and a new performing
technique. His originality was commented on by all his contemporaries. He was fortunate in having a public intelligent
and sensitive enough to see that his limitations were the essence
of his romanticism, and, paradoxically, the secret of his forceful
impact on his successors.

His very first works would not have led one to expect this.
The C minor Sonata, which Chopin himself did not publish, is
duller than Field's, if less technically inept. Chopin's attempt
to measure up to the classical ideal inhibits even his sense of the
keyboard. In his other apprentice works he avoids any approach
to sonata style, and confines himself to the episodic forms of
rondo and variation. A work such as the '*La ci darem*' Variations
betrays occasional flashes of Chopinesque personality, while
adding nothing substantial to its models, Hummel and Spohr.

Chopin's other early attempts at large-scale composition
founded on classical principles are much more interesting, if
only a little more successful. In the two piano concertos Chopin

---

* Cf. "You exaggerate the influence which the Parisian salons exerted on Chopin.
His soul was not in the least affected by them, and his work as an artist remains
transparent, marvellous, ethereal, and of an incomparable genius—quite outside
the errors of a school and the silly trifling of a salon. He is akin to the angel and
the fairy; more than this, he sets in motion the heroic string. . . ." Letter of Liszt
to Wilhelm Leng, 1872.

is a composer of genius who has not yet discovered the forms appropriate to his experience. The rondo finales are still salon music in which the butterfly impermanence of Field's or Hummel's virtuosity acquires a more subjective, slightly feverish flush. The slow movements too have their prototype in the concertos of the two older men; but Chopin translates Italian *bel canto* into pianism with greater refinement than Hummel, and with a luminous warmth such as we do not find in Field. Something of Field's chastity of line has gone; the delicacy of Chopin's ornamentation and pianistic texture is charged with a languishing sensuality. But these movements are the perfectly realized expression of a sensibility. Even Chopin's reticent handling of the orchestra here emphasizes the music's seductiveness.

The sonata movements are a different matter. Unlike those of the C minor Sonata, the themes are now memorably Chopin-esque; precisely because of this they are unhappy in their context. The classical notion of tonality and development meant nothing to Chopin. In the E minor Concerto his develop-ment section consists of harmonic improvisation by the soloist, into which the orchestra interjects, with hopeful perfunctori-ness, fragments of the themes. It is significant that although Chopin occasionally composed in large forms later in life, he never again attempted a compromise with sonata tradition. This was also the last occasion on which he permitted himself the redundancy of an orchestra.

One hardly needs, however, to consider the inadequacies of the piano concertos in order to understand why Chopin was essentially a composer in small forms: one needs merely to examine the nature of his melody and harmony. Chopin's melodies have two main roots: Italian *bel canto*, which, as we have seen, came to him both direct and by way of its pianistic metamorphoses in Hummel, Spohr, and Field; and Polish folk-music, which is responsible for his preoccupation with dance movement, especially triple rhythm. Yet his themes are a highly personal sophistication of his 'sources', largely because his melodies are so intimately related to his harmony. The justly celebrated melody of the E major Etude, for instance, has the external features of Bellinian *bel canto*, while being unmis-takably Chopin in that its rise and fall reflects the sensuously fluctuating tensions of the harmony. It differs from Bellini's

themes in that, when once we have heard it in its harmonization, we cannot even mentally hear it apart from its harmonic
implications.

Basically, Chopin's melodies are diatonic and, like Italian
bel canto, are constructed in regular eight-bar periods. But
the metrical periodicity is frequently disguised by elliptical
cadences, and by modifications to the pattern arising from the
improvisatory subtleties of his harmony. Moreover, his ornamentation (like Mozart's) is often chromatic, as it emulates the
operatic singer's portamento and rubato; and this creates a
link between the fundamentally diatonic melody and the chromaticism of the harmony. Recollections of Polish folk-music are
responsible for the frequent intrusion of the lydian sharp fourth
into his themes. This again is associated with one of his most
obsessive harmonic mannerisms—the use of the second inversion of the neutral diminished seventh. Folk-like thematic phrases
frequently proliferate into chromatic arabesques which suggest
the ornamental, sophisticated idiom of the nocturnes and
waltzes. Such arabesques lend subtle ambiguities to the already
rich harmonic texture: consider the oscillating thirds in opus
63, no. 2 (Ex. 2):

Ex.2. Chopin: Mazurka opus 63 No.2

Chopin's harmonic texture always offers the exile's nostalgic commentary on the direct vitality of folk-like tunes and rhythms.

It is perhaps already evident that although Chopin is a
distinctive melodist, the essence of his art is in his harmony.
This, again, is fundamentally diatonic; but the movements of
his hands on the keyboard, as he writes 'through' the technique
of his instrument, provoke him to continual fluctuations of
harmonic stress, complementing the emotional irregularities of
his melody. Pianistic figuration creates chromatic alteration:
indeed, there are so many 'altered' notes that the unresolved
appoggiatura may become a substitute for the 'real' note. Far
from establishing classical tonality, Chopin's harmony seeks
mysteriously to disguise it: the A minor of the second Prelude,

for instance, is present mainly by implication. Passing chords flow so rapidly beneath his fingers that they cease to have tonal significance, and become an effect of colour. The harmonic figuration in the middle section of the E major Etude modulates so rapidly that no sense of key survives: except in so far as we hear it as a protracted, mysteriously disguised dominant pedal leading to a restatement of the serenely diatonic melody with which the piece had opened. In this passage we can see how readily the tonally neutral diminished seventh lends itself to this harmonic chiaroscuro (Ex. 3):

but chains of dominant sevenths, chromatic and enharmonic side-steppings, and mediant relationships are used in much the same way. Many of the more extravagant sequential modulations in Chopin's music do not really imply a change of key: they are as much effects of colour as his chains of diminished sevenths.

So Chopin's nervous sensations flow into the behaviour of his hands on the keyboard, which precipitates the swiftly coruscating texture of his harmony. So fluid a harmonic movement could be applicable only to forms conceived on a small scale; and in his early works the self-enclosed nature of his melodies or the regularity of a dance rhythm suffices to give unity to his pieces. It is, however, significant that the first work in which Chopin attains consummate maturity should be a set of Etudes, opus 10. His discovery of himself is here explicitly related to his discovery of the keyboard; for the unity of each piece now comes not merely from self-enclosed melody or periodic dance rhythm, but from the consistent use of piano figuration, derived from a specific technical problem. This frequently suggests a kinship with some of the Preludes from Bach's *Well-tempered Klavier*. In the E flat minor Etude from opus 10, for instance, a consistent accompanying figuration supports a strong, unbroken line; and in this sense the piece is more classical in spirit than the disintegrative slow movements of C. P. E. Bach [1714–1788] or

W. F. Bach [1710–1784], who lived so much closer to the classical tradition.* Chopin's virtuosity, like J. S. Bach's, is never a platform manner. The technical difficulties of his music are a product of his nervous intensity; his exploitation of his instrument reveals his personal style.

Chopin's generative use of piano figuration enables him to achieve extraordinarily varied transformations of his simple ternary song or dance form; the growth of the figuration disguises the basic pattern in much the same way as the subtleties of harmony and rhythm disguise the periodicity of the themes. In the 'Revolutionary' study the surge of the figuration is so consistent and so cumulatively exciting that we are hardly aware of the primitive ternary structure which underlies it. More complicated instances are those in which a coda figure usurps some of the functions of the decorated repeat of the first section: in the B major Nocturne, for instance, the 'Wagnerian' drum-beat coda introduces a new emotional dimension which grows inevitably from the previous material.

Most subtle of all, perhaps, is a case like the isolated Prelude, opus 45, which is ostensibly in C sharp minor, though only the first bars and the last touch upon this key. The main theme is a distillation of Bellinian *bel canto* that starts in a sub-dominant-flavoured E major; the accompaniment is a pianistic figuration evolved from the conventional operatic arpeggiated bass. This accompaniment becomes much more important than the melody, generating a succession of dreamfully remote modulations which seem the more hazy since no basic key has been established. These culminate in a cadenza of dissolving tritones, which does not even hint at a key. Only after this disintegration does quasi-operatic recitative lead back to song melody: and to the long-delayed resolution into a sombre minor tonality.

Maturity also enabled Chopin to create works on a larger scale which do not deny the sensory, emotive roots of his art. The G minor Ballade looks superficially like a sonata movement, while no longer attempting to imitate sonata procedure. It opens with a slow introduction, followed by two subject-groups, one in the tonic minor, the other in the flat submediant major, both lyrical and in dance rhythm. Instead of a thematic development, Chopin builds up his climax by harmonic 'improvisation' travelling through a kaleidoscopic range of

* See Part III, pp. 590 et seq.

keys—a large-scale expansion of the effect of the cadenza in the C sharp minor Prelude. This leads, in a kind of mirror structure, to a restatement of the second group modified, a curtailed repeat of the first group, and a coda to balance the introduction. Still more remarkable is Chopin's treatment of the sonata in the only two mature works to which he gave that title. The B flat minor Sonata is a big piano composition in which unity is virtually derived from keyboard figuration. The motive which is stated at the opening in long-note values is expanded into different figurations in all the movements; and this pianistic extension of a single idea supplants the conventional dualism of sonata style. One might even say that the work represents a reversal of the sonata principle (which creates unity from the diversity of tonal conflict). Chopin's first movement is closest to an orthodox sonata, preserving a balance between song melody (the second subject) and the disintegrative force of piano figuration (the *agitato* first subject). In the scherzo classical tonality is broken by a dynamic assault of harmony and figuration. This is followed by a funeral march, in which song melody appears, in the trio, only retrospectively, nostalgically. Thus the fourth and last movement, which seems so oddly brief and immaterial as the conclusion of a large-scale work, proves to be inevitable. Here line itself becomes harmonic disintegration: for the movement is in unison throughout, and in effect entirely harmonic. During a considerable proportion of the piece, tonality disappears. The music becomes a fluttering of the nerves which tells us, in an intimate whisper, what *Tristan* tells us in its grandly impassioned lament: the battle between man and God, between man and the World, has been absorbed into the inner life of a single, hypersensitive soul.

This reference to Wagner is significant; for the force of Chopin's restricted genius is attested in the fact that so many of Wagner's harmonic processes are anticipated in Chopin's keyboard style. Of course, the originality of Chopin's talent exists in its own right, not as a preparation for something else. But it is revealing that so subjective and limited a style should so strikingly complement the titanic force that was to emerge later in the century; the Chopinesque preoccupation with the ego was to have consequences far beyond his reckoning. There is even a parallel between Chopin's development and Wagner's. It is often said that, having established its identity in the Etudes of opus 10, Chopin's music never developed. In a sense this is true, for opus 10 is a perfectly realized work of art which could not be improved. But we have only to consider Chopin's ornamentation to see that, as he grew older, he revealed the intimacies of the solitary heart with an ever-increasing precision.

In his first works quasi-vocal ornamentation is mainly decorative, as it is in much of Rossini. In his earlier mature works altered notes and chromaticisms in the ornamentation become an intensification of the line, as they are in Bellini. In his late works ornamentation becomes itself melodic, almost thematic; and creates the harmonic ambiguities typical of his sensory style. This is clear in the almost polytonal* arabesques and intertwining, subsidiary polyphony in his two last and ripest essays in pianistic *bel canto*—the *Berceuse* and, still more, the glowingly sensuous Venetian evocation of the *Barcarolle*. Here the irregular *grupetti* and swaying parallel thirds of Bellini's vocal *fioriture* become a pianistic quiver of sensation: a haze of light and water suggestive of, though more powerful than, impressionistic technique. Bellini's tendency to withdraw from operatic projection into the inner dream is here consummated in instrumental terms.

This thematic ornamentation is, however, only one aspect of the more linear style of Chopin's last years. We know that towards the end of his life he studied Cherubini's treatise on counterpoint, and the creative manifestation of polyphony in the preludes and fugues of Bach—as well as in the part-writing of his beloved Mozart. Although it would be extravagant to say that the last mazurkas are contrapuntal in Bach's sense, they manifest a more economical texture than his earlier works, along with a partiality for canonic devices. These canons (see, for instance, opus 50, no. 3) may have been suggested to Chopin by a traditional feature of peasant dance—the flight of the 'danseuse' before the 'danseur'; yet they become, in their context, highly sophisticated. The tightly-wrought part-writing throughout the last mazurkas would seem to be derived from harmony in much the same way as Wagner's 'new polyphony' in *Tristan* and *Parsifal* results from a horizontalization of chords.†
The mazurkas are small, reticent works compared with the searing passion of *Tristan*; but like Wagner's masterpiece they

---

* POLYTONAL: the use of more than one key simultaneously. Polytonality is not systematically exploited until the twentieth century.
† See Part III, pp. 755.

create, from the harmonic fluctuations of personal sensation, a whole world of thought and feeling. Wagner's elegy is passionately monumental; Chopin's is twilit and phantasmagoric. But Chopin's mazurkas already intimate a new approach to form. Though ternary song and dance forms still pervade them, their inner unity lies in the fact that the nervous oscillations of the harmony themselves generate the motives which build up the texture (Ex. 4):

Ex.4. Chopin: Mazurka in C# minor Op.50 No 3

From this point of view they are no longer dances, but miniature symphonic poems: so that we are not surprised when the opening pages of Chopin's last considerable work, the *Polonaise Fantaisie*, vividly suggest not merely the late work of Wagner, but also the ripe harmonic-polyphonic texture of Richard Strauss.

While the last mazurkas come closest of all Chopin's works to the spirit of Polish folk-music, they are not nationalistic. Chopin was fascinated by the modal and rhythmic ambiguities of folk-music because they both stimulated and complemented the harmonic and pianistic subtleties through which he expressed his nervous life; his deepest revelation of the self is also his most nostalgic evocation of a private dream-world. It is interesting to compare his last waltz (the A flat, opus 64, no. 3) with his last mazurka (the F minor, opus 68, no. 4). In the waltz the chromatic passing notes in the melody and the strange enharmonic modulation to E major flush the 'social' elegance with a slightly fevered wistfulness. In the mazurka the chromatic sequences and enharmonic transitions create a disintegration of the entire tonal structure; the pathos cannot be resolved, and the piece is left suspended, without even a final cadence. One might say that the melancholy of Chopin's waltzes comes from the sense of alienation that underlies his portrayal of a gracious aristocracy. The melancholy of the mazurkas is more profound, because whereas the world of Parisian vivacity did exist, or had existed, Chopin's Poland was 'real' only in the sense that some such nostalgia haunts every man, to the measure of his nervous capacity. The 1848 Revolution destroyed the only kind of society which Chopin could breathe in; and the final rupture with George Sand broke the one human contact that gave stability to his tremulous nerves. Yet we do no honour to Chopin's memory if we romanticize his biography. His consumption, like Bellini's, was symbolic in the sense that he died because he burned up his nervous vitality; yet he had a central source of strength of which he was well aware when he referred to himself as a minor talent, but a master. No artist was ever less the unconscious rhapsodist; his power lay in the precision of his realization of his inner life. The strength of the last mazurkas—more than of the big polonaises or scherzi—is in the crystallization of subjective melancholy into the timelessness of art. This is why his highly personal idiom foreshadows so much of the evolution of nine-teenth-century music; and is why his spell, having survived commercialization, is as potent to-day as ever.

It is odd that although there has never been an artist more preoccupied with personal sensation than Chopin, or one more chained to a specific environment, his music remains undated. In every bar of his work is the chivalrous aristocratic gesture, the rustling of silk in shuttered drawing-rooms; yet he is never enslaved to a time and place that are past. He becomes a mythical Pierrot-figure, symbol of our youthful yearning for the moon, and of the unappeasable cravings that remain when the years have taken their toll. He is unique in his perfection. Only the youthful Schumann may be said to parallel his achievement; and his case is more complicated, because he belonged to the German tradition.

Chopin came from a country that had lost or forgotten its musical tradition. The music he was brought up on was Italian; the language he spoke and the books he read were French. From the start there was little to distract him from his romantic individuality. Schumann [1810–1856] came of

respectable middle-class stock, was brought up on the Viennese
classics and on German romantic literature; and was intended
for the law. As a boy he was, like Chopin, moody and hypersensitive, oscillating between exuberant gaiety and a black
hypochondria. His earliest musical passion was for Schubert:
a significant fact, since whereas Chopin was always content to
live for his own passions, Schumann followed Schubert in
cultivating friendship as a bulwark against a hostile world. His
'Davidsbund' was not merely an artistic coterie directed
against philistinism: it was also an alliance of all solitary
Pierrots against those who would destroy them through misunderstanding, if not through wilful malice. But there was
nothing revolutionary about Schumann's circle. It was more
exclusive, more private than Schubert's: indeed, as it affected
his music it turned out to consist of himself, in various disguises,
and of the women he loved, who—because he loved them—
became at once a part of himself and a barrier between himself
and other people. This is why a kind of ideal domesticity is so
moving an element in Schumann's work. It is revealing that
while Chopin too was a passionate lover, his music seems independent of his loves. In listening to his music we may sometimes think of Chopin himself—the pale face, the fragile fingers,
the unexpectedly fierce eyes—but we do not think of George
Sand. Ernestine von Fricken or Clara Wieck are never far
from Schumann's most beautiful and typical music.

Schumann's opus 1 was inspired by love: or at least by a
passing fancy for a pretty girl he met at a dance. The young
woman's name, Abegg, happened to be a sequence of musical
notes. Out of them Schumann made a waltz tune, suggestive
of Schubert in its nostalgically rising and falling arpeggio, yet
strangely personal in the regularity of its clauses, which seems
to inhibit the music's flow. The bird would soar, were not his
wings clipped (Ex. 5):

Ex.5. Schumann: Abegg Variations Op.1

The variations that follow are less interesting, with a faint
suggestion of Hummel's drawing-room elegance; but they

establish the importance of variation technique througnout Schumann's formative years. No more than Chopin did he have any instinctive feeling for the sonata principle; variation was the only technique whereby he could create works on a reasonably extended scale. In a sense, all his works were variations on his own sensibility; his sequences of small piano pieces in simple ternary or binary form were free variations on an often latent theme. Each passing mood was related to the others, if only because all the moods were his.

This is already evident in Schumann's opus 2, the revealingly titled *Papillons*. Schumann gave this chain of waltzes a literary programme derived from the neurotically sentimental romances of Jean Paul;* but he also said, "When I play Schubert, I feel as though I were reading a romance of Jean Paul set to music," and the real impetus behind these pieces is Schubert's waltzes and polonaises. The difference is that whereas Schubert's dances, though idealized, were in fact *musique de société*, Schumann's exist only in the dream-world of Pierrot. In the first number we have again the upward-soaring phrase which then declines, twice repeated in four-bar periods. After the double bar come four bars of rapid sequential modulations which seek to destroy both tonality and symmetry; but are prevented by a repeat of the opening phrase. Two other Schumannesque features should be mentioned: a fondness for canonic devices in aggressively regular metre—a wilful discipline, in opposition to the lilting dream (consider the second dance); and a use of chromatically intertwining inner parts which create, through dissonant passing notes, a pathos that is acute rather than languishing (consider the fifth number).

Papillons, written in Schumann's teens, may be regarded as a preliminary sketch for *Carnaval* (1834), described by Schumann as *"scènes mignonnes sur quatre notes"*. The four notes in question (A-S-C-H) are also the place where Ernestine von Fricken was born; Schumann again unifies the sequence of fleeting moods by basing the movements on various permutations of these notes. Though the work is not strictly in variation form, it is another instance of Schumann's variation principle linked, once more, to autobiography. In this Carnival the characters are Schumann himself in his two contradictory personae—Florestan the extrovert, Eusebius the brooding

* Johann Paul Richter (1763-1825), German novelist of Sensibility.

melancholic; Estrella and Chiarina, who are Ernestine von Fricken and Clara Wieck—the woman he loved at the moment and the girl (then fifteen) who was to be his wife: and the traditional figures of the *Commedia*, joined significantly by Chopin and Paganini. The two latter were Pierrot-figures actually living in the early nineteenth century; and it is no accident that the mythical Pierrot who himself broods over the Carnival is portrayed in a piece which is the quintessence of early Schumann. The short, chromatically involuted phrase closes in on itself, and is obsessively repeated in regular clauses which contradict the bar-line (Ex. 6):

Ex. 6. Schumann: Carnaval Op. 9

Again, the metaphor of the trapped butterfly, the caged bird, springs to mind; but in this exuberantly youthful work he seems to fly free. The cycle ends with the march of the Davidsbundler against the Philistines which, in routing the vulgar and academic, reveals the interrelations between the themes. Only a certain fanatical quality in the rigid rhythm hints that the powers of darkness have not said their last.

The haunted and hallucinatory are certainly present in the sliding chromatics and rhythmic elusiveness of the *Kreisleriana*. The title was suggested by an autobiographical story in which Hoffmann described his own sufferings through the mask of an imaginary Kapellmeister. Schumann told Clara that the pieces were about himself, in relation to her; and significantly said the same about the *Kinderscenen*, which one might have expected to be less directly personal. He wrote these pieces, he said, because Clara had remarked that she sometimes thought of him as a child. This child is himself, and the self-sufficiency of the child's world is a refuge from the turbulence of adolescence. Again, the revocation of passed moods is unified by a free variation principle, since all the pieces are dominated by permutations of the phrase with which the work opens—the rising sixth (sometimes changed to a fourth), followed by a descending third and a slow turn.

Schumann's keyboard texture, his harmonic reverie, his fondness for dotted-note march rhythms, may owe something to Beethoven's 'transitional' piano sonatas, such as the A major, opus 101; but the originality of his style was rightly recognized by his contemporaries as hardly less potent than Chopin's. There is nothing Italianate about his melodies, which derive from the simple symmetry of German folk-song and the Lied. The pathos of his harmony, even when it is extremely chromatic, depends less on a rapidly coruscating texture than on the clear spacing of the part-writing which rounds off the sharpest discord in its resonance. Often these inner parts are precipitated out of a texture of richly flowing arpeggios; often again they are associated with the repetition of a rhythmic figure, as in the beautiful piece describing the child asleep. The lucid sonority of Schumann's part-writing may have something to do with his early enthusiasm for Bach, though his polyphony seldom betrays Bach's tension between line and harmony. Fundamentally, Schumann, like Chopin, thinks in harmonic terms; one might even say that the canonic passages in Chopin's last mazurkas are more Bachian in spirit than anything in Schumann.

The essence of Schumann's youthful fantasy is to be found in the pieces he explicitly called *Fantasiestücke*. We are told that Schumann liked to play to his friends at twilight; certainly the first piece of the set, *Des Abends*, reveals how intimately Schumann lives in half-lights and ambiguities. The time signature is 2–8, but the figuration is in 6–16. What we hear melodically, however, is a tune in 3–8; and this rhythmic equivocation leads to harmonic ambiguities created by the figuration: consider the transition, rather than modulation, from D flat to E major (Ex. 7):

Ex. 7. Schumann: Des Abends Op. 12 No. 1

In the second piece, *Aufschwung*, the romantic spirit soars in a more than normally extended ternary form, while the cross-rhythms imbue the bird's floating ecstasy with a certain fearful precariousness. In the exquisite *Warum?* the tenderly rising and drooping phrase never flowers; its question floats pathetically from voice to voice, leading into strangely shifting harmonies and keys that are no resolution. In *Grillen* the fantasticality lies equally in the rhythmic and tonal contradictions, which are not so much witty as weird. In *In der Nacht* we have one of Schumann's favourite whirling arpeggio figures, above which a melody strives to soar, but is pulled back by the appoggiatura in the middle part. When, in the middle section, the melody manages to free itself, the harmony becomes frustrated, because the decorative appoggiaturas in the arpeggios create an ambiguity between major and minor. Even the jovial *Ende vom Lied*, in which the *amici* make merry, contains some oddly abrupt enharmonic transitions in its middle section; and concludes with a slow coda which transforms geniality into dream. This is a beautiful instance of the harmonic nature of Schumann's counterpoint.

In 1840 Schumann turned from small piano pieces to songwriting, in a mood of lyrical expansiveness appropriate to a marriage that seemed to offer all he asked of life. The stream of songs which he created in this *annus mirabilis* stands with the finest of his piano works as his supreme achievement; but they add nothing new to the experience the piano works had expressed. The physical presence of the human voice inspired Schumann to some of his most moving melodies, and perhaps he never achieved in his piano works a melody which has the inevitable drive, the cumulative, wavelike motion of *Ich grolle nicht*. But both the periodic nature of this melody, and the relation of its melodic development to the tensing and relaxing of the harmony, do not radically differ from the idiom of the piano pieces: even Schumann's partiality for the turn (see, for instance, *Er, der Herrlichste von Allen*) comes as much from pianistic habit as from unconscious reminiscence of opera. Many of his songs, indeed, double the vocal line in the piano part, so that they could be played as piano pieces and still make sense. Moreover, the psychological interest which Schumann displays in his songs is implicit in his piano pieces also, for most of them have reference to a specific emotional situation, usually autobiographical.

It is significant that the majority of Schumann's songs should be love songs. Schubert too created his greatest songs when he discovered an identity between his poets and himself; but he still preserved a measure of classical objectivity in his ability to project himself into other, and very different, people. Schumann is musically moved by poetry only when the singer is himself— whether as Florestan or Eusebius—or Clara; and this spiritual identity between composer and poet is more important than the quality of the poetry, however highly developed his literary taste may have been. His settings of Heine, or even of Chamisso, are musically superior to his settings of Goethe, because in Heine especially he found a poet whose pathology was extra-ordinarily close to his own. Beneath the rosy languors of romantic convention there is in Heine's verse a masochistic melancholy that frustrates passion: a schizophrenia parallel to the break in rhythmic continuity, the sudden dissonance, the abrupt enharmonic transition that in Schumann's music may threaten the bloom of a melody that would sing in heart-easing, folk-like simplicity. Only in this light can we understand the obsessive quality in Schumann's rhythms. Initially, his fondness for square rhythms may have had something to do with his susceptibility to poetic metres, and especially to the simple stanzaic forms of folk verse. Ultimately, however, he drives his metrical patterns so hard because he is terrified of what might happen in the silence, were they to stop. The implications of this become evident only later, in his orchestral and chamber music.

The *Dichterliebe* cycle is one of the richest and most compre-hensive of Schumann's works because in these Heine settings the two contradictory sides of his and the poet's ego sing together. Although the songs show a profound understanding of the workings of the mind in love, they are lyrical reflections on, not dramatic presentations of, experience. The climax of the cycle is significantly the lovely piano postlude, which rounds off the passion in nostalgia. Perhaps one might say that the spirit of all Schumann's finest songs is nocturnal; in the tenderly resonant harmony of *Mondnacht* we find the bliss of sleep, in *Allnächtlich im Traume* we have night as the augury of dreams and phantoms. Schumann evokes the night, either because its darkness may lap him in warm security, or because obscurity is filled with uncertain fears, the nameless shapes that flit by owl-light. Chopin's music has no such external associations; knowing the limitations of his nerves, he has an inner strength denied to Schumann.

This becomes clear when we turn from Schumann's short piano pieces and songs to his attempts at large-scale composition. His greatest songs are all settings of short poems, especially those of Heine which have an epigrammatic, folk-like directness. His treatment of the text is often strophic; in any case, his structures in song-writing usually preserve the simple ternary or binary form of his piano pieces, and he achieves some of his most beautiful effects when the harmonic structure 'overlaps' the literary setting (consider the exquisite harmonization of the last sung note of *Mondnacht*; the dominant seventh is resolved in the postlude, when the voice is silent). But Schumann, unlike Chopin, was never completely fulfilled in his mastery of short forms. Partly, perhaps, because he lived within the German tradition, he felt impelled to tackle the sonata, even though his youthful attempts were written with a laboured anguish very different from the spontaneity with which he composed piano pieces and songs.

In 1835 he composed three piano sonatas, dedicating the first to Clara. While they are less convincing than his other big piano work, the *Etudes Symphoniques* of 1837, written in his free variation technique, they are certainly not negligible, like Chopin's C minor Sonata. The material is as vital as one would expect from Schumann at the height of his youthful powers, and all three slow movements are nocturnal songs of the richest beauty. The themes of the first movements, too, have an aphoristic quality which might have lent itself well to sonata development, had such development made any appeal to Schumann's imagination. But while enharmonic transitions and Schubertian mediant relationships fascinated him as a means to express his dreams and fancies, in tonality as a means towards dramatic argument he had no interest at all. As a result, he tends to substitute simple transposition for development; and however excitingly remote the transpositions may be, to repeat is not to develop. Indeed, the sonata principle is rendered nonsensical when Schumann repeats long passages of his 'development' in the recapitulation, as he does in the last movement of the G minor Sonata. In the first movement of this sonata Schumann evades his difficulties by way of the continuity of his figuration and rhythmic pattern, and through the use of canonic devices in the development. In remarking that the movement portrayed "the wild dance of a desperate couple, Florestan and Chiarina", Schumann admitted the auto-biographical genesis of the music; and while its stormy surge is not the less impressive for having little in common with the dualism of the classical sonata, it would have been still more impressive if it had been a little shorter. In these early sonatas he does not approach Chopin's inspired rethinking of classical precedent in his B flat minor Sonata. Schumann rather attempts to accommodate his genius to the past; and while genius would have told him when to stop, he preferred to listen to the spirit of tradition.

Very gradually, he came to realize what Chopin perceived intuitively: that he had not to copy, but to renew the past. In 1841 he consciously prepared himself to tackle the symphony itself by a study of the symphonies of Beethoven. Now Schumann's free 'variation' principle involves the metamorphosis of a motive into related forms; and Beethoven's symphonies involve, as we have seen, thematic growth and transformation. The difference is that whereas Beethoven's transformations are growth—the creation of an idea—Schumann's are variations on a mood. Thus when Schumann consciously takes over a technique which in Beethoven was in part subconscious, he creates an effect radically distinct from Beethoven's. Both derive their material from a basic motive or motives, usually stated in a slow introduction; but whereas in Beethoven the seed inevitably germinates, in Schumann the interrelation of the themes serves—often in association with obsessive rhythmic patterns—as a substitute for evolution. He links his themes *because* they have no inner capacity for growth.

Though this is often held to be a deficiency in Schumann's symphonies, it is not necessarily so. Greater stamina is needed to create a symphony, rather than a set of piano pieces or a song cycle, out of interlinked, mosaic-like moments of fancy; but we cannot simply say that Schumann lacked that stamina. We may love the Eusebius of the slow movement of the C major, with its almost Brucknerian soaring sixths and drooping sevenths and its ripe chromatic texture; we may be exasperated by the Florestan of the first movement, with its fanatically square rhythms, its rigidly reiterated motto, its 'development' by transposition. Yet each movement is an integral part of Schumann's contradictory nature; and if, like Mozart or Beethoven or even Schubert, he had created a classical synthesis from dualism, he would not have been Schumann. The fascination of his symphonies consists as much in their weaknesses as in their strength. In attempting to express all he had in him—and perhaps a bit more—he reveals his soul in a manner peculiarly touching. We see that his cosy domesticity is the inverse of his hypochondria: that his compulsive energy may at any moment flare into frenzy. We cannot claim his depth of feeling nor even perhaps, his integrity; but we can understand his troubles—and even forgive his orchestral texture which was dominated by the movements of his hands at a keyboard.* We are all heirs to romantic sensibility, all variously 'maladjusted' souls.

In the latter part of his life Schumann never relinquished his attempts to create works of symphonic stature. His three string quartets, for instance, show his technique of thematic interrelation in an even more extreme form: most of all in the lovely A major, which is significantly his most complex work harmonically. The texture at times suggests Chopin's last mazurkas, or even *Tristan* (Ex. 8):

Ex. 8. Schumann: String quartet in A major opus 41 No. 3

It almost seems as though in a work such as this, even more than in the D minor Symphony, Schumann was seeking a formal ideal of which he was but dimly conscious: a completely thematic unification of transitory moments of harmonic sensation, such as we find tentatively in Liszt's Sonata, consummately in the earlier work of Schoenberg.

In any case, the A major Quartet has no successor in Schumann's work. His most experimental works, though in some

---

* If one attempts to read one of Schumann's orchestral scores at the keyboard, the parts 'lie under the hands' with almost no modification. Berlioz's orchestral scores have to be radically rewritten before they make any sense in pianistic terms.

ways his most fascinating, are not those which wear best, if
frequency of performance means anything. On the whole, his
most convincing large-scale works are those which involve the
piano, because the improvisatory element suggested by the keyboard usually provokes some relaxation of his fanatical search
for unity. The Piano Concerto is largely a monothematic, even
a monorhythmic, piece, yet its vitality flows and sings. It
compels us, rather than forcibly compelling itself; even its
orchestration glows, shedding inhibition as it follows and
enriches the soloist's fantasy. Virtuosity for Schumann was
never exhibitionism (his piano studies on Paganini's Caprices
revealingly contrast with Liszt's from this point of view). Nor
was it nervous excitement, as in Chopin. It was an emotional
liberation; and it is no accident that both the Concerto and the
Phantasie, opus 17—perhaps Schumann's greatest work for solo
piano—should have been so closely associated with Clara.

In the face of works such as these it seems hardly valid to say
that Schumann, like Chopin, was essentially a master of small
forms. Yet it is true that an uninhibited outburst of passion on
the grand scale, such as the *Phantasie*, is exceptional in his
career; and that although the symphonies are a part of the
essential Schumann, respect for tradition prevented him from
creating a symphonic cosmos out of a kaleidoscope of moods.
Only Wagner could feel sensations so heroically that they
became a cosmos. Schumann revered Weber and sought for a
suitable opera libretto all his life; yet the failure of *Genoveva*
proves that he could never have been the creative link between
Weber and Wagner. The twilit fancies, the ardent loves, the
exuberant passions, the fireside simplicities, the nocturnal
glimmerings of his youthful piano pieces and songs faded as he
tried to build more from them than their nature warranted;
and while the later symphonies and chamber works have many
fine qualities, it is unquestionable that the later piano pieces are
a decline. Only fitfully—most of all in the haunting, pitiful
Bird as Prophet—is the old magic recaptured. Is it too fanciful to
think that what this solitary bird prophesies—we recall the
fluttering, pinioned birds and butterflies of Schumann's youth
—is the darkness that ultimately overwhelmed him: the silent
melancholy that proved too strong even for Clara's love? The
terror of his last years was that he, who had lived for feeling and
communion with the beloved, was caged in the silence of his

solitude. Feeling was followed by inertia; the dreams of his
youth became hallucinations. Schubert dictated to him sublime
themes which he could not, alas, remember; the obsessive
rhythms which had pounded through his youth became a single
hammered note reiterated in his head—sound and fury, now
signifying nothing. This German Pierrot's fate was more fearful
than that of the Franco-Polish Pierrot whom consumption
destroyed when his nerves were spent. For Schumann came to
live in a past which he could no longer believe in; in the dream
of his madness, the dreams he had lived for seemed a sham. His
music, if sometimes almost unbearably poignant, is never
tragic; but in contemplating the romantic myth which is his
life one certainly feels both pity and terror. It is difficult to
imagine anything more appalling than the letter which he
wrote to Clara from the asylum, asking her to send him the
little tune he had written for her, "long ago, when we were in
love". He was forty-two.

Schumann was a no less original artist than Chopin. None
the less, his desire to 'belong' to a tradition grew more urgent
with the years; his divided and distracted soul could not, like
Chopin's, be sufficient to itself. The kind of spiritual struggle
which he experienced would have been equally unintelligible
to Mendelssohn [1809–1847] or to Liszt, but for diametrically
opposite reasons. The hints of romantic sensibility in Mendelssohn do not disturb the conservatism of his nature; in many ways
he is closer to the eighteenth century than to Chopin. Liszt,
on the other hand, was from the start the romantic hero-
prophet, the conscious innovator whose work was a stimulus to
others. Moreover, as conductor and teacher he did everything
in his power to encourage other progressive artists—even when
their appreciation of his efforts was as scant as Wagner's.

Mendelssohn's father was Jewish and a banker. His wealth
was associated with a moralistic strain that found an only too
ready outlet when his son settled in Victorian England, where
material prosperity was considered the legitimate reward of
virtue. During Mendelssohn's childhood, however, the family
circle was cultivated and vivacious. He himself was intellectually precocious, and as socially amenable as Chopin was
isolated in his nerves, or Schumann in his dreams and his
personal affections. Thus although he too wrote little piano

pieces, he designed them to fit comfortably into the drawing-room, rather than to express his private fancies. Chopin's short piano pieces are an exploration of piano technique, which is also a harmonic (and emotional) discovery; even Schumann's domesticities, being personal rather than social, imply a new approach to keyboard style. In Mendelssohn's *Songs without Words*, on the other hand, there is no pianistic feature that suggests the pressure of new experience. Melodically, they compromise. The tunes are habitually andante, neither fast nor slow: neither operatic nor folk-like. The gracious melody of the first piece of the first book, for instance, domesticates the step-wise contours of operatic lyricism far more thoroughly than do Schumann's Lied-like themes (Ex. 9):

Ex.9. Mendelssohn: Song Without Words Bk.1 No.1

The quasi-vocal turn coos; the arpeggiated accompaniment purrs on the hearth; the tune sinks in the sweet contentment of its persistent feminine endings.

In harmony and modulation, the piece attempts no breach with classical precedent. The harmonic flow of the arpeggios is sensitively spaced, and the use of mediant relationships is touching; but Mendelssohn's modulations nowhere approach the visionary unexpectedness of Schubert's, or the dream-like fantasy of Schumann's. The limpness of the melody is here justified by a mood of exquisite relaxation. Sometimes, however, it droops into sentimentality because Mendelssohn's chromaticisms, though less frequent than those in the last works of Mozart, have little of Mozart's linear vitality. Mozart's chromaticisms stimulate movement; Mendelssohn's, like

Spohr's, tend to clog the growth of the line. A tiny song piece like the E major from Book 2 seems pretentious because the harmony gives a disproportionate stress to the slight, fragmentary tune. At our fireside, dreams may be encouraged, but pretence we must avoid at all costs.

There are no dreams in Mendelssohn's *Songs without Words*, though there are often charming fancies like the B minor piece from the sixth book, or the last of the Gondoliers' songs (in A minor, from the fifth book). To compare this last piece with Chopin's rich and strange evocation of Venetian· light and water in his *Barcarolle* is to see that the two belong to irreconcilable worlds. Chopin's unprecedented sonorities create a visionary Venice within his sensibility; Mendelssohn's prettily melancholic piece brings a picture postcard into our parlour. It is a tasteful, indeed a beautiful postcard; but it is not, and does not pretend to be, an imaginative revelation.

How far Mendelssohn is from Chopin and Schumann is revealed in the fact that the most successful pieces in the *Songs without Words* tend to be those which approximate to sonata form. In the B minor from Book 2, for instance, the energy of the repeated note figuration to some extent counteracts the periodicity of the clauses; the onward drive of the music even provokes abrupt, but convincing, modulations in the brief development. It is interesting too that although the piece is grateful to play, it is not pianistic; it rather suggests string technique, most of all in the coda, when the repeated notes gradually still themselves. This reminds us that in his earliest, adolescent works Mendelssohn had already used the classical symphonic convention with an authenticity unapproached by his contemporaries. The Octet for strings—written in his seventeenth year—pays homage to tradition by employing sonata form for all the movements. It recalls Mozart in its lyrical grace, the youthful Beethoven in its dramatic vigour, and Weber in its richness of sonority; yet in working within an inherited tradition Mendelssohn does not stifle his personality. Significantly, the movements in all his early works which most reveal his nature are the scherzi, in which the formalities and symmetries of classical precedent become a dancing play of fancy. Although these movements are formally strict, and tonally less adventurous than Haydn, Mozart, or Beethoven (let alone Schubert), they seem to suggest that tradition itself is dissolving into insubstantiality, so rapid is the movement, so feathery the texture. Mendelssohn's overture to *A Midsummer Night's Dream*, also composed in his seventeenth year, manifests the true classical spirit in creating an entity out of material as diverse as the fairies' gossamer-like frolics, the ceremonial theme for Theseus's wedding, and the grotesque 'translation' of Bottom. At the same time, its delicately poetic scoring eternalizes sensation in a manner comparable with that of Weber's fairy music. Mendelssohn, like Weber, still lives in the classical world, while admitting that it is now a world of exquisite artifice.

This is why his adolescent works remained in some ways his best. For a boy of sixteen, or even twenty, the sonata principle could legitimately become excitingly fanciful rather than dramatic. As he grew older, he became more aware that he had been born 'late'. Deeply though he loved Mozart's music, he could emulate only its surface elegance, not the intensity within the charm; greatly though he revered Beethoven, he could but fitfully recover the fire that had made his sonatas a revolutionary force. The *Hebrides* overture is probably Mendelssohn's finest work, because he here challenges middle-period Beethoven on his own ground, developing a pithy subject admirably adapted to sonata style, while attaining a strange immateriality in the hazily floating modulations at the opening of the development. The battle is thrilling, though the issues are no longer a matter of life and death. The Beethovenian trumpet-calls no longer summon one to action; they lure one away to a Hebridean fairyland.

Occasionally, the drama of the classical tradition lives again unambiguously in Mendelssohn's work. The first movement of the E flat Quartet, opus 44, for instance, has a powerful sonata theme incorporating a wriggling semiquaver figure which may become either a rhetorical gesture or an accompanying figuration. The subsidiary themes—especially a wailing descending figure in dotted rhythm—are also strong, and interlock with the first theme in a development at once exciting and spacious. The scherzo is even more impressive, since it combines sonata drama with the feathery, dancing texture which is the essence of Mendelssohnian fancy. The last work which Mendelssohn completed—the F minor Quartet—is even more nervously intense: so much so that Mendelssohn forgets his impeccable manners in creating a string texture that strains the medium.

He evens begins the recapitulation of the first movement anticipatorily, at what appears to be the climax of the development.

Music of such force is, however, exceptional in Mendelssohn's career. Perhaps the pent-up emotion of years was released by his sister's death and his own increasing physical frailty; certainly something more than the example of Beethoven's opus 95 in the same key is needed to explain it. More representative is the Mendelssohn of the symphonies, especially the 'Italian'. Here he handles classical convention more expertly than Schumann; yet the music fascinates less. The themes are often fetching, and if they lack the innately symphonic character of those of the *Hebrides* overture, they serve as well as the lyrical tunes of the average rococo symphony. The orchestration is as sensitive as Schumann's is gauche. Yet Schumann was striving to create a new symphonic ideal, approximating, perhaps, to the Lisztian symphonic poem; Mendelssohn was accepting a legacy from the past. Only seldom could he feel that past so powerfully that it became present. For the rest, he was content to manipulate his pseudo-classical material mechanically; and to rely on the fact that he was close enough to the classical tradition for its conventions to be still acceptable to a middle-class audience that then, as now, feared change.

It is revealing that although Mendelssohn could afford to be influenced by the dramatic rhetoric of middle-period Beethoven —most notably in the F minor Quartet—he failed whenever he attempted to imitate the lyrical or contrapuntal manner of Beethoven's last years. Both Beethoven and Mendelssohn studied Bach; and Beethoven developed in his late works a unique contrapuntal texture which yet resembled Bach's in effecting a tension between line and harmony. Mendelssohn's counterpoint is Bachian imitation, but even less than Brahms's or Schumann's is it Bachian in spirit. When successful, as in the Preludes and Fugues of opus 35, it hardly pretends to be genuine linear writing. The well-known E minor, for instance, begins with a richly arpeggiated prelude leading to a harmonically derived fugue subject; this reaches an almost Lisztian 'apotheosis' in a chorale, accompanied by a resurgence of the flowing arpeggios. The work is structurally convincing, and more romantically 'progressive' than Mendelssohn was wont to be; but it has no more to do with Bach than with late

Beethoven. This is not surprising, for Mendelssohn betrays no interest in, let alone knowledge of, religious experience.

His attempt, when he settled in England, to create a nineteenth-century version of Handelian oratorio and Bachian cantata was thus doomed to failure. The English still sang Handel; but the zest of the Chosen People in an age of mercantile expansion was by now wearing shoddy; and there had never been any organic connexion between the spiritual implications of Handelian oratorio and those of the Bach passion. There are moments of genuine and powerful dramatic feeling in Mendelssohn's *Elijah*; but one has to admit that his harmonic mannerisms—for instance, his fondness for inversions of the diminished seventh—are much more obtrusive in his religious than in his secular instrumental music: and that the weak periodicity of his phrases, with their limp feminine endings, is the more damaging in music which aims at drama and monumental grandeur.

During his visits to London, Gounod was greatly impressed by Mendelssohn's pseudo-oratorios. To us, perhaps, Gounod's sweetness seems preferable to Mendelssohn's solemnity; we can take a little Tennysonian honey, so long as we are not simultaneously bullied with a pietistic morality that seems to us irrelevant. It is significant that Mendelssohn should have reached the pinnacle of his fame in a rapidly and recently industrialized England. Our native musical tradition being moribund, we were the more prepared to accept a consciously archaistic style: and to welcome in musical convention a spurious religiosity which reflected the element of unconscious humbug in our morality and beliefs. George Bernard Shaw hit the nail on the head with characteristic trenchancy when he pointed out that Mendelssohn, "who was shocked at Auber's writing an opera in which a girl sang '*Oui, c'est demain*' (meaning 'To-morrow I shall be a bride') at her looking-glass before going to bed, was himself ready to serve up the chopping to pieces of the prophets of the grove with his richest musical spice to suit the compound of sanctimonious cruelty and base materialism which his patrons, the British Pharisees, called their religion."

We may think that Shaw was going a little far when he said: "Set all that dreary fugue manufacture, with its Sunday School sentimentalities and music school ornamentalities, against the expressive and vigorous choruses of Handel and ask yourself on your honour whether there is the slightest difference in kind between Stone him to Death and Under the Pump with a Kick and a Thump from Dorothy." He was none the less making a valid and important point. In an industrial society the values of art were becoming indistinguishable from those of commerce. It is not a question of the decline of a talent, for, as we have seen, Mendelssohn's last work, the F minor Quartet, was one of his finest, if not most characteristic. In a sense, Mendelssohn's case is sadder than slow decay, for he prostituted his gifts wilfully, and with the most high-minded intentions.

2

LISZT AND ROMANTIC VIRTUOSITY

Liszt [1811–1886] was born two years later than Mendelssohn: spiritually it might have been twenty. His acquaintance with Mendelssohn, if not extensive, was cordial; yet it is difficult to imagine a temperament more remote than Liszt's from Mendelssohn's socially 'safe', musically conservative gentility. It is interesting that for Liszt, as for Wagner, the Jews became synonymous with the triumph of the world of trade and mechanization. Wagner did not think of the Jew romantically, as the solitary outcast, like himself; the Jew was Meyerbeer, indecently successful, the degraded and degrading architect of a commercialized world. Liszt too—though it was not in his nature to hate—believed that the Jew was opposed to the Artist-Hero, whose duty was to preserve the aristocratic virtues, while striving for liberty both spiritual and political.

It is odd to think that during Liszt's childhood on the Esterházy estate many people must have been able to recall the days when Haydn was Director of Music. Much of the cosmopolitan glitter of the palace still survived; the vast grey wastes that surrounded the aristocratic oasis were certainly as unchanged as the gipsies who roamed the countryside. Years later Lizst wrote a book in which he contrasted the avaricious, factory-enslaved life of the city-dwellers, the Jews, with the 'poetical Egotism' of the gipsies. Possessed by "a mad love of Nature, the gipsy would enjoy his passions completely, fully, on every occasion and forever. He is not the passive instrument that reproduces the feeling of others and adds nothing to them"; in possessing the passions of others, he is always himself a creator, 'the natural virtuoso'.

Whether or no this is an accurate description of the gipsy— and whether or no Liszt had gipsy blood in his own veins—it certainly describes the kind of artist he himself wanted to be. But of course he was not in fact primitive. The world to which he gravitated was as aristocratic and cosmopolitan as that of the Esterházys. In the early 1830s he was living in Paris, a youthful prodigy of virtuosity who, through his talents, magnetism, and extreme physical beauty, became the intimate friend of the most brilliant group of poets, painters, and musicians in Europe: and the lover of a succession of women, all beautiful, mostly of noble birth. Unlike Chopin, he turned outwards to meet this resplendent society, becoming the prototype of the Artist as Hero. Aristocratic hauteur is fired by a primitive frenzy; unruly passion is rendered amenable by exquisitely gracious manners; the acceptance of cultural and intellectual aristocracy is reconciled with an ardent if unspecific enthusiasm for the ideals of the 1830 Revolution. The impact of Liszt on Europe is, indeed, something to which there is no musical parallel. Only in Byron do we find the same combination of aristocratic elegance with revolutionary force, of fearless sincerity with histrionic virtuosity. Even in youth, Liszt became a legend; the long mane of fair hair, the eccentric 'Bohemian' garb, became more familiar, as well as more interesting, than the private life of the most fabulous film-star. Medallions were showered on him, town bands turned out to meet him, riots accompanied his gladiatorial progress through Europe. Significantly, the only country where he was a relative failure was industrialized England. Distrusting his histrionics, we put our faith in, and money on, Mendelssohn.

But we must return to Liszt's early days in Paris, where there were three musicians Liszt knew who decisively stimulated his imagination. The greatest of them, Berlioz, affected him the least directly. Though he was impressed, even overwhelmed, by Berlioz's "Babylonian and Ninevehan imagination", his nature was much more egotistic.* Berlioz forgot himself in operatic pro-

---

* There is, however, another pianist-composer—Charles Henri Morhange, known as Alkan [1813–1888]—whose affinity with Berlioz is profound. His melodies, like those of Berlioz, have a poised grandeur deriving from the classical operatic tradition, while his harmonies—seldom chromatic, sometimes modal— have an enigmatic flavour arising from the fact that they are frequently prompted by an unexpected melodic progression. (Consider the Funeral March from the Symphony for piano in relation to that from Berlioz's *Symphonie Funèbre et Triomphale*.) Both composers combine their melodic, operatic approach with a deep understanding of Beethoven's dramatic architecture (consider the first movement from the Symphony for piano); and there is perhaps some similarity between Berlioz's orchestral virtuosity and the necromantic quality of Alkan's pianism. The highly original variation-set *Le Festin d'Aesope* suggests Berlioz not only in the aristocratic bearing of the theme, but also in the manner in which it "does coolly the things that are most fiery": consider the astonishing final variation and coda.

jection, whether or no he wrote for the stage. Liszt became his own actors, in life as in his art.

The impact of Chopin was more immediately significant; for he was a pianist-composer. Yet while his opus 10 studies certainly influenced Liszt's keyboard technique, the effect of Chopin's music on Liszt was neither lasting nor deep. Chopin, like Liszt and unlike Berlioz, was an egocentric artist. But whereas his egoism was introverted, Liszt's found expression in extrovert exuberance. Chopin's virtuosity became the revelation of his dreams; Liszt's was designed, exhibitionistically, for the platform. This is why the third musical personality whom he met in Paris was, for him, the most immediately important.

Paganini was not a great composer like Berlioz, nor a profoundly original minor master like Chopin. But he was one of the most phenomenal executants, on any instrument, who has ever lived; and his virtuosity—like that of Liszt's gipsies—was essentially creative. Few living violinists are capable of playing Paganini's unaccompanied Caprices—the only works he wrote down in a form approximating to what he played on the concert platform. Even from those players who can negotiate the notes, we can acquire but a shadowy idea of the effect of Paganini's performance on contemporary audiences. The music is not—in the medium it hardly could be—remarkable for harmonic experiment of the type associated with Chopin's emotional exploration. None the less, the audacities of its virtuosity translate its incisive, mordant lyricism into Hoffmanesque necromancy. The icy glitter of the music is the inverse of the hot blood of romantic harmony: just as the sinister, cadaverous figure of Paganini himself haunts the nineteenth century, transforming romantic glamour into the spectral and demoniacal.

In a keyboard-dominated nineteenth century it was no accident that this dark undercurrent to romantic afflatus should have exerted a greater influence on piano technique than on that of the violin. As a youth, Liszt had been famed not as a composer, but as a virtuoso and improviser of mythical powers. The first works to reveal his creativity are his pianistic transcriptions of Paganini's violin caprices, and his *Etudes d' Exécution Transcendante*, which were intended to be a pianistic complement to Paganini's work. In both, exhibitionism releases, rather than disguises, creative energy. Even when the youthful Liszt does not call for 'transcendental' virtuosity, his music usually implies exhibitionism. The first book of his *Années de Pèlerinage*, for instance, is a musical record of his tour of Switzerland with the first of his aristocratic loves, the Comtesse d'Angoult. The pieces—prefaced with literary quotations from Byron, Schiller, and other apostles of romanticism—express his reactions to the places they saw: the beauties of art and Nature. The most remarkable piece in the collection—*La Vallée d'Obermann*—has a long quotation from Etienne de Senacour, which indicates how Liszt's consciousness of place was, like his virtuosity, a stimulus to his egocentric imagination: "Vast consciousness of Nature everywhere overwhelming and impenetrable, universal passion, indifference, advanced wisdom, voluptuous abandon, all the profound desires and torments that a human heart can hold, I have felt them all, suffered them all, in this memorable night." In this piece keyboard technique becomes self-drama-tization; the transitory moods of the chromatics and the quasi-orchestral sonorities convince because they involve us in Liszt's rhetoric. Chopin communicates his dreams to us; Liszt 'presents' himself in a given situation. He could say, with Childe Harold, "I live not in myself but I become Portion of that around me"; and he acts with such aplomb that we are swept into the play, willy-nilly.

This is still more evident in the second book of *Années de Pèlerinage*, inspired by his visit to Italy in 1838–9. These pieces are all evoked by works of art, rather than by Nature. *Il Penseroso*, for instance, was inspired by the Michelangelo statue in San Lorenzo at Florence. The tenebrous gloom of its chromaticism and viscid keyboard texture is a romantic gesture. Yet this theatrical presentation of the Artist as Melancholic is profoundly felt: to dramatize oneself is not necessarily to be insincere. Indeed, this brief but oppressively powerful piece haunted Liszt's imagination for nearly thirty years, for recollec-tions of it crop up in later works. It both epitomizes Byronic melancholy, and anticipates *Tristan* by more than a decade. The difference is that whereas Wagner in *Tristan* had become a force that shook Europe, Liszt in this little piece is an artist acting a part: just as he acts, with equal conviction, an utterly different part in the *Eclogue* from the Swiss book, with its inno-cent, diatonic tune and exquisitely sensuous 'added notes' in the piano texture.

Since Liszt is a histrionic artist, it is not surprising that the basis of his idiom is operatic; he translates operatic gestures into pianistic virtuosity. Chopin's style, too, absorbed Italian *bel canto*; but his model was the most reticent, the most inward, in a sense the least characteristic of Italian dramatic composers. Bellinian lyricism could become a part of Chopin's inner life; Liszt, on the other hand, preserves, even enhances, the panache of the stage. He had no need of a theatre because, on the concert platform, he acted all the parts himself. We must remember that in his youth Liszt's creative work was centred in paraphrases and arrangements of other people's music, designed as a vehicle for his virtuosity. Sometimes—as in his masterly arrangement's of Berlioz's orchestral works—these were written in order to introduce the music of his friends to an audience that would be unlikely to hear it in its original form. Most often, however, they were potted versions of the operas that were his public's staple musical diet. These 'paraphrases' served much the same function as the gramophone record to-day, at least when they were not too difficult for the talented amateur. More exciting, and more significant, were the big *fantasies dramatiques* in which the well-loved operatic themes became no more than a stimulus to the virtuoso's improvisatory genius. As the actor needs the play to exhibit his talent, so Liszt needs the impetus of someone else's music. In the beautiful fantasy on Bellini's *Norma*, for instance, he is as though possessed by the themes; his virtuosity recreates Bellini's refined lyricism into full-blooded passion of almost Verdian directness. Chopin reveals the inwardness of Bellini's art; Liszt makes it almost more 'operatic' than Bellini's own operas. The fantasy on Mozart's *Don Giovanni* is an equally impressive, if more complex piece. Liszt chooses from the opera those aspects that appealed to his imagination—the Don's amorous abandon, the sepulchral horror of the graveyard scene—and created from them a tone-poem in which piano sonority is hardly less rich and multifarious than the sonority of the nineteenth-century orchestra. The work is not a tawdry substitute for Mozart; it is an aspect of Mozart, re-enacted by a consummate rhetorician.

The operatic nature of Liszt's talent is revealed most directly, of course, in his songs. His early setting of Goethe's *Freudvoll und Leidvoll* is highly Italianate in its persistent use of the falling sixth, of wide-spanning arpeggio phrases, and of the aspiring

turn: while the emotional sixths themselves generate the sobbing
alternations of major and minor, and the piquant 'Neapolitan'
alterations, in the arpeggiated accompaniment (Ex. 10):

Ex. 10. Liszt: Freudvoll und Leidvoll

The song acts itself, as it is sung, as much as a narrative scena like
Liszt's lovely, luxurious setting of *Kennst du das Land,* in which
the softly piercing dissonances of ninth and eleventh 'point' the
sobs in the melody. There is nothing here of the 'innig' quality
of Schumann's songs. If we compare Liszt's setting of Heine's
Anfangs wollt ich fast verzagen with that of Schumann, we can
see that whereas Schumann's song is lyrical reflection, Liszt's
is dramatic presentation. The lyrical phrases break under the
stress of feeling; the poem's bitterness is summed up in the
unexpected, inverted resolution from major to minor. The
tremendously powerful setting of *Vergiftet sind meine Lieder* is a
similar, but more extreme case. Liszt, unlike Schumann, here
dispenses with lyricism altogether; the dissonant appoggiaturas
of the opening and the ninths of the climax are as violent as
Tristan, and much starker, more abrupt (Ex. 11):

Ex. 11. Liszt: Vergiftet sind meine Lieder

When Liszt sets French words his style is usually less declamatory, more lyrical. But the tender contours of *O quand je
dors* are not less Italianate because they are relatively less
robust.

Liszt transformed three of his songs—settings of Italian

words—into piano pieces: the set of three Petrarch sonnets which appears in the second book of the *Années de Pèlerinage*. Though these ripely beautiful pieces bear a generic relationship to the style of Chopin's nocturnes, they could never be mistaken for Chopin. Chopin's melodies are often reveries which stimulate his harmonic and pianistic invention, without being in themselves significant. Liszt's *bel canto* themes are the essence of his passion: which is reinforced by the arabesques of his virtuosity and the luxuriance of his harmony. Consider, for instance, two of the finest pieces of Lizst's early maturity, from the collection *Harmonies Poétiques et Religieuses*. *Funérailles* is a heroic elegy, an 'oration' dedicated to the memory of friends who died in the Hungarian Revolution of 1849. It opens with a slow introduction exploiting 'orchestrally' the percussive depths of the piano, with dissonantly prepared diminished sevenths sighing frenziedly above the drums. This leads to a slow funeral march that suggests Berlioz in heroic grandeur, Verdi in robust vitality; the rising sixth, as so often in Liszt's themes, is prominent. A contrasting melody in the relative major, marked *lagrimoso*, brings Italian *bel canto* into its own: note how the chromatic alteration in the sighing, hypnotically repeated two-bar periods suggests the harmonic sob of the Neapolitan chord (Ex. 12):

Ex. 12. Liszt: *Funérailles*

Then follows a march section which builds up a terrific virtuoso climax over an ostinato bass, and leads to a 'triumphant' restatement of the funeral march. The passion explodes in recitative; the orator is so moved that his voice breaks. Then the piece concludes with a whispered reminiscence of the *bel canto* melody, *dolcissimo*, passing through sensuous mediant modulations: and a mysterious reference to the revolutionary ostinato. The *dolcissimo* recollection takes us into the realm of personal regret for our friends; the wild coda reminds us again of the epical significance of their death.

The other piece, *Bénédiction de Dieu dans la Solitude*, is even more remarkable. It is not deliberately oratorical, and therefore operatic, for it deals with God's power, through Nature, to soothe the turbulence of passion. The serene first theme is again, however, operatic *cantilena*, surrounded by a haze of 'added' notes in the piano figuration, warmly luminous in the key of F sharp major. The theme is repeated several times, ranging enharmonically through remote keys, and becoming more impassioned as the figuration grows more rich. Again, chromatic alteration in the melodic line suggests the emotional change in harmony, especially in the frequent transitions to the flat sub-mediant. A brief diatonic middle section in this flat submediant soon leads to an enormous expansion of the first song theme, with ever more opulent figuration; the ultimate climax comes in B flat—a second remove to the flat submediant. Finally, the figuration dissolves away in tensionless, pentatonic arabesques, leading to a consolatory statement of the 'middle section' in the tonic. A short retrospective epilogue both sums up the essence of the song theme and expresses elliptically the relation between tonic and flat submediant (Ex. 13):

Ex. 13. Liszt: Bénédiction de Dieu dans la Solitude

Many of Liszt's song-like pieces have this kind of valedictory coda, in which all passion is spent; not often, however, does he achieve so deep a serenity out of his operatic lyricism, his sensuous harmony and virtuosity. Whether or no the piece is religious in the orthodox sense, it certainly represents the romantic Artist's spiritual fulfilment; and the same is true of the two *Légendes*. St. Francis of Assisi speaks to the birds in tender operatic recitative; the birds chirrup in glinting pianistic virtuosity, their song being tonally ambiguous owing to a prevalence of augmented triads. In the companion piece ('St. Francis of Paola walking on the waves') the song theme is more hymn-like than operatic; but the virtuosity of the waves again threatens tonality with its chromatic sequences and seething diminished sevenths. The piece is a superb example of the colouristic and dramatic use of the piano. The music is not 'orchestral', for only the piano could create this astonishing sonority; yet it evokes a scene and a situation as vividly as could an orchestra, combined with the scenic resources of an opera house.

Perhaps one might say that operatic lyricism was the positive pole of Liszt's self-dramatizing talent, harmonic and pianistic experiment the negative. Certainly we find that in his middle years the Paganinian, demoniacal side of his virtuosity led him to create a number of works associated with the infernal: and that harmonically and pianistically these are often of breath-taking audacity. The *Fantasia quasi una Sonata*, composed "after reading Dante", is the earliest and one of the strangest of these excursions to Hell. More tightly wrought, less rhetorical, and therefore more frightening, are the first *Mephisto* waltzes, and the *Totentanz* for piano and orchestra—a series of variations, inspired by Orcagna's frescoes at Pisa, on the Dies Irae. Alongside lyrical reminiscences of opera we find here ferocious passages of metallic dissonance which, in their simultaneous use of appoggiaturas and the resolutions, suggest Bartók and Stravinsky (Ex. 14):

Ex. 14, Liszt: *Totentanz*

Even Liszt's fantasy on the waltz from Gounod's *Faust* seems dominated by the spirit of Mephisto; for Gounod's footling tune, as redolent of the tawdry, gas-lit glamour of the Parisian theatre as it is remote from Goethe, is transformed by Liszt's harmonic ellipses and sinister virtuosity into a devil-dance. In the haunted, tritonal metamorphosis of the tune in the coda and the hectic chromatic stretto, a world shatters in ruins. The showpiece designed to amuse Society acquires an almost Berliozian, apocalyptic quality: at least we can see that this piece of ostensible frivolity came from the same mind that created the

Mephisto waltzes and the appalling vision of chaos in the first section of the symphonic poem, *Hunnenschlacht*.

Whether as romantic Hero or as Mephistopheles—though especially in his Satanic role—Liszt betrays a fondness for harmonic processes (augmented chords, mediant relationships, whole-tone progressions, chromatically altered notes) which weaken tonality. A large-scale piece like the *Bénédiction de Dieu* is formally convincing because it is mainly an elaboration of a single melody; virtuosity becomes creative expansion. In the more demonic ranges of his imagination he cannot, however, rely simply on lyrical decoration; the stranger are his harmonic progressions, the more urgent is his search for a new formal criterion. From this point of view, the key-work in his career is the Piano Sonata of 1855. Liszt had long been fascinated by Schubert's 'Wanderer' Fantasia, which is a four-movement sonata built on transformations of a single theme, the keys of the four movements standing in mediant relationship to one another. In his own sonata, Liszt telescopes the movements into one, and builds all the material on four interrelated motives stated at the beginning. He expresses a much more violent alternation of moods than does Schumann in his cycles of piano pieces; and the wilder the alternation the more important is it that the moods should preserve their inner identity. So the work is unified not by the classical disposition of key centres, but by a vestigial 'serial' technique. The motives are transmuted into widely contrasted themes: the snarling, demoniacal phrase derived from the diminished seventh becomes nostalgically lyrical; the sinister repeated note figure is metamorphosed into cantabile grandeur, or into pathetic *bel canto* (Ex. 15):

Ex. 15. Liszt: Piano Sonata

The romantic lover and the devil are synonymous, for all the actors in this drama are aspects of a single ego; as were the actors in Wagner's later music dramas. Liszt's embryonic serial technique is, indeed, an anticipation of Wagner's creative method far more significant than the superficial resemblances between the chromaticism of the two composers. We may note how frequently—especially in the quicker sections of his sonata—Liszt employs a quasi-Wagnerian 'harmonic polyphony'; the music becomes a tissue of linear motives, derived from a harmonic progression.

The sonata is Liszt's greatest virtuoso piece; yet its formal discovery no longer necessarily entails virtuosity. Henceforth, pianism was in itself less important for Liszt than composition. His celebrity had been not merely European, but international. In a specially constructed, luxuriously appointed coach, with his medallions and insignia and his three hundred and sixty-five cravats (one for each day of the year), he had performed to the barbarians among the minarets of remotest Russia and Turkey. Now he voluntarily relinquished fame and riches and retired to Weimar, to devote his energies to composition and also—with un-Wagnerian altruism—to the cause of progressive musicians everywhere. Again, Wagner *is* the prophet, who can see and feel nothing but the force of his prophecy. Liszt acts the prophet, seriously and sincerely, becoming the guide and mentor of the rising generation. Whereas Wagner accorded to Liszt no more than a grudging homage in so far as he identified himself with the Wagnerian cause, Liszt reverenced Wagner with something approaching idolatry; he was prepared to abandon his own creative work if only he could raise adequate funds to finance a production of *The Ring*. Yet though Wagner's genius is self-justificatory, he himself admitted that "since my acquaintance with Liszt's compositions my treatment of harmony has become very different from what it was formerly". He added, characteristically, that "it is, however, indiscreet to babble this secret to the whole world".

This curious blend of self-advertisement with humility in Liszt's make-up is evident when, at Weimar, he took time off from conducting other people's music to work on his own compositions. At the age of thirty-six he returned, as it were, to school. He studied orchestration, for he realized that the formal conception inherent in his sonata could achieve a more satisfactory resolution in orchestral terms. His symphonic poems all have a literary basis which is also a musical idea: they deal with the Artist as Hero, his tribulations and ultimate triumph. The basis of the musical structure is usually a quite primitive and traditional ternary or rondo form; but the works adapt the technique of Liszt's sonata to the orchestra in being mono-thematic. The various aspects of the Hero's ego are separate, yet the same; and the form of the music is the revelation of their identity. Liszt does not create themes through conflict, as Beethoven does; his music, like Wagner's, is self-revelation rather than evolution. But although his substitution of repetition for development sometimes creates an easy alternative to composition, Liszt is not necessarily wrong in principle because he differs from classical tradition. Indeed, the closer he approaches to Beethoven the less convincing he tends to be; his 'apotheosis' codas, for instance, are usually an intention rather than creative realization.

Yet the historical importance of Liszt's symphonic poems can hardly be overestimated. He achieved Schumann's unconscious ambition, creating a technique whereby the fluctuating passions of the personal sensibility could be organized not merely in miniature, but on an extended scale. Perhaps it is not fortuitous that both Schumann and Liszt scored in a manner dictated by the movements of their hands at a keyboard. The difference was that Liszt's piano texture was itself of 'orchestral' richness and variety. Texturally as well as formally, he had more to teach his *immediate* successors than Berlioz. Although Wagner would have found his salvation in any case, it is hardly excessive to say that Liszt showed the way to all post-classical orchestral composers, and most of all to those who, like the Russian school, were the least deeply rooted in tradition.

The ultimate revelation of Liszt's genius comes, appropriately enough, in a symphonic version of Goethe's *Faust*—a supreme masterpiece that epitomizes at once the romantic yearning to make the ego self-sufficient, and the Satanic spirit of denial. The Faust theme of the first movement and its various mutations are Liszt as the arbiter of human destiny. The theme is significantly Wagnerian in being based on a series of augmented triads—and so almost entirely harmonic in its implications; the 'new man' brings with him a new tonal world. The Marguerite theme of the second movement is Woman in relation to Liszt—and the passive side of his own nature. In the last movement, portraying Mephistopheles, the same themes are metamorphosed into snarling venom. Frequently one feels in Liszt's music that the Satanic impulse is the strongest; in the companion symphony, inspired by Liszt's other literary hero, Dante, the Inferno is much more convincing than the Paradiso. The 'Faust' Symphony, however, is so deeply felt that the Devil does not have the last word. His malformations are restored to pristine beauty in a thrilling choral epilogue, where for once the apotheosis is justified. Perhaps it is precisely because Liszt knew so much about the Devil at first hand that the religious resolution impresses us. Certainly it points the way to the last phase of his work, when this surprising virtuoso, having relinquished the concert platform for the gospel of Art, dedicated his art to the gospel of God.

We cannot say that he experienced a religious conversion, for even as a youth he had been fascinated by the glamour of Catholic ritual. If there is an element of theatricality in his final admission to the Faith, we have seen that theatricality is the essence of his temperament, not to be confused with insincerity. Apart from Bruckner, most of the great composers of the nineteenth century—Schubert, Berlioz, Brahms, Wagner, Verdi— were agnostic. Liszt was genuinely a man of faith, according to his own rather lurid lights; his attempts to reform Catholic church music was thus a profoundly serious undertaking, whether or no it was successful. If he was sincere, he had to create a church music that grew from the demands of his own nature. The Church might be unchanging, as God certainly was. But man's attitude to it and Him changed inevitably; and one did no honour to God or the Church by pretending otherwise.

St. Elizabeth—the first of the gargantuan creations of Liszt's Roman period—is thus a very operatic kind of oratorio; and *Christus* employs a polyphony which is as harmonically rooted as that of the Piano Sonata or of *Tristan*. Liszt had already experimented with a highly chromatic polyphony in piano works like the *Weinen, Klagen* Variations and in the Organ Fantasia and Fugue on B-A-C-H. In these works he often approaches atonality—a chromaticism so extreme as to be without even an implied tonal centre. The pretence of strict fugal writing is not sustained much longer than in the Piano Sonata; but even more than in that revolutionary work it is the serial interrelations of the motives that keep the music from collapse. In Liszt's very last works this disintegrative, sensuous atonality is paradoxically combined with vocal, Gregorian modality, creating—especially in *Via Crucis*, a series of meditations for soli, chorus, and organ—a brooding, involuted ecstasy to which there is no parallel in nineteenth-century music. The glowing, continuous texture of *Parsifal* seems, in comparison, supremely self-confident. *Via Crucis* has some resemblance to the most advanced chromatic writing of the early seventeenth century; only whereas a composer such as Jacopus Gallus starts from vocal modality and disintegrates it into the chromatic *frisson*, Liszt works the other way round. Chromatic disintegration and whole-tone ambiguity seem to be seeking resolution in serene modality. Liszt seeks, and does not find. The poignancy of this music is conditional on its senile fragmentariness; and something the same is true of the single symphonic poem which he composed in these final years. The last movement of *From the Cradle to the Grave* is called "To the Tomb: the Cradle of the Future Life". Again a spare linear chromaticism and ambiguous whole-tone progressions create an atmosphere of hovering expectancy. The music lives between sleeping and waking; but what we are waking to is indeterminate.

We find the same disturbing fragmentariness in the small piano pieces and songs which are the secular counterpart of the ecclesiastical works of his last years. It would be difficult to imagine music superficially more remote from the flamboyance of his youth. In the third and last book of the *Années de Pèlerinage* the water-music of *Les Jeux d'Eaux à la Villa d'Este* has acquired a lucid precision that suggests Ravel; and while the two beautiful threnodies, *Aux Cyprès de la Villa d'Este*, preserve the operatic melodies and arpeggiated accompaniments, the texture is sparse, the harmonic progressions epigrammatic (consider the Tristanesque opening of the second piece). Liszt the romantic lover here recollects in tranquillity; the mane of hair has grown white instead of golden, but it sits well on the Abbé's robes. Mephistophelian fire may still dart from his eyes, too; the virtuosity of the last *Mephisto* waltzes is sharp, brittle, more scarifying in its restraint than the romantically 'horrid' rhetoric of the 'Dante' Sonata. The very last pieces are perhaps not so much fully-fledged artistic creations as sketches towards new worlds of thought and feeling. The *Czardas Macabre* suggests

Bartók in being based largely on barbaric parallel fifths. *Nuages Gris* is a keyless study in the impressionistic use of augmented triads; *Unstern* creates nightmare from whole-tone progressions and harmonic ostinatos. In the last songs, the vocal line is mostly in fragmentary, non-tonal recitative, while the piano part is exiguous. Usually the songs peter out on an unresolved dissonance. The most remarkable of them is (significantly) a setting of Musset's 'J'ai perdu ma force et ma vie'. The barless *parlando* vocal writing, the unresolved appoggiaturas, the aphoristic enharmonic modulations remind us that though Liszt was born two years after Haydn's death, he died only two years before the birth of Alban Berg.

The suggestion of Bartók in the last piano pieces is interesting in view of the fact that in old age Liszt developed an intense, perhaps nostalgic devotion to things Hungarian. The early Hungarian Rhapsodies are Liszt playing at gipsies. But the Hungarian element in the song *Die Drei Zigeuner* or the weird piano piece *Sunt Lachrymae Rerum* uses the stark texture and irregular rhythms of folk-music to effect a dissolution of traditional tonality and form. In discovering the folk, Liszt paradoxically discovers his own loneliness and disillusion. It is significant that the last pieces are not especially pianistic, nor do they suggest any instrument except possibly a spectre of the human voice. At the end of his life Liszt the play-actor no longer addresses an audience. He talks to himself, as did Bach in *The Art of Fugue* or Mozart in his last chamber works. Nor is it an accident that his fragmentary self-communing should seem—in comparison with the profound lucidity of Bach or Mozart—an old man's mumble.

It is revealing that the most artistically successful of these last piano pieces should be not one of the Hungarian evocations, but the two versions of *La Lugubre Gondole*, a queer, spectral elegy on a passionately operatic life. The piece opens with unisonal recitative, rocking on the neutral diminished seventh; the yearning upward sixths of Liszt's youth droop in fragmentary, linear chromaticism. When the arpeggiated barcarolle accompaniment tentatively appears it oscillates dreamfully between the major and minor triad, suggesting the enigmatic harmonic style of Liszt's great virtuoso successor, Busoni. But the waves of the arpeggios cannot flow. The music clogs in chromatically descending six-three chords, over which fragments of recitative

grind dissonantly. The music fades out in unison recitative, metreless, without tonality (Ex. 16):

Ex. 16. Liszt: La Lugubre Gondole

There is no music in the nineteenth century which disrupts tonality so completely as this linearly chromatic piece: for even *Tristan* implies a long-range tonal architecture, while Chopin's harmonic chromaticism is merely a transitory disintegration. It is ironic that Liszt should have thought of *La Lugubre Gondole* as a premonition of the death of Wagner, for whose cause he had sacrificed so much. Partly through Liszt's efforts, Wagner had found complete fulfilment; Liszt ends with this pathetic whimper. Yet it is Liszt, even more than Berlioz, who looks to the future: directly in the technique of the symphonic poem, which became the basic constructional principle that succeeded the sonata; more remotely in the 'expressionism' of his final epigrams. Berlioz preserved a visionary grandeur which we cannot aspire to. Liszt's ultimate fragmentariness goes home to us acutely, for we live in the wake of the disintegration he so honestly recorded. His honesty is the more impressive because he had been an actor all his life. When the play no longer interested him, he was no longer able to create an integrated work of art. But his stammered ejaculations are profoundly touching in their incoherence. We accept them as our birthright. We would complete them if we could.

3

THE RUSSIAN NATIONALISTS

Liszt, hero of romanticism, was also a great cosmopolitan, a citizen of Europe, as Lasso had been in the sixteenth century or Handel in the eighteenth. Lasso and Handel both lived and worked in three countries, spoke and thought in at least three languages. Even Byrd in the sixteenth century or Bach in the eighteenth—composers who did not travel widely and who worked within a relatively local culture—employed a musical language which was intelligible all over Europe. Haydn, living in seclusion on the Esterházy estate, was international in approach as well as in renown; Mozart, as much Italianate as German, would have considered an aggressive nationalism in music—or in life—bad taste. With the development of the 'democratic' sonata, however, we can detect the beginnings of a change. Beethoven, trained in the same European tradition as Mozart, hints that *The Magic Flute* is Mozart's best work partly because it is the most German. We have seen to what enormities this attitude was to lead in the career of Wagner.

Gradually, the cult of the individual nation grows alongside the cult of the individual personality. National differences complement the inexhaustibly surprising differences between human beings; and the nineteenth century becomes the age of cut-throat competition in both personal and political life. Naturally, a preoccupation with 'nationhood' is most vigorously evident in small countries which were just growing to political con-sciousness (we may recall Liszt's mild mania for things Hungarian during his last years): or in a large country which had no deep roots in the cultural heritage of Europe. Russia became the nerve-centre of musical nationalism because she had long been an outsider from the European community. Having been untouched by that vast, complex phenomenon we call the Renaissance, she had moved straight from medieval feudalism to eighteenth-century autocracy and, incipiently, to revolution.

In so doing, she had suffered a cultural bifurcation. The ruling aristocracy spoke and thought in French, and fostered French and Italian art; the peasant community spoke and thought in Russian and lived out their passions in an indigenous folk-art. In Elizabethan England folk-art and the European conventions of 'art' music mutually enriched one another, for Elizabethan society involved a homogeneous interrelation of all classes. Even Haydn and Mozart, living in a relatively heterogenous community, did not feel that their music was in any way opposed to popular music. But the European elements in eighteenth-century Russian music were simply importations. The music was created mainly by Frenchmen and Italians for Russians who wanted to become as nearly French and Italian as possible. The European could not be absorbed into the local culture, since, apart from folk-music—which the aristocracy despised—no local culture existed.

The tradition of Russian 'art' music, like the Russian literary tradition, thus begins to appear only when revolution is incipient. Consider the career of Glinka [1803–1857], whose hypochondria was perhaps a sign of senility in a world that had had its day. He was the son of a rich landowner. After a pampered childhood, he moved to St. Petersburg, where he lived the life of a young man of good birth, fashion, and fortune. He dabbled in musical composition, as one among many mild diversions; and the music he wrote, reflecting the brittle merriment of serenades, balls, and opera parties, was inevitably amateurish in technique, Italian in manner. He then travelled briefly in Germany, where he gained some acquaintance with the music of Mozart, Cherubini, and Beethoven: and more extensively in Italy, where he revelled in the delights of Bellini and Donizetti. At the height of these frolics, however, "homesickness led me to the idea of writing in Russian". Italian opera, he felt, needed the Italian sun; he had to create a music which belonged to his moody and volatile people ("for us it is a matter either of frantic merriment or bitter tears . . . love is always linked with sadness"). Naturally, he chose to write an opera, because opera was the only form he was familiar with; naturally, with the amateur's enthusiasm, he began to compose it *ad hoc*, before he had even seen the libretto. The opera which finally emerged, on his return home, was *A Life for the Czar*; in 1836 it was produced at court with considerable pomp. Superficially, with its mingling of big choral numbers and dance scenes, it resembles a French grand opera: while the vocal writing for the soloists and most of the instrumental accompaniments are—for all their technical gaucherie—charmingly Rossinian. Yet the essence of the work lies not in its fashionable emulation of Western manners, but in its portrayal of peasant life. Somewhat to the dismay of his aristocratic audience—and possibly some-what to his own consternation—Glinka had produced an opera about peasants rather than about Czars; for in the choruses and the orchestral dances he recalled the folk melodies and rhythms which he had heard in his country childhood. His opera had been prompted not by aesthetic ideals, still less by a desire to express himself, but by the observation and imitation of the life around him. Only he was discovering, perhaps painfully, that 'real' life was not the world of fashion to which he had been committed. It was the Russia remotely remembered from his childhood: which seemed to be as eternally unchanging as the rhythms of the folk-songs that sinuously wound themselves around a single note; which was in fact being changed in the process of becoming articulate.

Glinka's only other attempt at opera, *Russlan and Ludmilla*, is a great advance on the first, partly because the fantastical subject suits his empirical methods, partly because his technique has improved with experience. The well-known overture, for instance, shows that he could on occasion control classical form effectively, without sacrificing his incidental delight in harmonic surprise and in rhythmic or colouristic excitement: the whole-tone passage for trombones in the coda provides a genuine, if unorthodox, climax to sonata drama. On the whole, however, *Russlan* is a more subversive opera than *A Life for the Czar*, technically if not politically. The fantastic subject suggests the use of more barbaric, sometimes Oriental, kinds of folk-song, far removed from traditional diatonicism; and this in turn influences the harmony. In particular, the use of folk-scales with the sharp fifth encourages the Russian partiality for aug-mented triads, for false relations,* and for 'colouristic' oscill-ations between tonic major and relative minor (the third of the subdominant minor triad becomes enharmonically identical with the seventh of the relative minor). Many of Glinka's most

---

* FALSE RELATIONS: the simultaneous or closely adjacent sounding of two notes a semi-tone apart, usually the major and minor third. See Part II, p. 314.

astonishing harmonic passages are directly modelled on peasant-band music: for instance, the telescoping of tonic and dominant in the Caucasian *lezginka* in Act IV. This harmonic effect—like the orgiastic dances or choruses in five-four or seven-four time, and the sharp, barrel-organ acidities of the orchestration—lead on directly to the early work of Stravinsky. Glinka may have learned something from Weber in creating a music of fantasy; yet the core of this opera lies not in its unreality, but in his pungent imitation of sounds he had actually heard.

It cannot be said that the idiom Glinka creates is self-consistent, since the two main roots of his music would seem to be mutually irreconcilable. Folk-songs are melodies complete in themselves; Russian folk-songs, in particular, tend to move in short reiterated periods, and to oscillate around a fixed point. They can be repeated, incrementally, in varied orchestral colours; but they cannot be developed, either through lyrical expansion (as in operatic melody) or still less through the tonal argument of the sonata. Hence a desire to compose nationalistic music almost necessitates an episodic technique, while encouraging an interest in orchestral titillation. The episodic method of composition may be convincing, and would seem to be intimately related to the Russian approach to life as well as art. But it is bound to depend largely—and dangerously—on 'inspiration'. The composer who creates from moment to moment, from bar to bar, may lose sight of the whole in his preoccupation with the parts. We know from accounts of Balakirev's teaching that the Russian nationalists habitually criticized each other's works in this empirical fashion, commenting on a chord here, a modulation there. They wanted their music to be effective, exciting, at a given moment. They trusted to genius to see that the moments, put together, made sense; and genius sometimes, not always, obliged.

Balakirev himself [1837–1910], the senior member and perhaps the most powerful personality among the Big Five, is the most conspicuous exponent of the Russian principle of hit-or-miss. By the time he started to compose, German symphonic music, as well as Italian and French opera, had penetrated to Russia. His symphonic works have, however, little in common with the classical tradition. In his early B minor *Overture on Russian Themes*, for instance, he simply strings the tunes together in the manner of Glinka's fantasias. The themes are brilliantly treated and decorated in harmonic and orchestral terms, for Balakirev is technically much more adept than his predecessor; but they do not make a whole. In *Russia*, on the other hand, Balakirev uses virtually the same method in treating folk-songs: only genius takes possession. Though the themes do not develop, they coalesce in a structure of extraordinary power.

Much the same is true of the fantastic virtuoso piece for piano, *Islamey*. The work is modelled on the virtuoso pieces of Liszt, who made so deep an impression when he visited Russia. But Balakirev's Oriental folk-themes are much more static than Liszt's Italianate melodies; indeed, the themes are less important than the profusion of harmonic and pianistic 'colour' they provoke. Pianistic decoration—an aural titillation—becomes itself a creative act. Balakirev's two symphonies, which he tinkered at over a period of thirty years, are not radically different in approach. The motto theme of the introduction to the C major is extended in monothematic elaboration, in varying contexts of harmonic and orchestral colour. The music has a tremendous barbaric power; but it is not a dramatic argument, however logical its thematic structure may be. The technique has something in common with that of Liszt's symphonic poems; and there is a similar relationship between the method of Liszt's Piano Sonata and Balakirev's remarkable Sonata in B flat minor. Though Balakirev's work is in four separate movements, it is impregnated with thematic relationships which are varied repetitions, rather than development. The first movement is a most striking fusion of sonata and fugue, in which the subject— a long, sinuous Russian *cantilena*—is equally remote from classical notions of fugue or sonata, while being superbly devised for creative elaboration. Whether it is conceived in orchestral or pianistic terms, Balakirev's music thus owes its power to its rhythmic momentum, to its bold scoring, and to the power of the themes to proliferate in ornamental arabesque. Balakirev's obsessional partiality for side-stepping modulations (especially from D major to D flat major and from B flat minor to B minor, the four keys being interrelated) is relevant in this connexion. The modulations are an incidental intensification: an elaboration rather than a point in an argument.

The First Symphony of Borodin [1833–1887] is an even more remarkable example of this anti-traditional tendency. He too was an amateur who worked at his compositions over a number of years. In small works, such as the exquisitely written quartets or his French rather than Italianate songs, he proves that he had command of an assured, even polished European technique. Indeed, if we compare his use of unresolved seconds in the song *The Dark Forest* with that in the song *The Sleeping Princess*, it would seem that he was perhaps the first composer to reveal the subtle relationship between empirical primitivism and a sophisticated nervous impressionism* (Ex. 17):

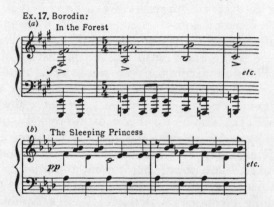

Ex. 17. Borodin:
(a) In the Forest
(b) The Sleeping Princess

Moreover, whereas Balakirev's themes are usually derived from folk-song or are relatively undistinguished, Borodin's themes attain—within a restricted range, oscillating around the fourth, third, and augmented second—a most personal, expressive pliancy. Any apparent oddities in his symphonic technique are therefore unlikely to be due to deficient inventiveness or skill. If the first movement of his E flat Symphony looks superficially like an orthodox classical sonata, but does not in fact behave like one, we may suspect that the reason is that Borodin did not intend it to.

The terrific rhythmic impetus of this first movement of the E flat Symphony carries the music onwards; while the modulations tend to have an almost contrary effect. Sharing Balakirev's partiality for the side-stepping modulation, Borodin will make the most abstruse enharmonic transition, only to return to the chord and the ostinato rhythm form which he had started; anything approaching the Beethovenian notion of evolving tonality is avoided. When we examine the movement

---

* For instance, between Debussy and the Stravinsky of *The Rite of Spring*.

in detail we find that it is in fact no longer a dualistic structure. The first and second subjects are not after all contrasted; they are interrelated fragments which are varied and integrated until finally they become a theme. This is different from the technique of Liszt's symphonic poems, which thematically unify widely disparate feelings; for whereas Liszt's themes do not—any more than Balakirev's—grow, Borodin creates a theme in the course of the movement. Beethoven sometimes does this, but never stops there. More normally, the process which takes place in Borodin's movement has gone on in Beethoven's mind and sketch-books before the composition begins—and the composition is the revelation of the themes' destiny. In this sense, Borodin's technique in this movement is as original in its primitivism as is Beethoven's in its maturity.

The other movements of Borodin's E flat Symphony make no attempt to establish any organic relationship to the first; they might be part of a pleasing, more than normally competent, Russian suite. Nowhere else, perhaps, did he approach this deep discovery of Russian primitivism. The implications of the technique of incremental repetition are, however, apt to crop up in his most civilized sonata movements. Even his opera, *Prince Igor*, is not so much a drama as an epic, presented episodically in a series of tableaux; and Borodin achieves an unexpected cohesive force by using throughout the score a number of motives, derived from the contours and rhythms of folk-music. They are not leitmotives; they are an application to opera of the technique whereby motives in themselves static are varied, as they are in Balakirev and in Borodin's own instrumental works. To achieve this unity out of episodic moments is even more difficult in a large-scale work like an opera than it is in a symphonic piece, though the composer has, of course, the element of theatrical illusion to help him. In *Prince Igor* the conventional Western operatic elements are not musically integrated with the Russian and Oriental elements, masterly though the score intermittently is. Perhaps one might say that the years which Borodin spent on *Prince Igor* found their ultimate justification in his B minor Symphony, a work which expresses, with epigrammatic trenchancy, the opera's essence. The unisonal opening, with its reiterated notes and its oscillations between flat second and the major and minor third, seems to epitomize Borodin's creative personality (Ex. 18):

Ex. 18. Borodin: Symphony No.2

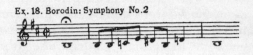

Borodin thought more convincingly in instrumental than in operatic terms; but the greatest—and most revolutionary—work of Russian nationalism was to be àn opera of precisely the epical and episodic type which Borodin had struggled with. Moussorgsky's career [1839–1881] was also a struggle, both creatively and spiritually. In his case, however, the vindication of the amateur's empiricism is his genius. In no composer are genius and ignorance so inevitably linked.

Born in 1839, he came of a wealthy landowning family and was intended for the Army, though he resigned his commission in 1858. As a youthful dilettante he composed a little piano music in the style of the minor romantics. The realization that he was a composer came simultaneously with the realization that he had not the slightest interest in the kind of music he had been writing. He was not merely anti-academic; he was also anti-artistic in the sense that he believed, or affected to believe, that art was simply the revelation of truth. "That object is beautiful", he said, "which speaks to us of life." He sought "not beauty for itself, but truth, whatsoever it may be". And the cosmopolitan society into which he had been born was neither life nor truth. Now that he had cast off his cosmopolitan past he felt "reborn; everything Russian" was close to him. Life, as opposed to make-believe, was the life of the Russian peasants. In his fragmentary autobiography (written most significantly in the third person) he said: "Under the influence of his nurse, he became familiar with the old Russian folk-tales. It was mainly his familiarity with the very spirit of the life of the people that impelled him to extemporize music before even knowing the most elementary rules of piano-playing." This may or may not have been true. It was certainly what Moussorgsky wanted to think; and it was certainly true that he developed so deep a love for the peasants that he seemed to be identified with them, moving "in another world, in a far-away past". But in thus revealing the collective spirit of his race, he would destroy a degenerate world and, like Tolstoy, create a new, instinctive life from the ashes of the past. This was why, for him as for Tolstoy, art could never be an end in itself, but must be communication, of the most direct kind possible. He could not be content even with Balakirev's abstract racialism; after his juvenalia, all his music is inherently dramatic.

His concern with 'reality' implied too a passionate desire to free his country's music from Italian and German slavery. Nothing could better indicate the connexion between nationalism and individualism than Moussorgsky's comment that his *Night on the Bare Mountain*—an operatic scena without voices— was "Russian and original": it would never have occurred to Handel or Mozart to claim either nationality or originality for their compositions. In creating a "Russian and original" style he did not have to work entirely alone. He had the example of the popular elements in Glinka's operas, the early symphonic works of Balakirev, and Dargomyzhsky's rather pedestrian attempt, in *The Stone Guest*, to create a melodic line from the inflexions of speech. Interest in the contours of peasant speech became the most positive influence on Moussorgsky's attempt to slough off tradition; we can see the immediate result of his efforts in the short opera, *The Marriage*, based naturalistically on Gogol's brusquely comic tale. Moussorgsky said that he had here tried to note down those changes in intonation which crop up in human conversation for the most futile causes, on the most insignificant words. . . . I should like to make my characters speak on the stage exactly as people do in real life, without exaggeration or distortion, and yet write music which will be thoroughly artistic. . . . What I foretell is the melody of life, and not of classicism. . . . I call it well-thought-out, justified melody. Some day the unexpected ineffable song will arise against classical melody, intelligible to one and all."

In *The Marriage* Moussorgsky has hardly succeeded in his ambition to make speech-melody 'artistic', for the piece is not much more than a play in music, with speech sometimes intensified to chant, harmonized with a deliberately rudimentary starkness. These harmonies were arrived at empirically at the piano, usually prompted by the words or dramatic situation: consider the notorious coruscation of parallel seconds suggested by the word 'nasty'. But if Moussorgsky fails to achieve artistry in his first attempt at the complex art of opera, he soon does so in the medium of the song. His earliest songs preserve some

contact with traditional lyricism; his mature songs have become
dramatic scenas in miniature. In all of them his startling originality manifests itself in an un-Wagnerian forgetfulness of self;
he finds himself in becoming identified with people utterly
remote from his own personality. The seven Nursery Songs, for
instance, use the incantatory rhythms and pentatonic formulae
of folk-song and have the direct, unsentimental simplicity of the
nursery jingle. Yet they are profound studies of the workings of
a child's mind, which only a man of Moussorgsky's intuitive
imagination could have written. One cannot say that the
parlando vocal parts are 'accompanied' by the piano; the song-
speech is involved in the drama of the piano's fragmentary
ostinatos, its abruptly changing rhythm, its grammatically unrelated concords, sevenths, and ninths. Even the most abstruse
dissonance is used empirically, as in the middle-period works of
Debussy. The suggestion of Debussy is even more potent in the
cycle called *Sunless*, where the *parlando* line reflects a Dostoevsky-
like introspection instead of a childlike innocence: consider, in
the second song, the weird use of the pedal D, and the unresolved six-three chord which leaves the singer's pain suspended
in the void of his solitariness (Ex. 19):

Ex. 19. Moussorgsky: *Sunless*

But the greatest of Moussorgsky's songs are undoubtedly
the *Songs and Dances of Death*. If we may still call these dramatic
scenas, they are so starkly 'truthful' that no stage presentation
could ever do justice to the honesty of Moussorgsky's imagination. The meeting of the drunkard with Death on the lonely
road has the same simple, impersonal acceptance of reality as
the children's songs: yet nothing could be more frightening than
the gradual intrusion of the chromatic wriggle into the mono-
tonous pedal note under the wailing folk-lamentation; or more
desolate than the peace of the empty fifths at the end. The
Cradle Song is a colloquy between a mother and Death, fighting
for her sick child. The two characters are sharply differentiated

in this tiny operatic conflict. Death's hypnotic lullaby to the
child droops caressingly from the tonic through a tritone, then
a fifth, then a sixth, on to the third of the minor triad: an
unexpected, ambiguous 'resolution' after the warmly sinister
chromatics. The final descent, in the last repeat, to the low
tonic instead of the third conveys with uncanny simplicity
Death's last, tranquil word. There is no more to be said; yet
this minor triad reverberates in the memory (Ex. 20):

Ex.20. Moussorgsky; *Cradle Song*

One finds the same impersonality in the grinding dissonances
that accompany Death's appearance on the battlefield in
Field-Marshal Death: or in the effect of the ninth chord, followed
by the nagging, diminishing tonic pedal, that occurs in Death's
dreamy, wooing, modal incantation in the *Serenade*. In the
context, we are not sure whether that ninth is the bliss of peace
or the honey of corruption; fear is inextricably twined in our
welcome. Such 'moments of truth' are certainly among the
most remarkable manifestations of instinctive genius in music;
yet Moussorgsky's greatness, and the intensity of his imagination, are revealed still more in the fact that, from a concaten-
ation of such moments, he was able to create an episodic yet
cumulative work on a vast scale. *Boris Godunov* is both a psychological drama of guilt and conscience and an epic of destiny
and race. Moussorgsky understands 'history' because he knows
that history is made of the experience of individual human
beings. To create *Boris* called both for Moussorgsky's imaginative insight and for his detachment.

If one looks at any particular passage in the score, the
technique seems much the same as that of the songs. Yet the
various episodes form a whole, without calling on the recognized
methods of achieving tonal and theatrical coherence. Consider,
for instance, the scene of the Clocks. Boris, grimly reflecting on
his guilt, is interrupted by the wild flurry of the squabble
between the nurse and his young son's parrot. Feodor, left alone

with his father, offers to explain what happened. He tells the story in a simple folk-monotone, in rigid periods alternating between three-four and five-four. The phrases tend to be pentatonic, harmonized with simple diatonic concords, often without the third. When he begins to describe the hubbub itself the centre of 'modality' shifts abruptly from F sharp to F, and the droning phrases are now harmonized with instable seventh chords, with a bass rocking between a tritone. Boris then sings—in G flat, the major of his son's initial modal F sharp—of his hopes for his son. His melodic line moves largely by step rather than by pentatonic thirds, within a very restricted range; it is accompanied by smoothly flowing triplets over long pedal notes on D flat and G flat, as opposed to the harmonic unrest of the parrot episode. Boris ends by warning Feodor of Councillor Shuisky's deceit. Meanwhile, Shuisky has entered, to tell Boris of the threat of rebellion. Boris rounds on him, his *parlando* phrases now accompanied by diatonic triads enharmonically related, then by seventh chords embellished with trills; the tonal instability increases the sense of shiftiness. Shuisky's phrases are also restricted in range, close to speech inflexion, but incline to be pentatonic, like Feodor's. As melody, they look innocent; but their innocence is belied by the fluctuating sevenths of the harmony; they are sweetly lyrical, cooing in their repetitiveness.

When Shuisky at last names Dmitri as the pretender, Boris utters a yell, and orders Feodor out of the room. He leaves, to the accompaniment of skirling chromatics that recall the parrot's flurrying. Boris tries to brush aside his fears, decrying the supernatural. The flowing triplets that accompanied his vision of Feodor as Czar return, in distorted chromaticism, in frenzied contrary motion. He pleads with Shuisky to confirm that he had in fact seen the boy Dmitri, dead: while the chromatics in contrary motion have become sustained, fateful minims. The contrary motion scales lose their chromaticism and become slowing moving crochets while Shuisky describes the dead boy, "a smile most gentle" on his lips, a toy still in his hand. The tonality is a modal C sharp, pentatonic in the more tender moments.

Boris's frayed nerves can sustain it no longer. He dismisses Shuisky—with an outburst of the contrary motion triplets; and at this moment the clocks start chiming. The pendulum swings between the notes of the tritone (the domestic madness of the

parrot episode has become a spiritual frenzy); the violins wriggle
in snake-like chromatics; brass and woodwind interject polytonal fanfares. This ghastly whirring and clanking accompanies Boris's strangled cries until an apparition of the dead
Dmitri appears before his fevered eyes. The pedal E flat returns
below string tremolandos; and provides a transition to the
wonderful close when the whirring is stilled in Boris's chromatically descending prayer for forgiveness. His voice finally sinks
to rest on the major third, over the timpani's pianissimo A flat.

Moussorgsky was certainly conscious of some of the subtle
interrelations that give cohesion to the sequential episodes of
Boris; but in most cases one suspects he was conscious only after
the event. *Boris Godunov* is a miracle of art almost fortuitously.
Moussorgsky rehashed it several times, accepted the advice of
Rimsky-Korsakov and of other people incompetent to give it,
worked simultaneously on other opera projects, none of which
came to fruition. His art has a frightening ludicity; his life is
chaos: and this is perhaps related to the fact that there is nothing
in his art that can be called love. The second version of *Boris*,
which develops the theme of Boris's personal crisis, is deeper
than the first, which considers the story mainly in national
terms; but in some ways the first version is more typically
Moussorgskian. In his art, he loses himself so completely in
becoming other people that he has nothing left to give. The
search for reality entailed a loss of identity that is almost
delirium. Moussorgsky drank himself to lunacy and death in
bringing a new world to birth.

The old world did not die easily. Throughout the nineteenth
century the two streams that flowed from the stylistic 'bifurcation' in Glinka's music ran parallel. The Russian revolutionary stream culminated in Moussorgsky's empirical genius; at
the same time the cosmopolitan cult of Italian, French, and
German art found in Tchaikowsky a personality intense, if not
strong, enough to recreate it in Russian terms. Nor is it an
accident that Tchaikowsky's work should centre around a
feverish search for love—around the attempt to mend the
sundered personal relationship.

Tchaikowsky [1840–1893] came from much the same background as Glinka, but both his nervous sensitivity and his
musical talent were more potent. He could not be content to
forget his nervous instability in vapid distractions; nor could

he accept an intermittent dilettantism in his creative work.
Glinka was the passive creature of a world in decay, his talents
vitiated by inertia. In Tchaikowsky, decay flares into neurosis.
His Chekovian anguish at times approaches insanity. Whereas
Moussorgsky, who probably suffered from the same psychological perversion, preserved his impersonal art free from the
contagion of his lunacy, Tchaikowsky used his art as a
safety-valve. Only in his music could he escape from the prison
of his pathological devotion to his family—above all, to his
mother. Schumann too had sought in domesticity a refuge from
a hostile world. But his domesticity was the normal, grown-up
relationship of man and wife. Tchaikowsky never grew up; the
desire to regress to the womb, which we all have in varying
degrees, remained the strongest impulse through the years of
his harried life.

His mother died when he was fourteen; this negative event
coloured his whole future. Almost immediately afterwards, he
began to compose; and when he said "undoubtedly I should
have gone mad but for music" we may—in the light of later
events—take his words as literal. For the rest of his days he
sought a substitute for the maternal relationship. His strange
relationship to his patroness, Mme von Meck, was the closest
he came to finding it; and both he and she were aware that their
weirdly passionate association could be sustained only so long
as they did not meet. He was the artist-son of her neurotic
imagination; she was the lover-mother he had lost—with the
additional advantage that she provided a comfortable income.
Debarred by his identification with mother and sister ("those
angels come down from Heaven") from normal relations with
women, Tchaikowsky became a homosexual: and a homosexual
obsessed by feelings of guilt. He embarked on his marriage
partly to stifle slander, partly to quiet his own sense of sin. The
result was an almost complete mental breakdown. After having
tried to commit suicide by contracting pneumonia, he was
unconscious for forty-eight hours. He never saw his nominal
wife again. Significantly, this second crisis in his life was associated with his supreme period of creative activity. He saved
himself from madness in creating *Eugene Onegin* and the Fourth
Symphony.

For, unlike Chopin and Schumann—also introverted artists
—Tchaikowsky had the pronounced histrionic streak which

often accompanies homosexuality. Involved in his nerves, he instinctively dramatized himself, whereas Moussorgsky shed the burden of self in identifying himself with others. Only by being, or pretending to be, proud of his oddness could Tchaikowsky save himself from the self-revulsion—and the doubts about his creative ability—which periodically over-whelmed him. The desire to be loved was inevitably involved with self-pity: and therefore with self-hatred, because of what he described as the 'Thing' in him that held love at bay.

Tchaikowsky's histrionic sense found an immediate echo in the music on which he was brought up, for this was almost all theatrical. In a sense, Tchaikowsky loved most the music that was furthest from his own introversion. The more subjective of nineteenth-century composers he disliked. Wagner he con-sidered a bore, maintaining that *Götterdämmerung* was inferior to the ballets of Delibes; even for Beethoven he had no more than a grudging respect. But Mozart was for him "the Christ of music"; and the Mozart he adored was the Italianate Mozart who, in opera, objectified passion in lyricism. Bellini, Rossini, and Verdi he admired ardently; Massenet, more understandably, moved him to tears. Among other French composers, he loved the ballets of Delibes: and considered Bizet's *Carmen* to be the greatest work of his time. *Carmen* was the kind of music he would liked to have written himself; for it was vibrant with life, colour-ful, passionate, dominated by a sense of fate; yet at the same time elegant, emotionally detached.

The detachment of Moussorgsky seemed to him barbarous; he set out to write music based on the very Italian, French, and German models which the nationalists had rejected. Yet because he was a Russian—and not the less because he belonged to a de-generating world—the music he created was very different from his models. Like the nationalists, Tchaikowsky had, as a child, been brought up on folk-song. For Moussorgsky folk-song had become the symbol of a new world; he loved folk-song as the expression of the 'collective soul' of his race, beyond personal feeling. For Tchaikowsky, the significance of folk-song was almost entirely personal; he loved it because it reminded him of his childhood, of his mother and sisters, of the security of home. For this reason his musical approach to folk-song is quite different from that of the nationalists. They felt the songs so inwardly that they could evolve techniques whereby folk-song became the basis of substantial works. Tchaikowsky, on the other hand, naturally thought in terms of Italian *cantilena* or the French dance tune; when he introduces folk-songs into his symphonic works they seem unhappy in their context. This is not because they are insensitively treated, but simply because they conflict with the melodic, harmonic, and orchestral language that came to him most naturally.

None the less, at a level below consciousness folk-song influenced Tchaikowsky profoundly. Folk-melody is not the essence of his thought, as it is with Balakirev or even Borodin; but his French and Italianate melody was modified by his nostalgic recollection of the folk-music of his childhood. This we can see most immediately, and most expressively, in his songs. In *Had I only known*, from opus 47, for instance, the singer is ostensibly a Russian peasant girl who has fallen in love with a dashing young man and been jilted. In the poem she recalls her love story—her tremulous desires, her joys, her despair. The song is both dramatic and lyrical. It opens with a piano introduction—a tootling little balalaika tune that seems to have no connexion with the song itself, though it is in fact thematically related, and a masterly piece of dramatic craftsmanship. For it sets the scene, providing the background of everyday trivialities, at once carefree and care-laden, against which the girl's personal experience is to be seen. Her opening phrase is broken, brief, folk-like in its continually drooping fourths. It is interspersed with a hypnotic repeated figure on the piano—a drone-like folk monotone which suggests the nagging thrust of her sorrow. The phrases rise sequentially, in cumulating despair, but always tend to droop back nervelessly to the piano figure's subdominant (this and other flatwards modulations are significantly more important in Tchaikowsky's music than modulations to the dominant and sharpwards). The drooping interval expands, the phrases grow more lyrical: until they lead into a 'middle' section in which the same phrases are transformed into a frenzied waltz. This is the familiar waltz-song of the cosmopolitan Tchaikowsky—the evocation of the glittering gaiety from which he is shut out. The phrases are still brief, obsessively repeated, but are now carried forward by the swirl of the rhythm. The climax comes in a tremendous cry of pain, in an unexpected irregular (five-bar) phrase, followed by a piano interjection based on feverish descending appoggiaturas. Thus the music returns to a retrospective, yearning repeat of the first section. The drooping phrase rests inert, on repeated Gs: until a wonderful lyrical arioso consummates the girl's passion. Then the balalaika tune sounds again, tinklingly, from afar. The world goes on, oblivious of our sufferings.

We can hardly doubt that the strange power of this song comes from Tchaikowsky's identification of the young woman with himself. Moussorgsky would have become the woman. Tchaikowsky makes the woman become himself, while at the same time his histrionic sense enables him to present his (her) suffering in quasi-operatic terms: from this point of view, the transition from folk-lamentation to operatic waltz and back is especially interesting. The larger part of Tchaikowsky's working life was spent on the creation of theatrical music. If he is not on the whole as successful as an opera composer as he is as a writer of songs, the reason is that he needed a libretto that—like this song—offered him a character and a situation close to his own. In this he is utterly distinct not only from Moussorgsky, but also from Verdi and Bizet—the two composers who, superficially, influenced him most.

When he did find such a libretto, however, he created, in *Eugene Onegin*, his masterpiece. Tatiana was a character with whom Tchaikowsky could—and on his own admission did—identify himself; and if we remember his dreadful account of the circumstances leading to his marriage, it would seem that there was more than a little of Onegin in his make-up also. It is interesting that he deprives Onegin of the sympathetic characteristics which Pushkin had given him, making him merely a negative foil to Tatiana's tender, hopeless passion; he is the hard world's dusty answer to the need for love. The setting of Pushkin's drama—the world of the small provincial land-owners—took Tchaikowsky back to his childhood, and enabled him to introduce both nostalgic folk-melodies and the gay, melancholy waltzes and mazurkas of the world of fashion. The central preoccupation with Tatiana's character naturally lent itself to the intimate lyrical style which Tchaikowsky adapted from Massenet and Bizet. The letter scene—which was the starting point as well as the core of the opera—achieves the direct simplicity which Tchaikowsky admired in Bizet. Its unbroken lyricism is harmonically more heavily charged, more scented, than that of the French composer, but it nowhere impedes the growth of the drama. The harmonization of the descending phrase with the chord of the flat sixth creates a pathos which seems, in the context, as Russian—but Chekovian rather than Pushkinesque—as it is inimitable (Ex. 21):

Ex. 21. Tchaikowsky: *Eugene Onegin*

A cliché of theatrical lyricism becomes related to the nagging iterations of the folk-lament. Something the same is true of the theme of the slow movement of the Fourth Symphony, on which Tchaikowsky was working at about the same time.

Only on one other occasion did Tchaikowsky find a libretto which, avoiding the historical or fantastical, dealt with a world he knew at first hand, and with a character sufficiently like himself to stimulate his interest. Pushkin's original story, *The Queen of Spades*, was much sharper, more satirical, more eighteenth-century in spirit than the libretto which Modest Tchaikowsky made from it. Yet the adaptation provides in Hermann a dark, frustrated lover who can become Tchaikowsky, while the merely potential union of Hermann and Lisa stands as a symbol of the desire for love, which remains unfulfilled. What frustrates fulfilment is the macabre figure of the aged Countess, a projection of the nervous frenzy of a world in senile decay. Although the opera is not as a whole convincing, the scene in the bedchamber, in which Hermann and the Countess confront one another, touches a nerve of neurotic horror which came from deep in Tchaikowsky's being, yet is magnificently realized as art. The hysteria is the more pointed by contrast with the snatches of a Grétry air which the Countess croons to herself as she makes her toilet. In the Countess the eighteenth-century aristocratic world has grown corrupt and nightmarish; in the Grétry tune we have an evocation of rococo elegance as it once was. Perhaps we can understand why Tchaikowsky adored Mozart. He once wrote in a letter to Mme von Meck: "You say that my worship of Mozart is quite contrary to my musical nature. But perhaps it is just because, being a child of my time,

I feel broken and spiritually out of joint, that I find consolation and rest in Mozart's music."

As it happens—and, of course, these things do not really happen by accident—the action of *The Queen of Spades* provides an opportunity for Tchaikowsky to introduce a masque in what is usually described as Mozartian pastiche. If the term is supposed to imply that the music is patched together from the ragbag of Mozartian cliché, it is unjustified; but the music is certainly a most exquisite and personal act of homage in which formulae of the rococo age merge into Tchaikowsky's lyricism, and into the chromatic extensions of his harmony. The eighteenth century becomes for Tchaikowsky a fairyland. Perhaps it is significant that the rococo scenes are a masque, not an opera. The voices are silent, or sing with stylized formality; the action becomes pantomime, a game. This helps us to understand why Tchaikowsky was supremely successful as a writer of ballet music: why all his ballets are based on fairy tales: and why the greatest of them, *The Sleeping Princess*, tells in dance and mime one of the fairy myths of the classical age. Nor is it an accident that Perrault's beautiful legend concerns the miraculous renewal of life by love.

Tchaikowsky's adagio melodies in *The Sleeping Princess* recall not so much Bizet and Massenet—nor even their immediate models, Delibes and Adolphe Adam—as Bellini, in whose elegiac lyricism operatic action was transmuted into an inner dream. It is almost as though, for Tchaikowsky, the fairy tale of Russian ballet seemed truer than life, because life itself was so strange. In precisely following Petipa's instructions—which were hardly less exacting than the mathematically measured schedule of the modern film score—Tchaikowsky could forget his neurosis in projecting emotion into the physical movements of the human body. There has never been music that more intimately provokes, as it is provoked by, the dance. Consider how in the famous waltz the conventional hemiola rhythm— the cross-accent of $3+3$ against $2+2+2$—grows from bodily movement while being the source of the superb momentum of the cantabile melody; consider still more how in the Rose Adagio physical gesture flows into such serenely balanced lines that it creates from movement a paradoxical immobility. At last, the mythical lovers of Tchaikowsky's imagination are united in a world of calm and grace. But their union is only make-believe; for Tchaikowsky's most perfect music depends on the admission of theatrical illusion. This eternal-seeming bliss is only mime, the artifice of movement which Petipa evokes from Tchaikowsky's muse; and the end of this greatest of classical ballets is musically most queer. After the penultimate, ecstatic restatement of the Rose Adagio which Beauty, awakened, dances with her Prince, everybody joins in an exuberant, fanfare-dominated mazurka. This can only be—one thinks—the end; as in all good fairy stories, everyone lives happily ever after. But it is not the end. The mazurka is followed by a coda which, though it may be majestic, is certainly not joyful. The tonality changes from resonant major to a stark minor, with a slight flavour of 'Russian' modality; the rhythms lose their extrovert flow, becoming frigidly symmetrical, austere. There is not the slightest hint, in this severely disciplined music, of the hysteria that we find in Tchaikowsky's more subjective symphonic and even operatic music. None the less, the effect is oddly—and on Tchaikowsky's part quite unconsciously—chilling. As the curtain falls the music dispels illusion. The stage lights are obliterated by the dark of reality; and what our eyes blink at, as we emerge from the theatre, is neither merry (like the mazurka) nor (like the Rose Adagio) serene.

Tchaikowsky was proud of his ballet music, and rebuked those critics who complained that his symphonic works were too reminiscent of the dance. Yet he also took himself very seriously as a symphonist: and believed that in his symphonies he was dealing with the reality which the illusory world of his ballets evaded. He could not understand that criticism of the ballet element in his symphonies did not discredit ballet music in general, let alone his own: that Taneiv was justified in pointing out that lyrical dance themes were no more suitable than folk-tunes for development in classical symphonic style; and were perhaps still less amenable to the kind of organization which Balakirev and Borodin explored in their symphonic works. Tchaikowsky hardly attempts to use folk-song symphonically, though he shares the nationalists' partiality for side-stepping modulations. He does, however, attempt to incorporate into his symphonies the big, self-contained song or dance tune; and he was only too sensitively aware that his problems as a symphonist derived from that fact. "The seams", he said, "always show, and there is no organic unity between the episodes." With careful revision, he can to some extent disguise this; but though he can superficially improve the form, he cannot fundamentally alter it, for he cannot alter the "essential qualities of my musical nature". Whether he wrote symphonies or overtures or symphonic poems, Tchaikowsky's compromise with classical tradition was almost always the same. He begins with a slow, atmospheric introduction; then follows an allegro, with a first subject, usually rather frantic, extended into sequential repetitions. Then comes a long bridge passage; and a second subject, strongly contrasted, usually slower and more lyrical (in *Romeo and Juliet* it is an operatic *cantilena*, in the Fourth Symphony a waltz). This, again, is sequentially extended. Then there is another long bridge passage, followed by a recapitulation of both themes and a coda, based on the introduction, or on a modified version of one of the allegro themes. This structure is essentially an alternation of episodes. In the classical sense there is no development at all, because the themes, though opposed, do not interact. The trouble lies, of course, in the bridge passages. Apart from the ubiquitous sequences, Tchaikowsky relies on ostinato figurations, agitato rhythmic motives, and sustained pedal points to create an illusion of continuity. Along with the sensationally modified scoring (the cantabile theme is almost always 'recapitulated' by all the strings in octaves, accompanied by skirls on the woodwind and brass chromatics), these devices certainly heighten the hysteria. But they do not make it less mechanical; they suggest, indeed, that Tchaikowsky's histrionics, divorced from theatrical projection, are partly self-induced.

Nor is there normally any relationship between the movements of Tchaikowsky's symphonies, as there is between the movements of a symphony of Mozart or Beethoven. The most completely successful movements are unadulterated ballet music, like the pizzicato movement from the Fourth (whether it was inspired by Delibes' *Sylvia* or by a balalaika orchestra), the waltz from the Fifth, or the bedraggled, slightly tipsy waltz in five-four from the Sixth. Only in this sixth and last symphony does Tchaikowsky begin to create a kind of symphony which is relevant to his nature; and this significantly proves to be closer to operatic techniques than to the classical ideal. It is not merely that the second subject resembles Don José's D flat aria from *Carmen*, nor that the excited semiquaver figuration of the first subject is strikingly similar to that in the final bedchamber scene of Verdi's *Otello*, both of which operas must have been fresh in Tchaikowsky's memory. Much deeper than this is the fact that there is now much more thematic interrelation both within the individual movements and in the work as a whole. In the first movement, for instance, the transition from the first to the second subject seems to consist of a banal sequence of descending scales; these, however, generate the declining phrase of the second subject, and its continuation proves to be a free inversion of the agitated semiquavers of the first subject. This and many similar transitions may not be very impressive as musical architecture: but as dramatic transitions, similar to those between the episodes of his *Eugene Onegin*, they would be entirely satisfying. Perhaps we may say that if Tatiana is a mask for Tchaikowsky himself, in the Sixth Symphony he dispenses with the mask and offers us self-dramatization in a strictly comparable technique. We may think that he writes better when he has the human voice and a theatrical situation to canalize his emotion. We may even think that he writes best of all when he accepts the limitations of the dance and lives in the illusion of mime, for his ballets, especially *The Sleeping Princess*, are undoubtedly his most consummately realized music. Yet not even the loveliest illusion is in the long run preferable to reality. So his richest, most rewarding music is in *Eugene Onegin*; and we can at least say that in the Sixth Symphony he was beginning to understand how the symphony might express his own strange, very partial, truth.

Moussorgsky, who intended to create a people's music which was anti-academic and even anti-artistic, proved a dead end in musical history; for he had virtually no influence on any composer except Debussy in his middle years, when he became the supreme musical representative of the cult of the Ivory Tower! Tchaikowsky, on the other hand, who was an artist of personal neurosis if ever there was one, and highly professional at that, has become the most popular of all 'classical' composers among the vast, musically illiterate public of industrialized Russia, Britain, and America; and has become so, moreover, on the strength of his most hysterically self-indulgent works. We do not need to deduce from this that industrial democracy has produced a society of psychopaths, for the potency of Tchaikowsky's melodic appeal is self-evident, and we all enjoy self-dramatization. We have none the less to admit that it is curious, if but obscurely revealing, that Tchaikowsky should thus have become equated with the Common Man. It is difficult to decide whether he or the Common Man would be the more appalled, could he see the other as he really was and is.

In some ways, at least, the plain man's partiality for Tchaikowsky is encouraging, for it is better to be alive and hysterically kicking than dead and canned. The real mechanized music of our mechanized society derives not so much from Tchaikowsky as from Rimsky-Korsakov [1844–1908], whose technical expertise is exceeded only by his spiritual nullity. He acquired a brilliant technical equipment comparatively late in life, and then spent years rewriting the works of the empirical Russian geniuses in order to "remove the crudities of the originals". We may think his labours misguided; but they were certainly as disinterested as they were strenuous. He omits 'ungrammatical' passages in Moussorgsky, adds bars where he thinks the original too elliptical, corrects the harmony and part-writing and smoothes off the sharp edge of Moussorgsky's orchestration. Some of his alterations were essential if the music was to be performable at all; most of them can be defended on the grounds that, but for Korsakov's revisions, the music would never have gained a hearing in the nineteenth century. None the less, one cannot avoid the suspicion that the revisions are evidence of their perpetrator's imaginative poverty. He quite genuinely could not see that Moussorgsky's incompetencies were never *simply* incompetent. His own mechanical competence makes a curious appendix to a musical tradition which had been nothing if not truthful or heartfelt.

Rimsky-Korsakov, though the most prolific Russian creator of operas, was not essentially an opera composer at all, for he had no interest in human beings. His most conventionally dramatic operas are the least successful. *Ivan the Terrible* is a weak imitation of *Boris*, and even the character of Krishka in *Kitesh* owes his power more to the dramatic than to the musical conception. In so far as his love-scenes are usually feeble, Rimsky-Korsakov resembles most Russian composers other than Tchaikowsky: but it is certainly not fortuitous that his invention sounds most spontaneous when he is dealing with pantheistic or inhuman experience. His *Snow Maiden* seems a prettily decorated,

synthetically concocted fairy-tale compared with the poignant
nostalgia of Tchaikowsky's *Sleeping Princess*. But if we are looking for decoration, Rimsky-Korsakov's is delightful; and he
certainly understood a heroine who was tormented because
her heart could not melt to human love. Most of his best music
is associated with beings—such as Lel and Sadko—who sym-
bolize the power of art, as opposed to life.

Throughout his long career, Rimsky-Korsakov handled
expertly all the 'artistic' ingredients of Russian opera—folk-
song, realistic speech inflexion, choral dances in irregular metres,
quasi-medievalisms, Orientalisms, Italianate lyricism, 'colouristic' orchestral effects. He added some mannerisms of his own:
melodic formulae to which he returned all through his life,
harmonic and orchestral devices which he experimented with
at the dictates of fashion. His music is recognizable by its
mannerisms, while seldom speaking with an authentic voice.
Symphonically, his operas are always sectional, however much
he may have picked up from Wagner; they are most convincing
when they pretend to be nothing more, as in the deliberately
non-dramatic, masque-like 'tableaux' of *Sadko*, with its sonorous
evocation of the sea. Rimsky-Korsakov never, like Moussorgsky
or even Borodin, creates a cumulative logic from the sequence of
episodes. The 'situation' which impresses him is used over and
over again, from opera to opera: just as, within each work, his
musical repetitions are simply repetitions—a labour-saving
device rather than a constructive principle. The repetitions are,
indeed, as systematically contrived as the elaborate cycles of
keys; and this is most evident in the realm of the fantastic, where
so much of his music pretends to live. Even in *Sadko*, which
contains much wooingly lovely music, the underwater world of
fantasy is expressed by way of a most unfantastic (because
deliberate and excessive) exploitation of the harmonic neutrality
of augmented fifths and whole-tone progressions. Rimsky-
Korsakov is here a conjurer, rather than a genuine magician of
music; he produces water-sprites, but it might just as well have
been rabbits. He creates illusion, knowing it to be illusion:
whereas the illusion of Tchaikowsky's ballets becomes, for the
time being, truth.

Yasterbtsev reports that Rimsky-Korsakov once said to him:
"You would scarcely find anyone in the world who believes
less in everything supernatural, fantastic, or lying beyond the

boundaries of death than I do—yet as an artist I love this sort of thing above all else. And religious ceremonial—what could be more intolerable? And yet with what love have I expressed such ceremonial customs in music! No, I am actually of the opinion that art is essentially the most enchanting, intoxicating lie." Nothing could be further removed from Moussorgsky's belief that art is reality: or for that matter from Tchaikowsky's belief that art is the overflowing of the full heart. A sceptical magician is a contradiction in terms—unless he be the degenerate modern type who performs on the seaside pier. Certainly there is nothing in Rimsky-Korsakov's music to disprove his statement; for while *Kitesh* contains the most sensuously beautiful, even moving, music he ever wrote, this music is all associated with the pantheistic forest creature Fevronya, and especially with her final dissolution into earth, air, and trees. To admire her vocally sustained, exquisitely scored lullaby is not to support those who would claim *Kitesh* as 'the Russian *Parsifal*'. Music can be manufactured, but not the human heart—nor the kind of experience to which *Kitesh* pretends. It is appropriate that Rimsky-Korsakov's last work should have been not *Kitesh*, but *The Golden Cockerel*: a fantastic allegory of which no one today knows the meaning, and of which one suspects Rimsky-Korsakov did not know the meaning himself. The reason is simple: there is nothing to know. Beneath the carapace of orchestral scintillation and of 'advanced' chromatic and enharmonic devices, the bird is a mechanical toy. The only dawn his crowing heralds—in a manner far more sinister than the emotional orgies of Tchaikowsky and Puccini—is the slick fatuity of Hollywood.

4

THE NATIONALISTS OF CENTRAL EUROPE

THERE is something to be said for the view that the Russians are the only true musical nationalists. Russia's geographical vastness and her remoteness from the culture of Europe meant that the nationalism of Balakirev and Moussorgsky could be largely an indigenous growth. Bohemia, on the other hand, had been for centuries an integral part of Europe: so much so that she was, in the early nineteenth century, under both the political and cultural domination of Austria. Her 'nationalism' was a rebellion against tyranny; but she was not and could not be spiritually or culturally distinct from her oppressor. Perhaps this is evident even in Czech folk-music itself. The dances have none of the irregular rhythms characteristic of Russian or Magyar dances; and while the songs are sometimes pentatonic, they never employ the chromaticized scales—with sharp fourth or fifth—typical of eastern Russia; on the whole, they tend to a straightforward diatonic major. They can thus be readily incorporated into the traditional language of Western classical music. They neither suggest any disturbing rhythmic or harmonic alterations, nor imply a different approach to form.

Living in such intimate contact with Austria and a centre of European civilization, Czech composers naturally have little of the primitivism of the Russians. Indeed, the most obvious characteristic of Smetana's music is not its national flavour, but its technical maturity. His first works, it is true, are rather characterless in their cosmopolitan style; but it was not long before he developed a masterly control of the two techniques which, in Vienna, had long been interrelated—Italian opera and Austrian sonata. At the same time, Smetana's respect for tradition was modified by his progressive independence. He sought the acquaintance of Liszt not so much because he too was a virtuoso pianist as because he admired the creative enterprise of Liszt's mind. One who fought spiritually for the future of his country could not ignore one who fought so strenuously for the future of music.

Trained in the Austro-Italian tradition, Smetana [1824–1884] began by composing in the idiom of the classical sonata. He soon came to realize, however, that "absolute music is impossible for me"; for fundamentally he was not concerned with inner strife. Living in a predominantly rural community which was, for all its yearning for freedom, in itself stable, he instinctively tended to express himself in operatic terms. Indeed, self-expression was hardly his creative intention; opera for him was a social act, rather than an excuse for autobiography. He wished to give his society an opera in every *genre*; and in these operas personal drama was to be seen against the background of communal life.

The work which made Smetana a celebrity—the comic opera known to us as *The Bartered Bride*—was an unpretentious affair. Its success was due partly to the fact that it is the most obviously nationalistic of Smetana's operas, in that it deals directly with peasant life, and includes many dance numbers of exuberant vitality. But it is not a peasant opera, like Moussorgsky's *The Marriage*. Melodically, harmonically, and formally its technique is Austrian and Italian; the popular element merely injects fresh virility into its cosmopolitanism. In conception, the opera is closer to Mozart than to Moussorgsky. Smetana may not embrace the variety and complexity of experience which Mozart crystallizes into the lucidity of *Figaro*, but he is Mozartian not merely in technique, but also in his compassionate feeling for human beings. His opera deals with the interplay of real people in action, living in his own community and also in a self-consistent world of art. It is significant that ensemble numbers are frequent in Smetana's operas, as in Mozart's. In Russian opera, the ensemble is both infrequent and unimportant. Tchaikowsky's best operatic music goes into monologue, in which the individuality of each vocal phrase is somewhat exasperatingly emphasized by being echoed by an instrument. Moussorgsky's most typical music is in the monologues and the epically elemental choruses. Neither in Moussorgsky's nor in Tchaikowsky's case is this due to defective contrapuntal skill. The Russians were not greatly interested in people in their social relationships, as were Mozart and

Smetana. Primitivistically, they were concerned with the People generically: with individual creatures who were, like Boris, in one way or another outcasts from society: or, in Tchaikowsky's case, with themselves.

In his tragic opera, *Dalibor*, Smetana finds a revolutionary theme from Bohemia's past which was capable of a contemporary interpretation. The medieval setting means, however, that he is not much concerned with the evocation of a regional environment. The only element in the style which suggests folk-music—apart possibly from the energetic rhythm of some of the quicker arias—is Smetana's partiality for passages built over a tonic or dominant pedal, or over a single chord employed like a bagpipe drone. In these passages—often associated with some ceremonial or ritualistic episode, like the first appearance of Vladislav—the unmodified tonality, the repeated phrases and rhythmic patterns, the brilliant scoring in contrasted groups of brass, woodwind, and strings, seem to suggest the simple power, the unchanging stability, of the agrarian community. But their significance is dependent on their context: for they are startlingly opposed to the complex, fluctuating linear and harmonic texture in which the interplay of the principal characters is expressed. Smetana is a man of the nineteenth century, though his sophistication lives in the context of a peasant world.

We can examine the essence of his operatic style in Dalibor's D flat aria towards the end of Act I. There is, perhaps, the slightest hint of folk inflexion in the pentatonic tail to the opening phrase; but the lyricism is Italianate, and of Verdian directness. The harmony, however, is much richer than anything Verdi had written in the 1860s: note how the augmented triads and ninth chords shift the melody slightly askew, so that the tonality rises from D flat through D major, E flat, and E, gaining in exaltation until it reaches the subdominant, G flat (standing for F sharp in the scale-wise ascent) (Ex. 22):

Ex. 22. Smetana: *Dalibor*

It is interesting to compare these step-wise modulations with those in Balakirev or Borodin. With the Russians, they are a momentary effect of colour, unrelated to tonal argument or line. With Smetana, they lead progressively to the climacteric G flat: from which point the melody descends chromatically, over a sustained tonic pedal which balances the tonal unrest of the first section. The aria concludes with a triumphant choral and orchestral assertion of tonic and dominant.

No less thrilling is the love-duet at the end of the second act. Here the enharmonic changes and mediant relationships are an ecstatic intensification of the lyricism rather than, as in Schubert, a nostalgic relaxation of tension. Even at its most chromatic the music has a melodic and rhythmic drive which preserves its positive vigour. For instance, if one compares the chromatic meandering at the opening of the prison scene with the similar passage at the beginning of Moussorgsky's *Cradle Song*, it is evident that whereas Moussorgsky's passage exists in its own right as a manifestation of desolate vacillation, Smetana's passage owes its effectiveness to its context. Moussorgsky reveals a 'moment of reality'; Smetana, portraying characters in action, makes us aware of chromaticism in relation to the tonality it disrupts. Indeed, all the elements of his technique reveal the development of emotion and of character. As Milada approaches the prison, chromaticism gives way to fluent cantabile lyricism; but if the lyricism expresses her joy, the fluctuating sevenths of the harmony, the repeated notes of the bass, the intertwining orchestral texture, suggest the excitement, the fearful expectancy, with which she approaches the lover who is also the murderer of her brother.

To Smetana's deep disappointment, *Dalibor* was not a success, partly because the chromaticism and rich orchestration provoked the charge of Wagnerism. While the music may occasionally recall the more Italianate Wagner of *Tannhäuser* and *Lohengrin*, it is closer to Verdi: and is in any case most remarkable for its independence of mind. If Smetana was directly influenced by any composer, it was by Liszt rather than by Wagner. A passage such as Ex. 23 betrays a Lisztian fusion of ripe Italian lyricism with luxuriant enharmony, and there is a deeper relation to Liszt in that the formal conception of *Dalibor* has much in common with that of the Lisztian symphonic poem. The noble, slowly rising theme which is first stated in the overture appears throughout the opera in innumerable, emotionally varied metamorphoses. Few nineteenth-century operas have a structure so closely knit: so musically self-subsistent and at the same time so intimately related to the dramatic argument. Thus at its appearance

Ex. 23. Smetana: *Dalibor*

the theme's rising aspiration is given an expectant uncertainty by the freely sequential enharmonic modulations: whereas at the end of the love-duet it is resolved into serene diatonicism. This tender transformation is not merely 'brought in' as a cunning dramatic reference; it is a genuine musical resolution of the material of the love-duet and therefore—since the duet is the climax of the act—of the structure of the act as a whole. The simplified, rarefied version of the theme sung by the women's voices as a counterpoint to Jitka's consolatory aria at the original end of the third act is the ultimate resolution of the opera's revolutionary force. It is indeed a pity that Smetana did not remain true to his instinct and his formal logic. In response to criticism, he added a further scene in which Dalibor's death is presented on the stage.

Each of Smetana's operas represented a different kind of experience and a different social function: and therefore involved a different problem of form. *The Bartered Bride*, being a simple comic opera designed to entertain, could employ the relatively episodic technique of traditional *opera buffa*. *Dalibor*, being a heroic and tragic opera concerning personal conflicts within a national theme, called for more complex and stringent organization. *Libuše* is a large-scale festival opera which deals with an episode from Bohemian history in a visionary, almost mythological way; to it the Wagnerian technique of the leit-motive therefore seems appropriate. A late comic opera, such as *The Secret*, uses elements derived from *buffo* style, from the leitmotive technique, and from the Lisztian serial principle explored in *Dalibor*; for in such an opera the relatively external vivacity of *The Bartered Bride* is deepened by something of the strength and tenderness which characterize Smetana's tragic and heroic operas.

Although Smetana was fundamentally an operatic composer, he considered it a part of his self-appointed task to create an orchestral literature for his people. This he planned—with the same intellectual probity that he manifests in his operas—as a national epic. He described the sequence of orchestral works known collectively as *Ma Vlast* as symphonic poems, and gave them a literary programme which stresses their dramatic, rather than abstract, nature. But the works are musically as self-contained as the operas, and are in some ways more traditional in approach, for they do not employ Lisztian techniques. Thus *Vyšehrad* is in a vast ternary form, *Vltava* is a rondo, *Šárka* a telescoped sonata, *Z Ceskych* a classical suite consisting of prelude, fugue, chorale, and polka, all thematically related, and *Tábor* and *Blaník* form together an enormous variation-set or chorale prelude.

In later years, after he had more or less discarded the sonata principle as irrelevant to his experience, Smetana composed few chamber works. The two string quartets are, however, impressive instances of the application of a large-scale dramatic conception to an intimate form. The well-known First is auto-biographical not so much in the sense that it deals with subjective drama as that it evokes the scenes of Smetana's youth. The late Second Quartet, which is supposed to describe the struggles of the deaf composer to capture the themes that elude his fallible ears, is perhaps the only introspective work which this vigorously operatic composer ever created. Even so, it achieves objectivity in its laconically aphoristic language. No wonder that Liszt said that Smetana was harmonically in advance of Wagner; for this weird, moving piece is prophetic of the

Moravian master who, following Smetana, linked his rich sense of communal tradition to the spiritual isolation of the twentieth century.

Smetana has, indeed, more in common with Janáček than with Dvořák [1841–1904], with whom he is conventionally coupled. Smetana and Janáček both impress by the positive virility of their art; if Dvořák has Smetana's spontaneity, he has but little of his strength. A smaller personality, he is more reliant on the past; and while from one point of view he was able thus to rely on tradition only because of the vitality of the agrarian society in which he lived, from another point of view his adherence to the past stood between him and complete artistic realization. This is evident in what one might call the positive and negative poles of his relation to the Austrian classics.

The positive pole is his relationship to Schubert, whose lyrical spontaneity and harmonic instinct he inherited. But his was a simpler, less subtle nature. In Schubert, the mediant relationships and enharmonic changes may suggest a passive luxuriance in the senses; but we experience them with an acute poignancy, since we hear them in relation to Schubert's dramatic intensity. In Dvořák there is normally no such conflict; he enjoys his lyricism and his sensuous rhapsody for their own sake. Something the same is true, we saw, of Smetana's enharmony: only in his case sensuous experience is one part of a powerful intellectual and dramatic organization. Such organization is not in Dvořák's nature. He sounds most completely himself when he admits this and adopts a rhapsodic approach to composition, as in the movements based on the emotionally volatile folk-rhapsody of the dumka.

Unfortunately, he was not always content to be himself. He could not, like Smetana, free himself from the inheritance of the sonata; nor had he, like Schubert or Bruckner, the creative vitality to evolve a sonata style at once lyrical and dramatic. But he felt he had to measure up to the classical ideal; and the negative pole of his traditionalism was his admiration for Brahms, to whom he turned in later years as the progressive Smetana turned to Liszt. Dvořák's attempt to produce large-scale works in symphonic style sometimes—notably in the D minor Symphony—led to music of remarkable power; but it is undeniable that in writing such music Dvořák was forcing his nature. The grandiose peroration of the last movement of this symphony wears less well than the pastoral quietude of the slow movement: or than the more relaxed, less 'symphonic', movements of the Fourth Symphony in G, or the Third in F. Even the last movement of this symphony, however, sounds self-conscious when it attempts to provide a convincing culmination by recapitulating earlier themes: especially if one considers it alongside the transmuted codas in Smetana's *Dalibor*. Self-consciousness is disastrous in a composer as instinctive as Dvořák. It is significant that he found it so difficult to finish his symphonies. The true symphonist is always getting somewhere; the essence of Dvořák's temperament is that he is content to be and to enjoy.

Dvořák seems to have come to realize that although, as a nineteenth-century composer in the classical tradition, he ought to write symphonies, his talents did not naturally tend in that direction. After his visit to America, he turned from the symphony to the symphonic poem; yet he was hardly on happier ground here, for the monothematic Lisztian symphonic poem allows less for discursiveness than the symphony. Dvořák provided himself with a detailed literary programme and conscientiously illustrated it in music, forgetting that for Liszt the programme was no more than a general evocation of mood or atmosphere. Dvořák's symphonic poems are full of the most ravishing sensuous moments; but they do not wear well because they fall, structurally, between two stools. They relinquish classical precedent, while showing no understanding of the thematic techniques practised by Liszt and Smetana. Nor has Dvořák any grasp of the more complex structural techniques of Wagner, whose harmonic and orchestral luxuriance fascinated him no less than the economy of the anti-Wagnerian, Brahms.

It is no accident that Dvořák's most convincing large-scale instrumental work is the 'Cello Concerto. The virtuoso nature of nineteenth-century concerto style permits some relaxation of dramatic logic; and the 'cello is a singing instrument, sensuously mellow, which—unlike the piano—does not readily lend itself to rhetoric. Dvořák's own Piano Concerto is a fiasco because the soloist's rhetoric is not merely unrelated, but even opposed, to the lyrical essence of the music. In the 'Cello Concerto, on the other hand, the heart-easing warmth of the melodies is matched

by the inevitability of the music's rhapsodic growth. Schubert
wished, in his music, to resolve his distractions in love. Dvořák,
less distracted, has less to resolve; but the love is hardly less
potent. When a composer can create a theme such as this—in
which the relaxed pentatonic arabesques of folk-song are
absorbed into a flowing lyricism reconcilable with the richest
harmony, scored with a magical instinct for the sonority of
each instrument—we can but return his love in gratitude
(Ex. 24):

It is sometimes said that the pentatonic inflexions of themes
such as this—or the hardly less beautiful one from the slow
movement of the G major Symphony—were prompted by
Dvořák's experience of Negro music on his visit to the United
States. It would be truer to say that acquaintance with Negro
music emphasized a proclivity inherent in the folk-music of his
own people (and indeed in all folk-music): and that the innocence of such melody was consistent with his own temperament,
irrespective of racial considerations. In this connexion it is
interesting to compare Dvořák's use of the interval of the sixth
with Smetana's. For Smetana it usually implies an emotional
expansion, with the higher note on the strong beat, accompanied
by an increase of harmonic tension (as in Verdi); for Dvořák the
sixth often becomes an inversion of the pentatonic third, floating, relaxed, with the higher note on the weak beat. The effect
—consider the opening phrase of the 'Nigger' Quartet, and the
use of the sixth in the approach to the recapitulation—is of
softly-smiling, sensuous abandonment (Ex. 25):

and although this comes more naturally to Dvořák than the

stilted solemnity he sometimes affects in his symphonies, it has its own dangers.

Pentatonic melodies, indeed, being without a leading note, are not likely to prove convincing as the *basic* material for a sonata movement. They can serve as relaxation; but there must first be something to relax from. The charming irresponsibility of Dvořák's lighter chamber works bears only a superficial relationship to Haydn's wit. Occasionally—for instance, in the delicious E flat Quartet, opus 51, especially the last movement —he approaches the 'intense levity' which Haydn habitually achieves, because dramatic tension is implicit in his frivolity. In the average run of Dvořák's lighter works, however, vivacity has lost the edge of wit—the classical awareness of "other modes of experience that are possible". It would be curmudgeonly to complain of deficiencies in such delightful café music as the A major Quintet or the opus 96 Quartet. It would none the less be stupid not to recognize that such music represents a lower level both of human experience and of 'entertainment' than the ostensibly comparable works of Haydn.

Only rarely did Dvořák attempt 'symphonic' drama in his chamber music; the F minor Trio is unique in the manner in which Dvořák modifies his improvisatory, sonorously expansive keyboard style to create a Brahmsian trenchancy, even ferocity. It is a powerful, but hardly characteristic, work. At the end of his life, however, Dvořák at last managed to reconcile his sym- phonic ambitions with the instinctive sensuousness of his nature —in the two string quartets, opus 106, especially the Second, in G major. The luxuriantly lovely slow movement of this quartet is significantly a dumka. It is formally unpretentious, being a rudimentary kind of rondo. It is unambitiously reliant on the past—on the pentatonic inflexions, drone effects, and reiterated phrases of folk-music, and on such Schubertian features as an oscillation between the major and minor triad, a climacteric modulation to the flat sub-mediant, and a quasi-orchestral sonority in the string writing. Yet in being thus relaxed, Dvořák reveals his original genius most clearly; and creates not merely his most appealing, but his most poignantly imaginative music. Perhaps the major-minor alternation—which is far less habitual in Dvořák's music than in Schubert's—is mainly responsible for this pathos. It is interesting, however, that the minor is here a momentary disturbance before the radiant major: whereas in

Schubert the minor key is usually the stronger, making major seem sadder than minor, because illusory.

While Dvořák creates his most convincing music in a rhapsodic style, one can hardly say that he is incapable of handling large forms. Symphonic idiom was not congenial to him, except in an occasional lyric compromise, like the 'Cello Concerto; but both his operas and his church music are formally adequate. He is not innately an opera composer, for he has none of Smetana's objective awareness of human character. But his spontaneous flow of melody, his command of orchestral colour, and his instinct for the picturesque serve him well when he deals with peasant life, or still more with Nature, and with magical rather than human creatures. One has only to compare the music of the Nature sprites in *Rusalka* with any example of Rimsky-Korsakov's supernatural music to see the difference between the creative magician and the conjurer.

Equally beautiful are Dvořák's large-scale liturgical works; for here he has a text to discipline him, while having no need of the opera composer's response to character and situation. It is interesting that Dvořák was a sincere Catholic, whereas Smetana, like Schubert, was agnostic. His Catholicism was not an ardent, mystical exaltation, like that of Bruckner. It was rather synonymous with his easy-going temperament, which, unlike Smetana's sturdily independent or Schubert's acutely divided nature, accepted traditional dogma in religious belief, as in art. It is not therefore surprising that the *Te Deum* and the *Requiem* exhibit the same technical features as the instrumental music, though their structure is more coherent. This is particularly true of the big *Requiem*: for the sinuous unaccompanied chromatic phrase with which the work opens pervades the entire score. While it does not subtly change its identity, like Smetana's *Dalibor* theme, it provides a link between, on the one hand, the pentatonic folk-like lyricism, the simple choral homophony, and the luminous, rustic scoring (especially the parallel thirds for woodwind): and, on the other hand, the more conventionally Italianate lyricism and the caprice of the enharmonic modulations. (Consider the tremulously fluctuating 'In Memoria aeterna', or the Tristanesque opening to the 'Tuba Mirum',—Ex. 26.) Both in its pastoral and its sensuous aspects, Dvořák's attitude to his God would seem to be pantheistic rather than dogmatic; it is significant that the only weak passage in the score is the 'Quam olim', a conventional oratorio fugue of Mendelssohnic squareness. Smetana could still think and feel naturally in fugue, even

Ex.26. Dvořák: Requiem

within the apparently light-hearted context of an operatic overture like that to *The Secret*, not to mention the magnificent full-scale fugue in *Z Ceskych*. Dvořák could not. He merely felt that a fugue was expected of him at this point, just as he felt that a symphony 'ought' to end with a heroic peroration. In this connexion, it is interesting to contrast the richly spontaneous pagan opening of Dvořák's oratorio, *St. Ludmilla*, with the depressing academicism that sets in with the arrival of Christian redemption!

Smetana was born in 1824, Dvořák in 1841, and Janáček—the third and last of the great Czech nationalists—only nine years later. Dvořák lived until 1904, but was not temperamentally prone to experiment. Janáček lived (and composed) until 1928, and experimented throughout a long life. Like Smetana, he was brought up in a peasant community. His father was a village schoolmaster who encouraged him—with his numerous brothers and sisters—to play in the village band, as well as introducing him to the Viennese classics. At the age of ten he went to a local monastery school, where he gained his first formal instruction in music and heard the plainchant which, along with folk-song, was the most important musical influence on his youth. When he moved to Prague Conservatory, he acquired a sound Austrian technique similar to Smetana's. Born thirty years later, however, he was more consciously artistic in his nationalism. He began to feel, as the Russians had felt earlier, that a national style implied the rejection of cosmopolitanism; to be Moravian was to be original. Eventually he founded at Brno his own conservatoire, which was deliberately opposed to the conventionally academic. It is easy to deplore the time that Janáček wasted in apparently fruitless bickering with the members of more orthodox academies; but one cannot separate the development of his attitude to his art from the art itself. It was during these years that he wandered around the countryside listening to the cries of birds and beasts, the ripple of streams and the whining of wind—above all, to the voices of the peasants, the different rhythmic and tonal traits they assumed under the stress of varying emotion. The theories which he based on his observations were also a deduction from his creative practice. If a no less powerful, he was a later, more self-conscious revolutionary than Moussorgsky; he had to understand intellectually what, in emotional terms, he was trying to do.

Later Janáček said: "The study I have made of the musical aspects of the spoken language has led me to the conviction that all the melodic and rhythmic mysteries of music can be explained by reference to the melody and rhythm of the musical motives of the spoken language." From this point of view, folk-song was a sublimation of speech; and Janáček believed, with Moussorgsky, that the speech-song of simple people, living close to the earth, was both more musical and more 'real' than that of sophisticated people. He did not, however, follow Moussorgsky in equating art with the 'moment of reality'. This was not merely because he had, like Smetana, a background of traditional technique; it was also because, like Smetana and unlike Moussorgsky, he saw life as growth. *Jenůfa*—the opera which made his name—shares with Smetana's operas the positive vitality of a folk-culture and a rich inheritance of Austro-Italian technique. But Janáček's explorations into peasant speech and into the sounds of rural life more profoundly modify his sophistication. The flexible vocal lines approach speech without ceasing to be powerfully lyrical; the orchestral texture emulates the sounds of Nature while creating an elaborate network of interrelated motives. Consider, for instance, how the figuration suggested by the sound of the mill becomes a musical motive related both to an abstract concept like fate, and also to the development of pathological obsession within a character. Janáček's music becomes more 'realistic', less formally conventional, because he aims to embrace in his opera all the complexity and perversity of life. His greatness consists largely in the fact that he preserves something like Smetana's positive strength, even in expressing the abysmal depths of guilt and conscience. *Jenůfa* and *Katia Kabanova*—though one ends happily, the other tragically—involve an awareness both of the terrors within the human mind and of the will to live. Folk-vitality merges into Christian abnegation and a Dostoevskian sense of sin: just as peasant community and monastery school had moulded Janáček's childhood, and folk-song and plainsong meet in the contours of his melodic lines.

The essence of Janáček's originality lies in his approach to rhythm, which was influenced by his study of speech and of the sounds of Nature. Most of the chords he uses are in themselves simple—he is more sparing of sevenths and ninths than Smetana. But the complex and elliptical nature of his rhythm means that he discovers unexpected relationships between the chords; exploiting the acoustical 'period of reverberation', he sometimes dispenses with the normal grammatical transition. His conception of incremental rhythm also modifies his conception of form, as we can see most convincingly in an instrumental work which, while moving within a more restricted range than an opera, employs an exactly comparable technique. The third movement of the late *Sinfonietta*, for instance, opens with a lyrical phrase comparatively richly harmonized (Ex. 27a):

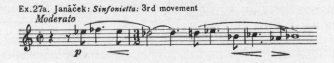

Ex.27a. Janáček: *Sinfonietta:* 3rd movement
Moderato

this music belongs to Smetana's world. The rising semitone and falling tone with which the piece opens gradually expands until it becomes an ascending fourth and descending fifth, then a sixth: at which point a violently contrasted, syncopated rhythm on the brass, interspersed with wild squeals of flute and piccolo, destroys the melody (Ex. 27b):

Ex.27b. Ibidem:
Con moto   Piccolo

The lyrical theme then reappears, rondo-wise, but is not allowed to sing. The brass interjections and the woodwind skirls are now telescoped with it, so that it becomes a frenzied dance, growing increasingly panic-stricken until the syncopated motive barks ferociously on horns and trombones, and the music explodes in a flute and piccolo scream. In the ominous silence that follows, fragments of the melody sound forlornly. This kind of structural technique has little in common with nineteenth-century symphonic methods; we hardly need the comparable examples from Janáček's operas to see how powerfully it suggests a dramatic or psychological crisis.

The fourth piece is similar, only this time it begins, not with a lyrical song motive, but with a folk-like dance tune, hypnotically repeated. The brief phrase is decorated with chromatic skirls on the violins and telescoped into ever more elliptical rhythmic patterns: until suddenly the chromaticism, which we had thought of as an embellishment, becomes the core of the music. A wailful descending phrase, starting high on the woodwind, splinters the folk-like vivacity (Ex. 28):

Ex. 28. Janáček: *Sinfonietta:* 4th movement

The little tune tries pathetically to re-establish its identity, but fails. The movement ends with an abrupt, almost hysterical assertion of dance metre, built on reiterated fourths. In these two strange, frightening movements the simplicities of a peasant world are transformed into a 'modern' nervous frenzy. The disruptive originality does not, however, bring a loss in power. The work opens and concludes with a broad ceremonial movement, mainly pentatonic in line, scored for brass and drums. Despite the intrusion of chromatic elements and elliptical rhythms into the pentatonicism, this has the extrovert exuberance of a peasant festival. The oppositions of tonality may be violent, but Janáček's music has none of Smetana's tonal fluidity. Even in his operas, Janáček will often maintain a single key until some external event occurs to destroy it; and his association of certain keys with specific emotional states (for instance, the D flat major he habitually uses for love scenes) reminds us of the statically symbolic use of tonality in the old heroic opera.

In all Janáček's music we find this balance between the vitality of an agricultural inheritance and the introspective exploration of the Freudian bugaboo. In the series of experimental operas that followed *Katia Kabanova*, the stress tends to fall increasingly on the disruptive elements. Yet even the last of the operas—*The House of the Dead*, which has a libretto freely based on Dostoevsky—has a virility that belies the brutality of the melodies, the strange orchestration, the fantastic rhythmic complications of the trombone and percussion parts. However complex the detail, the operatic 'projection' is so vivid that the effect of the music is extraordinarily simple, and simply extraordinary. This is true not only of the operas, but of Janáček's work in any medium—the tremendous revolutionary choruses, the two string quartets (both of which have programmatic subtitles), and the *Diary of a Young Man Lost*, for tenor, soprano, women's chorus, and piano. This work, an opera in miniature, provides a microcosm of every aspect of Janáček's technique —the plastic, *parlando* line, the rhythmic complications, the lugubrious dissonance, the nervous texture. There is no more sensitive portrayal of the agonies of adolescence than this work of a sixty-three-year-old composer; and it is significant that the piece was prompted directly by life, rather than by art. The young man of the title was not imaginary, but a peasant boy who left the safety of home for the wild love of a gipsy. After his disappearance, the folk-poems in which he described his experience were found and published in a local newspaper, where Janáček saw them. His music makes the story live again; and because he wanted us to live through the experience as we hear the music, he said that the cycle should be performed, as nearly as possible, in the dark.

In his seventieth year Janáček said, speaking of his new Wind Sextet, which he called *Youth*: "I listen to the birds singing, I wonder at the manifestations of rhythm in its million different forms in the world of light, colour and shapes, and my music remains young through contact with the eternally young rhythm of Nature." No finer testimony to this could be imagined than his last, and possibly greatest, work—the Mass for soli, chorus, orchestra, and organ. Intended for performance in the open air, like the medieval Slavonic festival mass, this is at once a Catholic act of praise to God and a pagan act of homage to the earth. But again the technique resembles that of the operas; the aphoristic lyrical phrases, the pentatonic contours, the compulsive metrical rhythms erupt volcanically, so that the powerfully positive music seems to contain the cataclysmic upheavals and inner torments of the twentieth century. Yet for all Janáček's genius, and for all his modernity, this music is inconceivable except in relation to a world we shall never see again. If Janáček does not belong to the nineteenth century, we can only say that he is *sui generis*. He has had and can have little influence on the music of the twentieth century; and though he may not be the greatest of contemporary composers, there is a sense in which he makes most twentieth-century music seem impotent.

5

THE DECLINE OF NATIONALISM

JANÁČEK is the last *great* composer whose music is inspired by a folk tradition. Bartók was born in an agrarian community; but folk-music was for him not so much a positive influence in itself, as a stimulus to exploration. For the rest, the national composers who followed the great Russian and Czech schools are minor figures. There is no successor to Moussorgsky; and even the successors to Tchaikowsky's Europeanized Russian idiom could not recapture his neurotic energy. Medtner [1880–1951] the most musically distinguished of these composers, adopted a style Teutonically Brahmsian rather than Russian, while attaining a discreet originality by way of his pianistic invention. Rachmaninov [1873–1943], one of the great virtuoso pianists of history, was not unnaturally even more wedded to the keyboard in his technique as a composer. The original and evocative moments in his music—for instance, the development section and cadenza of the first movement of the D minor Concerto (No. 3)—are almost always expansions of harmonic devices suggested by the behaviour of his hands at the keyboard. So it is not surprising that his large-scale, Teutonically constructed works are seldom convincing as wholes.

Perhaps they do not need to be. Rachmaninov's lyrical sense, caressingly drooping like Tchaikowsky's, makes it possible for him to create songs as insidious as, if less powerful than, Tchaikowsky's; and this nostalgic lyricism, in combination with the sultry chromatic embellishments of his harmony and his mastery of pianistic ornament, even suffices to make his formally inconclusive concertos hypnotic in their appeal. Some part of Rachmaninov's fascination for the vast popular audience may come from his very insecurity, his hypochondria, his lack of self-confidence. "If ever I believed in myself, it was a very long time ago, when I was very young", he wrote in 1912 from his self-imposed American exile. There was always a fight in him between material success and creative ambition. Small wonder that this finds an echo in our hearts, living as we do in a society dedicated to material gain.

For all the Russian quality of his pessimism, nostalgia, and instability, Rachmaninov is hardly a national composer. More typical of the latter-day nationalist is Grieg [1843–1907], whose distinction is closely related to the smallness of his talent. Norway, like Russia, was cut off from Europe; but there was little in her history to promote an 'epic' operatic or symphonic music comparable with that of the Russians. A certain cosy sweetness, rather than barbaric grandeur, was typical of Norwegian society; and except for the fact that his country was not much industrialized, Grieg's position was comparable with that of a composer in nineteenth-century England. Like Delius—and most British composers of his generation—Grieg studied in Germany, for there was no local tradition in which he could have been trained.

His first attempts to write large-scale symphonic works in the German tradition were failures. Even the later Piano Concerto is not a symphonic work, but a series of charming salon pieces strung together, and his only formally convincing large-scale work is the Piano Ballade, which is in non-developing variation style. He had nothing like Smetana's powerful sweep or Dvořák's spontaneity; nor had he Moussorgsky's ability to build up, through an inner dramatic momentum, a big structure from small components. Grieg habitually thought in two-bar periods, and his tunes, like Norwegian folk-songs, moved through a narrow range. The pentatonic flavour resulting from a fall of a tone followed by a descending minor third is as characteristic as the tendency of his themes to avoid the leading note.

Though this folk-like flavour is connected with Grieg's restricted emotional range, it certainly does not mean that he felt with primitive vitality. The composers he most admired were Chopin, Schumann, and—for his chromaticism and elegance rather than for his dramatic power—Mozart; Chopin's mazurkas were the model for his treatment of folk-melodies. Since folk-songs do not develop and are relatively devoid of harmonic implications, the simple repeated phrases could be harmonized with seductive chromaticisms and enharmonic sequences which are no more than a momentary distortion of tonal perspective.

The harmonic progression moves very slowly, if at all; the Wagnerian sevenths and ninths become sensory moments, chained to the two-bar phrases, instead of a cumulating passion. This static conception of harmony has melodic consequences also; Grieg is especially fond of themes consisting of chains of thirds—horizontalized chords of the seventh or ninth.

The nostalgic flavour of Grieg's little piano pieces comes largely from the odd way in which simple folk-like tunes thus come to terms with sophisticated harmony. The effect is much more artificial than that of Chopin's mazurkas, in which there is an interpenetration of the primitive and the sophisticated. Chopin's harmonic-polyphonic epigrams are much deeper in their yearning. Yet the superficial quality of Grieg's music is inseparable from its later date. He could not become part of a folk-tradition—as Chopin did, ideally and retrospectively; he could only offer an emotional commentary on it. Chopin is a highly emotional composer who is never sentimental; the *flow* of his harmony preserves an inner vitality. Grieg's static sequences, anchored by internal pedal points, are frequently sentimental. Revolving around themselves, emphasizing their pathos, they seem in excess of the object—the simple, un-developing tunes.

Grieg is most successful as a song-writer, partly because a vocal line prompts greater pliancy and subtlety of contour, partly because the folk-inspired poetry of the *Vinje* or *Haugtussa* songs released hidden depths in his nostalgia. It is interesting that Grieg's finest music looks not backwards to the days when nationalism was a creative force, but forwards to some of the 'disruptive' techniques from which twentieth-century music was born. Especially in some of the songs dealing with Nature, the harmony becomes almost as statically impressionistic as Debussy's; the evocation of a folk-culture has been transformed into a private world of the senses. Grieg's music was significantly fashionable in Paris during the 1890s.

On the other hand, Grieg now accepts the primitive as primitive. He sees in the unself-conscious integrity of folk-techniques potentialities that may extend the boundaries of 'art' music. The late *Slåtter* for piano, for instance, can be legitimately compared with the folk-song arrangements of Bartók. Here Grieg attempts neither to sophisticate nor to sentimentalize the bagpipe drones, the telescoped tonics and dominants, the acrid tritonal arabesques of Norwegian fiddle music. He transfers the sharp, crackling sound of the village fiddler with miraculous skill to the piano (Ex. 29):

Ex.29. Grieg:

and although the little pieces are as undeveloped and as undevelopable as the folk-tunes themselves, they suggest techniques which greater European composers were to use to revitalize convention. Grieg's approach is quite different from Janáček's. For all his urgent modernity, Janáček was still a part of the folk-tradition whose idiom he remade. Grieg in these little pieces is already, like Bartók, the folk-song collector, consciously preserving a dying art.

The decline of nationalism is most comprehensively illustrated, however, by the phenomenon of Spanish music. Like Britain, Spain had a great musical literature in the Middle Ages and the Renaissance. During the eighteenth and nineteenth centuries the Spanish tradition had withered like the British, though perhaps for the opposite cause. We were the progressive nation; too rapidly industrialized, we lost contact with our spiritual roots. Spain, on the other hand, was so backward that the past ceased to be creative; the roots themselves dried up. Both countries lost the essential balance between tradition and creativity.

The decline of both traditions is symbolized in the failure to create a national opera. There is a close parallel between, on the one hand, the music-hall opera of the English Restoration and the ballad opera of the eighteenth century and, on the other hand, the Spanish *zarzuelas** and *tonadillas*.† In Spain, however, the popular tradition, even in its urbanized forms, remained vital when 'serious' music virtually disappeared and

---

* ZARZUELA: a comic operetta, usually in one act, and satirical in character. Some of the dialogue is spoken and improvised. Often the *zarzuela* was a musical guying of a popular play.
† TONADILLO: a sung interlude in a spoken play.

most of the talented composers were voluntary exiles in France. Britain's John Field went to Russia, Spain's Arriaga [1806–1826] began the migration to Paris. Ever since, the cultural connexion between Paris and Spain has been intimate: consider the cases of Picasso, Debussy, Ravel.

Spanish music, like British, re-emerged at the end of the nineteenth century in association with a self-conscious folk-song revival. Though folk-music in Spain was still a living tradition, cultural decay had gone so far that composers of 'art' music were unable to use folk-music to regenerate their work. There is no Spanish complement to Janáček or Bartók; hardly even a Spanish complement to the later work of Grieg. The cult of folk-music became a kind of escape. Thus Granados [1867–1916] composed an enormous quantity of picture-postcards in sound, incorporating Spanish folk-rhythms and melodic formulae into a conventional pianistic style founded on German salon music. We remember him, however, because on two occasions he rediscovered, almost fortuitously, the real soul of Spain.

Almost, but not quite, fortuitously: for the first of these works, the *Tonadillas* for voice and piano, were based directly on the eighteenth-century popular tradition. Nineteenth-century harmony is rejected in favour of a simple, guitar-like piano texture, while the vocal line has the vivacity of eighteenth-century popular opera; it is no longer necessary artificially to graft a native idiom on to the style of the salon. In the other work, the piano suite, *Goyescas*, Granados finds himself through the stimulus of an immeasurably greater artist—the painter Goya. The piano style, founded on Liszt, is now ripely exuberant; and the liberation of technique is a liberation of feeling. These tone poems for piano are too long in their opulence: yet depend on their opulence for their emotional effect. Though their chromatic sequential writing is powerfully nostalgic, it is at least nostalgic for the real Spain, not the picture-postcard version.

Albéniz [1860–1909] is a similar but still odder case. His output of picture-postcards for piano was even more prolific than Granados's, and even less enterprising harmonically and pianistically. Then, in the last few years of his life he created the piano works, *Iberia* and *Navarra*—perhaps the most impressive Spanish music since the Italian Scarlatti. Indeed, these pieces have much more of the spirit of Goya than Granados's *Goyescas*. The haunting modal themes have the true *flamenco* spirit,* the unsentimentalized *cri de cœur*, and are no more nostalgic than Spanish folk-music itself. The pianistic arabesques suggested by *flamenco* music are likewise fierce and hard, not 'picturesque'; and although the harmonic concept was greatly influenced by Debussy (whose *L'Ile Joyeuse* was a revelation to Albéniz), the effect of the harmony is altogether un-Debussyan. Harmonic side-steppings off-key, similar to those in Debussy's misty pieces, become a background to strong melodies and violent rhythms, so that they are almost percussive in effect. Percussive unresolved appoggiaturas and acciaccaturas† relate back to guitar technique and to Scarlatti's harpsichord style. Albéniz's immediate, vibrant music thus becomes deeply traditional. Inevitably more self-conscious than the much greater art of Janáček, it may be an exercise in Spanish style. None the less, an exercise so positively felt left virtually nothing for Spanish nationalism to say.

In the music of Falla [1876–1946] Spanish nationalism is already singing its swan-song. In Albéniz's *Iberia* impressionistic techniques become percussive, embellishing strenuous lines and rhythms. In Falla's *Nights in the Gardens of Spain* (1907) regional vigour dissolves away in an impressionistic haze of harmony and orchestration. The music is poetic, and technically interesting in its guitar-like use of the piano as concertante instrument. But this is already the exile's Spain, viewed retrospectively, as in Debussy's *Ibéria*. All three movements sound much alike and are too long for their content: as is almost all Spanish national music, even Albéniz's masterpiece.

Perhaps the only exception to this emotional inflation or dissipation is a late work of Falla, the Concerto for harpsichord, oboe, clarinet, and 'cello (1923). Falla's preoccupation with traditional Spanish subjects in his operas and ballets stimulated an interest in the music of Spain's great traditions. In this masterly little work, Falla fuses folk-song, medieval liturgical music, Renaissance polyphony, eighteenth-century popular music, and the harpsichord style of Scarlatti and Soler into a twentieth-century evocation of Spain's spiritual history. The

---

* FLAMENCO: a version of traditional Spanish songs of lamentation, as sung by gipsies in the nineteenth century. The melodies are elaborately ornamented and often employ intervals smaller than a semitone.

† ACCIACCATURAS: a discordant ornamental note struck almost simultaneously with the principle note—like a very rapid appoggiatura.

harsh, unsentimental clatter of the street band meets the clangour of church bells in this terse score, which provokes comparison with Stravinsky's *Soldier's Tale*. But whereas Stravinsky's Russian fairy tale was a prelude to a reborn, European style, Falla's miniature incarnation of Spain's forgotten glory was a *post mortem*. It reminded us that Spain had once had a great culture; no more than Albéniz's *Iberia* did it create a new tradition. Falla had made the past present; for the later stream of Spanish nationalists the past has been no more than a period-piece. The figures in the postcards may be togged up in eighteenth-century, instead of nineteenth-century, costume; that does not make them more alive. The point about Stravinsky's Russian puppets, from *Petrouchka* onwards, is that they come to life. The Spanish puppets mimic real people, while deceiving no one—not even, perhaps, those who jerk the strings.

I

TWO SONG-WRITERS

THE paradoxical poignancy of Schubert's music, we saw, came from the way in which his reverence for the classical tradition—and all that it implied in terms of social stability—was undermined by nostalgia. He wished to 'belong'; yet he was aware that, isolated within his private dream, he could claim solidarity only with a few kindred spirits. Wagner inflated the private dream into a new mythology, becoming himself God and Society: in this sense he is the *ne plus ultra* of romanticism. Now Hugo Wolf [1860–1903] was Schubert's natural successor, and at the same time the idolator of Wagner. Far more completely than Schubert, he was centred in his nerves, subject to alternating bouts of exuberance and melancholia, composing in hectic fits of inspiration, or not at all. Like Wagner, he was an egoist ready to sacrifice anyone to the behests of his genius and —despite his petty irascibilities and pomposities—was personally so fascinating that people vied with one another to be sacrificed. Yet although part of him yearned to make a quasi-Wagnerian universe out of his feelings, he could never accomplish this. His obsession with Wagner involved hate as well as love: his *alter ego* held him back from self-deification. On the contrary, he rather sought, like Schubert, to find his own personality in losing it in the minds of others. The classical spirit won its most impressive victory in the man who, in the most obvious sense, was the typical romantic artist.

Wolf's future destiny was already implicit in the extraordinary String Quartet, which, started in 1878, was his first large-scale work. He was then in his nineteenth year, and had already come under Wagner's spell. Yet more significant than the Wagnerian influence in this music are its classical affiliations. The key (D minor), the expectant, tremolando opening, the epic proportions, suggest Beethoven's Ninth Symphony; while the gigantic leaps of the melodic lines and the 'orchestral' texture of the string writing resemble the Beethoven of the *Grosse Fuge*. Beethovenian, too, is the strife between the wild power of the imagination and the recalcitrant medium; though Wolf's Quartet, being a young man's music, cannot attain to Beethoven's strenuously won wisdom and serenity.

For if the Quartet is Beethovenian in intention, it is Schubertian in effect. The resonant chordal writing, the D minor tonality, and the fevered *moto perpetuo* of the last movement recall the death-haunted finale of Schubert's 'Death and the Maiden' Quartet; the wide melodic leaps and ambiguously oscillating tonalities of the slow movement remind us of the fight between lyrical dream and oppressive reality in Schubert's prophetic work in G. Listening to Wolf's Quartet, we are not surprised that it was the only composition, apart from student exercises, that he completed during adolescence. He felt that he had burned himself out in it; and it seems certain that madness would have overtaken him in early youth, but for the ability he discovered to objectify his sufferings in the passions of others. His experience was too vehement, too searing, directly to be embodied in instrumental terms. He became a song-writer because, in submission to the poet, he could find release from the burden of personality.

In Mörike Wolf found the poet who could unlock the clogged contortion of the nerves which had gone to make his Quartet; the noble, Beethovenian song which stands at the beginning of the Mörike volume—*Der Genesene an die Hoffnung*—was intended as a tribute to Mörike, through whom Wolf's creative spirit had been reborn. The extreme nervous intensity of the verse of this Protestant pastor with a Catholic imagination was controlled by ironic detachment; his religious feeling was infused (in the autobiographical Peregrina poems) with fervent eroticism. He was closer to Wolf than Müller was to Schubert; for whereas Müller was a minor poet who offered the themes which Schubert wished to transfigure, Mörike was a major poet who was Wolf's equal in range and depth. He was the first of Wolf's Masks; only in becoming Mörike could Wolf bring his creative energies to flower. Subservience to the poet certainly did not mean that the composer had to forget he was a musician.

Wolf's approach to song-writing is Wagnerian in the sense that the text generally speaks itself, while the meaning of the words creates thematic or harmonic ideas which are developed

symphonically in the piano part. The parallel with Wagner must
not, however, be pushed far. Wagner wrote his own words
which amounted to little more than a literary illustration of his
symphonic drama; if they were to be intelligible in the theatre,
they called for a spacious, rather than an incidentally subtle,
treatment. The words which Wolf set were usually great poetry;
the vocal lines into which they flower must be the core of his
songs, however minutely they reflect the nuance of the text,
however complex are the motives which the words generate
in the piano part. Consider, for instance, *Erstes Liebeslied eines
Mädchens*, which Wolf said "would lacerate the nervous system
of a block of marble". The piano opens with a fierce figure
characterized by an abrupt drop at the end. The 'symphonic'
structure is a continuous development of this figure, while the
voice phrases its words breathlessly, "with the utmost force and
passion". For all its speechlike disjointedness, the vocal part
builds up into a coherent line, which coalesces with the piano
line, while overlapping it rhythmically. The agitation and the
suffering—the psychological insight—become the musical
form; just as the girl who sings exists in herself, yet is at the same
time Wolf.

Though this approach to song is common with Wolf, it is not
habitual. He seeks, always, the musical corollary of the poem,
so his musical structures are as varied as the poems he sets.
If *Erstes Liebeslied* is a declamatory song, *Um Mitternacht* is
entirely lyrical. The poem is in two stanzas, each presenting the
same idea: that of the streams singing to the Night of the Day
that is over, while Night broods on the oneness of Time, which
is beyond diurnal change. Symphonic evolution would clearly
be inappropriate here: so Wolf adopts the strophic form and
allows both stanzas to be pervaded by the continuous rocking
figure suggested to him by the images of the 'golden scales' and
the evenly balanced yoke of the hours. Yet the two stanzas of
the song are not quite identical; a climax within this quietude is
created by the heavenly felicity of the expanded lyrical arch at
the words "ihr klingt des Himmels". Response to verbal nuance
again becomes the essence of the musical structure, even in this
lyrical, rather than dramatic, song.

Another formal concept is implicit in a song like *Nixe
Binsefuss*. Superficially, this is in the tradition of the fairy ballads
of Loewe. Its naïve, whimsical humour becomes in Wolf's hands

highly sophisticated; personal passion dissolves into the glinting
tenuity of the piano part. Far from being simply strophic,
the structure is characteristically subtle. The piano part works
out two figures, the first associated with the descriptive introduction, the second with the words the nixy speaks. The first and
third sections are in triple time, the second in duple: so that the
form is an ABA structure, the speaking nixy being framed by
the two descriptive pieces. The song resembles a miniature
operatic scena; and perhaps the same is true of so utterly different a song as *Das verlassene Mägdlein*, at least if Wolf's setting be
compared with Schumann's. Schumann becomes the desolate
girl who sings through his lyricism. In Wolf's song the mono-
tonous rhythm, the bare texture, the prevalence of neutral
augmented fifths, project both character and scene; we feel
the chill, wan dawn, in the house, in the heart.

Every element of Wolf's genius is present in the Mörike songs,
except his command of a broad symphonic architecture. This
becomes evident in the Goethe songs of the following year, 1889.
In *Grenzen der Menschheit*, for instance, Wolf accepts Goethe's
literary organization, in which each of five stanzas presents an
idea complete in itself, though related to the central idea of the
limitations imposed by God on man. But Wolf transforms this
literary concept into a large-scale principle of musical order.
Thus a minim pulse dominates the first and fifth sections, which
deal with the gods in relation to man. The three middle sections,
which describe man's vain attempts to transcend his limitations,
introduce a more restless crochet pulse, and a harmony more
chromatically contorted than the god-like diatonicism of the
first section. But in the final stanza the agitated rhythm and
harmony of man are fused into the minim pulse of the gods,
since we are now concerned not with man in himself, but with
man against the background of eternity. Even the directly
'pictorial' elements become, as with Bach, devices of musical
organization. The repeated hammering note which portrays
man's attempt to steady himself on the solid earth provides a
transition from the restless harmony of the second section to
renewed stability; and the symbolic wave movement carries the
music forward into the final stanza, in which the vast leaps are
at once illustrative and a climax to the song's growth.

The Goethe songs conclude the first phase of Wolf's career.
With the Spanish song-book of 1890 the 'objectivity' which had

counterbalanced his Wagnerian egoism becomes explicit in a preoccupation with Latin themes. Even the fanaticism of some of these Spanish folk-poems that fascinated him in Paul Heyse's translations acquires a Mediterranean lucidity. The Calvary songs may be related to Wolf's self-laceration; yet the implicit identification of Wolf with Christ imbues the theme of crucifixion with tragic severity. The vocal phrases have an almost plainsong-like austerity, but are splintered by chromaticism, with El Greco-like distortion. The piano parts touch an extreme of Tristanesque dissonance such as Wolf approached nowhere else and, in this spare texture, the tension is not mollified by the continuity of the harmonic flow (Ex. 30):

Ex. 30. Wolf: Herr, was trägt der Boden hier

At the further extreme from these Calvary songs stands a group about the Holy Family: tender, limpidly diatonic, unrhetorically lyrical. In the secular love-songs the fervour of the Mörike songs is both raised to fever pitch and modified by a mordant irony. Erotic passion is now adult, no longer (however ardently) adolescent.

Irony, as opposed to the fey whimsicality of some of the earlier German songs, pervades the last phase of Wolf's work, the Italian song-books; even the tragic and lyrical songs have an epigrammatic concision. This aphoristic quality characterizes the verse forms of *rispetti* and *velote* which Wolf set in Heyse's translation. His misunderstanding of the mannered conceits of the poetry was the highest inspiration of his genius; the most impersonal poetry he ever set provoked what he himself called his most original and artistically consummate music. The Mediterranean clarity would have been little without the pressure of experience behind it; without the lucidity, however, the pressure of experience would have driven him mad before he had left, as his legacy, some of the greatest songs in European history.

The range of technique and experience in these miniature compositions seems inexhaustible. *Geselle, woll'n wir uns in Kutten hüllen*, for instance, is character-portrayal of a subtlety which an opera composer would need several scenes to establish: the hypocritical monk's *parlando* line tells us what he says, with vivid realism, while the piano part's mincing seconds and thematically evolving, pawkily insinuating motive tell us what he means. On the other hand, a song such as *Nun lass uns Frieden schliessen* is the purest lyricism; the falling sevenths that mark the emotive points in the verse are the more touching because the vocal range of the song is normally so restricted. The incidental nuances suggested by the words do not disrupt the music's flow: on the contrary, they give it momentum—consider the cross rhythm provoked by the words "ein Paar zufriedner Herzen", or the hint of pain beneath the tenderness created by the piano's chromatic appoggiaturas at the cadences (Ex. 31):

Ex. 31. Wolf: Nun lass uns Frieden schliessen

Such music is gracefully elegant, like the poem: yet it epitomizes at once the happiness and the pathos of love. There is a similar quality in that exquisite vision of the transitory bliss of love, *Wir haben beide lange Zeit geschwiegen*. After the hesitant chromaticism of the opening, the diatonicism of the piano's E flat melody seems transfigured. Only to a spirit as tortured as Wolf could this swaying lullaby mean so much: even here a chromatic intrusion in the vocal line provokes a heart-breaking return from sub-dominant to tonic by way of the flat supertonic (Ex. 32):

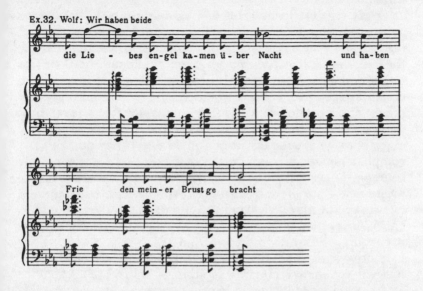

Ex.32. Wolf: Wir haben beide

die Lie - bes en-gel ka-men ü - ber Nacht und ha-ben

Frie den mein-er Brust ge bracht

The momentary peace of love seems heavenly because, in loving, one suffers so much.

In other songs the playful element which is inherent in the poems disappears completely from Wolf's setting. In *Der Mond hat eine schwere Klag' erhoben*, for instance, a conventional conceit becomes a universal lament. Each vocal phrase climbs slowly upwards and then droops through a wide interval, usually a seventh. The piano preserves one figure throughout—widely spaced falling thirds in dotted rhythm, often clashing acutely with the repeated notes of the vocal line. The voice part reaches its climax at the end of the poem, in a wonderful phrase which telescopes the slowly rising third and the falling seventh which dominate the song: while the piano's tension crystallizes into a grinding dissonance which softly uncoils itself not on to the tonic chord, but on to the flat submediant. In this setting the conventional conceit associating the moon with the 'starry' eyes of the beloved seems to be obliterated, in Wolf's imagination, by the profound mythological associations of the moon with solitude. No doubt it was his awareness of his own isolation which gave to the song so tragic an intensity; yet feeling could hardly be more objectified than it is in the austere progression of this piano part, or in the voice's reticent response to the inflexions of the words.

In his greatest songs Wolf is a miniaturist who epitomizes a dramatic situation in the lyrical moment. Yet the part of him that nursed Wagnerian ambitions pursued, or was pursued by, the desire to create a large-scale opera. At the same time he was half afraid of his desire. In his heart he knew that if he was to create a big work, its basis would be different from Wagner's. He sought a comic—and Mediterranean—subject, as opposed to Teutonic gloom, because in such a theme he could find the objectivity he sought in his songs. If *Der Corregidor*, his only completed opera, is a failure the reason is that he had not the courage of his convictions. The Wagnerian treatment is appropriate neither to the subject nor to Wolf's professed intentions.

Though the libretto is confused and dramatically intractable, one suspects that Wolf came to approve of it precisely because it encouraged him to compose from point to point, using the leitmotive technique—as Wagner did not—as a substitute for musical coherence. He was capable of thinking in extended terms, as is proved by his adolescent quartet and by the superbly rich, if over-complex, symphonic poem, *Penthesilea*. Presented with a dramatic situation, however, his instinct was to crystallize it into a moment of musical and psychological illumination. Thus *Der Corregidor* contains some magnificent music, which occurs whenever isolated incidents fired the composer's imagination. The Tio Lukas and Frasquita duets have the glow of Wolf's Latin love-songs, while the continuous thematic evolution of the orchestral parts acquires, within the surge of Wagnerian harmony, an almost Bachian lucidity. Such music, however profound in its tenderness, is a part of the opera's comic world. Lukas's tragic monologue of jealousy, on the other hand, is not; and Wolf noticed no discrepancy because he was interested only in the climacteric moment which summarized a situation. In this sense *Der Corregidor* is less an opera than a Wolfian songbook with orchestra. It is interesting that Wolf showed not the slightest concern over the theatrical aspects of opera production; he never even noticed when changes were made, let alone offering any opinion about them. His operas were projected in his mind as completely as were his songs. For him, the stage was a redundancy.

Manuel Venegas, however—the opera which he had recently started when mental breakdown finally overtook him—suggests that he might ultimately have created the kind of opera he wanted and needed to write. The fifty pages of score which he completed do not reach the dramatic core of a libretto as powerful as *Der Corregidor* was ramshackle; but there is enough music to give promise of a new, impressive operatic technique. Though there are still leitmotives, the texture of the music is now quite un-Wagnerian, as simple as it is passionate. The change that has come over Wolf's operatic style exactly parallels the change that occurred between the Spanish and Italian song-books. Manuel's part is, as Wolf said, "a part to tear a cat in"; precisely because his passion is so violent, it is objectified in simple, lyric grandeur, as in the noble diatonicism of his invocation to his home town. Even the love music, though more chromatic, is strong and direct in its contour, with none of the orchestral proliferation of *Der Corregidor*; Wolf significantly said that he was going to orchestrate the opera "like Mozart". Whether he would have been able to sustain continuity throughout the whole drama we cannot tell. We can say, however, that the surviving fragment, dealing mainly with introductory matter, has a cumulative sweep that Wolf did not approach in his earlier opera.

Whether or no *Manuel Venegas* could have been an operatic complement to Wolf's mature songs, it is fitting that his last completed work should have been the most intimate songs he ever wrote. In setting Michelangelo's sonnets he identified his own bitter lot with that of the sculptor, expressing his disillusion in what he called a "truly antique simplicity". The bare, skeletonic *Alles endet, was entstehet*, with its grinding ninths and diminished sevenths, would prove unbearable in its pessimism, were not the 'Bachian' texture of motives in both voice and piano parts a paradoxical germination. The muffled wail of the single semitone swells to the stepwise rise and fall of a third, then to the arch of the third prepared by the tense diminished fourth, then to the rising sixth followed by a scale-wise descent, then to a combination of several of these metamorphoses in various rhythms (Ex. 33).

Wolf's life had been a tension between potentially overwhelming passion and the discipline of art; in the tightly wrought, monumental simplicity of this song he finds freedom in submitting to the ultimate discipline of death. He was, he said, "really scared" by the song and, contemplating it, feared for his reason. Indeed, there was nothing further he could say.

Ex. 33. Wolf: Alles endet

He lingered for several years in the mental home, his mind and spirit destroyed. Megalomaniac delusions could at last reign unchecked.

There is a strange appendix to Wolf in the work and career of Henri Duparc [1848–1933], who composed all of his exiguous output sporadically between 1870 and 1885. He shared with Wolf a pathological nervous intensity and a devotion to Wagner. His response to verbal inflexion is hardly less sensitive than Wolf's, though his melody—deriving from Bizet's *opéra comique* and the delicately sensuous curves of Gounodesque *cantilena*—is less declamatory, more spontaneously lyrical. The intensity of his personality, however, carries his melodies far beyond the range of conventional French charm. The suave curves grow ample, the resonant spacing of the piano's Wagnerian dissonance gives to the themes a noble passion.

Formally, Duparc has a more direct relation to classical tradition than Wolf. Compare, for instance, Wolf's Calvary song, *Herr, was trägt der Boden hier* with Duparc's setting of a prose translation of Tom Moore's *Elégie* on Emmett. Both have in common a preoccupation with the Wagnerian appoggiatura; but whereas in Wolf the dissonances painfully shatter the line, in Duparc they serve rather to underline the melody's growth (Ex. 34). The 'hidden resolutions', the rising sequences, do not destroy the simple architectural tonality, which moves from tonic minor (with a suggestion of major deriving from the insistence on the dominant seventh of the subdominant) to relative major, and then back to tonic minor (with the major feeling rather more strongly defined). Even in *Phidylé*, where the tonalities range far from the home tonic, the mediant relationships are both broadly and symmetrically

Ex. 34. Duparc: Elégie
(Voice)

planned. The effect is quite different from that of Wolf's more fevered, tonally ambiguous epigrams.

In some ways the spaciousness of Duparc's periods is—for all his architectural classicism—more Wagnerian than Wolf's intimate precision. The big dramatic songs, such as *Le Manoir de Rosamunde* or *La Vague et la Cloche*, have a compulsive sweep like that of Wagnerian opera: consider the transition, in the latter song, from the clanging bare fifths to the pulsing chromatic accompaniment to the voice's soaring phrase at the words "Pourquoi n'as-tu pas dit, O rêve". Even a song such as *Au pays où se fait la Guerre*, in which the texture is less obviously Wagnerian, depends for its effect on the fact that the beautiful modal melody develops under the stress of a dramatic situation; it gains intensity from the increasingly chromatic part-writing of the piano, until the grandly 'operatic' peroration in the final strophe. Such music seems to call for theatrical presentation as Wolf's music—even in his opera—does not. The purely lyrical songs, like the wonderful *Invitation au Voyage*, also have this Wagnerian amplitude; for although incidental chromatic and enharmonic subtleties abound, the basic progression of the harmony is extremely slow, moving over and around sustained pedal points. The piano parts are beautifully written and a delight to play; but they are all orchestral in the sense that they suggest the 'pianistic' orchestration of the nineteenth century. Floating arpeggios approximate to a haze of strings, pedal notes to sustained horns.

From the depths of his introspection, Wolf had found, through the Mediterranean lucidity of his art, a vision of the bliss of love. Similarly, the quintessence of Duparc's passion leads to his invocation to the "ordre et beauté" of art, the "luxe, calme et volupté", which is Baudelaire's heaven. And the discovery killed his mind and spirit, as it killed Wolf's. Having created thirteen compositions which are the greatest achievement of French song after Berlioz, Duparc lived on for nearly fifty years, creatively mute, imaginatively dead. The paralysis that afflicted him was perhaps more dreadful than the delirium of Wolf's last years, both because it was so prolonged and because the creative flame had produced, from him, so little. He was not mad; his spirit simply withered into inanition. His life and death are, even more than Wolf's, a parable of the terrors of moral isolation.

2

FRANCK AND HIS DISCIPLES: WITH A NOTE ON SKRYABIN

W E have noted that, during the nineteenth century, French culture did not suffer the disintegration that afflicted German culture—possibly because the French had experienced their revolution in fact. Yet the preservation of a façade of orthodoxy could not suppress dissensions within the mind. Composers such as Berlioz, or even Fauré, are not less original for maintaining a classical objectivity. Minor figures such as Gounod and Saint-Saëns can remain creative while being guardians of academic respectability; though they may not be great composers, they are musical personalities, in a way that the 'academic' composers of Germany or of this country were no longer.

While French composers of the generation following Berlioz were conservative in a very different sense from that revolutionary autocrat, the French none the less had their minor masters of romantic isolation. Duparc was such a composer, in whom Wagnerian passion was controlled by classical lyricism. Only in one composer, perhaps, does this discipline break down; and it is no accident that at the end of the nineteenth century César Franck [1822–1890] became a Myth which modestly parallels the Wagnerian legend. Franck's music, according to Vincent d'Indy, was the natural successor to Beethoven's *Missa Solemnis*, which had been written in 1822, the year when Franck was born! Nowadays, we are suspicious of the halo of stained glass with which the disciples adorned Franck. We cannot see much connexion between his music and the *Missa Solemnis*; and if we can see that there is a relationship between Franck's music and *Parsifal*, we doubt whether that makes him a saint and a mystic. *Parsifal* is the inverse of *Tristan*; renunciation and eroticism are inextricable: and in Franck's chromaticism and enharmony there may be a similar equivocation. A passionate and simple nature struggles against circumstances—the oppressive influence of his father, the subtler domination of his no less monstrous wife, the bad taste of his time, the adulation of his disciples, and possibly a certain innate lack of intelligence.

Though these would seem to be formidable obstacles, we cannot merely regret them, for they called forth Franck's latent genius. The music of what d'Indy dignified as Franck's First Period was written between 1841 and 1858, while his father was trying to launch him as a piano virtuoso. It is salon music almost entirely destitute of personality. When in 1858 he was appointed organist of St. Clotilde's, he deserted the salon for the church; but his music did not radically alter. This was a bad period for French church music, for, in a materialistic world, the average liturgical work could not be spiritually committed. The music's chromaticism was in itself neither good nor bad. An eighteenth-century composer such as Couperin could write—in the Elevation settings from his organ masses—music as chromatic as anything in Gounod, or—in the "Recordata est" from the *Seconde Leçon des Ténèbres*—could compose an aria operatically ripe in its lyricism, voluptuous in its dissonant suspensions. Yet the music remains pure, strong, spiritually valid: perhaps because the seductions of harmony reinforce a nobly sustained line. Gounod's pretty pieties and sanctimonious eroticisms fall into tepidly disintegrative two-bar periods. Franck's oratorios live on a higher plane of creativity; yet the passages in which his harmonic imagination catches fire are hardly frequent enough to discount the conventionalities. Significantly, when Franck tries to portray Satan he relapses into musical comedy.

Mme Franck would have liked her husband to compose hymn-book insipidities all his life; it was not the flights of harmonic genius which she admired in *Les Béatitudes*, but the tracts in which the salon composer donned a surplice. When, in his middle fifties, Franck finally discovered the springs of his creative energy, it was not through the agency of the Church, nor from the example of his revered master. Even in the later oratorios, in which Gounod was his ostensible model, the deepest formative influence was Liszt—and indirectly through him Schumann, Beethoven, Wagner, and the German tradition. The dominance of an alien culture led to his becoming one of the Originals of the nineteenth century. Like Wagner himself, he took a long time to discover what he wanted to say; if he took even longer than other hyper-individualist composers, such as Moussorgsky and Delius, this may have been because he

could not start *ab ovo*, but had first to live down a tradition that
was, for him, moribund.

However this may be, the real Franck emerges when he aban-
dons the search for the sublime and allows his sensuous imagination free play. The symphonic poem, *Les Eolides*, strives after
no religious ideal and emulates no academic model. It is
deliberately episodic; chromaticism breaks up the lines into
fragmentary phrases which create a shimmering texture, scored
for divided strings and cooing woodwinds, in a manner that
already suggests Debussy's impressionism. Yet although *Les
Eolides* intimates a new technique it is not in itself a decisive
turning-point. This comes in the Piano Quintet of 1879, in
which for the first time we have the direct expression of the
Franckian ego. We are not surprised that Mme Franck loathed
it ("César, I do not approve of that music you are playing");
that the respectable Saint-Saëns objected to playing it in public;
that it even brought a blush to the cheek of so experienced a
sensualist as Franz Liszt. Whether or no it was composed in the
heat of a (suppressed?) passion for Franck's pupil, Augusta
Holmes, it sums up the essential Franckian theme: eroticism
curbed, or rebellious passion that struggles to break free.
Franck's most typical melody—oscillating chromatically around
a single note, or see-sawing between the tonic and the
mediant—embodies precisely this desire to escape from fixation:
as does the extreme chromaticism of the harmony, as contrasted
with the metrical rigidity of the four-bar periods (Ex. 35):

Ex.35. Franck: Piano Quintet (first movement)

The more remote and enharmonic the modulations, the more
metrically strict the prison of the sequential periods becomes; or

alternatively, the more rigid is the periodicity, the more abstruse become the tonal relationships, as compensation.

In this particular, Franck offers a more extravagant version of a technique which we saw to be characteristic of Schumann. Enharmony—the static point that changes its meaning, striving to become something else—has as crucial a significance in Franck's psychology as it has in Schumann's; and Franck's cyclic form, even more than Schumann's thematic recurrences, becomes a prison for the waywardness of harmony and melody. Beethoven transforms his themes in the course of the creative life of his compositions; Franck brings his themes 'back' as a protest against his instinctive harmonic and modulatory licence. Both Franck's and Schumann's cyclical processes are an *idée fixe* in a sense more frightening than their overt intentions. Indeed, all Franck's 'weaknesses'—his repetitive clauses, his artificial transitions, his chromatic sequences, his cluttered texture—are part of his essential experience. Beethoven was the rebel who strove to create a new world. Franck was the unwilling rebel whose only desire was to be able to accept.

This quintet—a work of genius, of however hectic a character —let loose the creative flood. For the remaining years of his life Franck poured out a series of works which seemed to his disciples *sui generis*, and a spiritual illumination. At this date, looking at his large-scale piano works, we can see that Franck derived his 'motivic' conception and his piano technique from Liszt: his harmonic polyphony from Wagner: his philosophical solemnity from Beethoven: his interest in counterpoint and to some extent his chromaticism from Bach—or at least from Liszt's mutation of Bach's chromaticism in his *Weinen, Klagen* Variations. Yet Franck's contemporaries were justified in thinking him a profoundly original force. For what he learned from Liszt concerned only the superficies of his art; what he has in common with Wagner is more an innate affinity than an influence; and his relationship to Bach and Beethoven is a creative misunderstanding. Bach's counterpoint depends on tension between linear independence and the dramatic logic of harmony; Franck's counterpoint is always dominated by harmony. The fugue subject of the *Prelude, Chorale, and Fugue* has a generic resemblance to the subject of the B minor Fugue from Book I of Bach's *Forty-eight*. But whereas Bach's theme—chromatic though it is—creates a continuous line through all the vagaries of tonality, Franck's soon becomes an excuse for harmonic passage-work (Ex. 36):

Ex.36. Franck: Prélude, Chorale et Fugue

Franck's method is not 'wrong'; it merely suggests that, whereas in Bach personal feeling is absorbed into a creative act, in Franck the quasi-mystical sublimity of the contrapuntal opening is absorbed into subjective passion. Franck's technique is here, as elsewhere, not so much Bachian as Wagnerian, without Wagner's heroic stature.

In his Symphony Franck thought he was emulating the evolutionary form of Beethoven's last years. Yet the Symphony's most impressive moments are purely sensuous, as in the haunting allegretto. Cyclical form is here not so much growth as imprisonment, as it had been in the first of Franck's truly representative works, the Quintet. Once more the main theme is tied to a naggingly reiterated mediant; and its Lisztian apotheosis in the last movement sounds more like neurotic obsession than a hard-won victory over the self. The only work of Franck which has any real resemblance to late Beethoven is his String Quartet, in which his melodic sense is freer and more expansive, less anchored to obsession. The harmony, being conceived in terms of four equal-voiced melodic instruments, achieves orchestral luxuriance without being crabbed or cluttered. The thematic transformations may be quite unlike Beethoven's; but here, perhaps for the first time, the senses sing and flow, so that the music's evolution becomes creative fulfilment. Much the same is true of *Psyché*, his last orchestral work, which stands as a companion piece to *Les Eolides*, the first creation of his maturity. The earlier work had been momentary impressionism; the last work is more linear, more transparently scored, more continuously generative. Inhibitions of more than usual severity had first pricked Franck's muse into activity. He triumphs over them in the opulence of his Quartet and of this symphonic poem—to which Mme Franck refused to listen.

In his very last works, the Organ Chorales, Franck tries to

epitomize his new sense of power by creating works in which the form *is* the generation of the theme—as it is in the first movement of Borodin's E flat Symphony and in some movements of Sibelius. D'Indy thought that these pieces contained the best of Bach, Beethoven, and Wagner in one! It would be more appropriate to say that they combine the improvisatory virtuosity of Franck's youth with the eroticism of his old age; but that they suffer, in comparison with the Quartet or *Psyché*, from a suggestion of keyboard rhapsody. They are freer, formally and texturally, than the Quintet, which ten years earlier had provoked the swelling tide of Franck's passion. But though the emotion screams less stridently against the barriers of inhibition, it is perhaps more febrile. When Franck no longer feels repulsion at his own desires, we find ourselves feeling it for him.

Once more we react against an element of pretence in Franck's sublimity. We can be swept away by his passion, but not by his grandiloquence; and we return with most affection to his most spiritually modest works. In the Symphonic Variations for piano and orchestra, for instance, he took as his model Schumann, a composer whom we have seen to have an even more intimate relation to Franck than has Wagner; and he found in the variation style of Schumann's *Etudes Symphoniques* an idiom that suited him to perfection, for it offered free fantasy without an oppressively dramatic purpose. He further showed intuitive insight in devising a double subject, each part of which approximated to one of the contradictory aspects of his nature—submission and rebellion. Franck could not be content that the loveliest, most sweetly sensuous music he ever wrote should be the first appearance of the Acceptance theme. Each part of the subject must have its own development, and the two must coalesce in the spiritual radiance of an apotheosis Finale. Yet perhaps the most revealing feature of Franck's art is that this does not, in fact, happen. Instead, the Finale returns to the climate of Franck's youth, being delightful salon music, better than Saint-Saëns, utterly remote from Bach, Beethoven, or for that matter Wagner. The Variations are not so consistently fine a work as the Quartet. But their deficiencies, as much as their virtues, make them perhaps Franck's most representative, and most moving, work.

For a composer's power over his auditors depends on the

authenticity of his experience, even when authenticity involves damaging limitations. This is obvious enough if we compare Franck with two of his younger contemporaries, Chausson [1855–1899] and d'Indy [1851–1931]. In ultimate achievement, Chausson is probably a finer composer than Franck. Though he learned much from both Franck and Wagner, his elegiac nobility is without Franck's hysteria, largely because his lyrical line has an almost Berliozian power and span. One can see this in a fervently nostalgic song like *Le Temps des Lilas*, in the cantabile violin writing of *Poème*, or in the broad opening theme of the symphony (Ex. 37):

Ex.37. Chausson: Symphony in B♭

and one has only to compare his Symphony with Franck's to appreciate the difference between true nobility and the grandiose intention. Chausson's Symphony, like Franck's, is cyclical: yet is at the same time genuinely Beethovenian in its thematic evolution. Even d'Indy, though melodically less distinguished than Chausson, shares with him a nobility of conception derived both from Beethoven and from the French classical tradition. The massive drama of his Symphony or Piano Sonata, the *Parsifal*-like harmonies of his operas, acquire the dignity of an inherited ideal of civilization. This is perhaps still more strikingly evident in the work of two of Franck's younger disciples, Albéric Magnard [1865–1914] and Paul Dukas [1865–1935]. Both were highly personal composers whose dramatic potency had more real affinity with Beethoven than with Franck; and both had an instinctive feeling for the serene grandeur of Rameau and the French classical age. Yet Franck's neurotic music has had a greater influence on European history than the civilized, imaginatively felt art of Chausson, d'Indy, Magnard, or Dukas. Its lure is insidious; and this may be because, in his divided sensibility, he is not only less French than his younger compatriots, but also more deeply representative of something that happened, during the nineteenth century, to 'the mind of Europe'.

From this point of view, there is an odd appendix to Franck's career in that of Skryabin [1872–1915]—a cosmopolitan Russian who settled in Paris. Skryabin's early music shows an affinity with Tchaikowsky in the drooping pathos of its lyricism: with Chopin in its fondness for enharmonic progressions and for a languishing decorative elegance: and with Liszt in its exploitation of the bravura possibilities of the piano. In the larger works, such as the early piano sonatas, the strenuous quality of the quick movements and the conception of sonata as a dramatic conflict suggest continuity with the methods of Beethoven and Brahms. By 1903, however, the date of the Fourth Sonata, the wealth of higher chromatic discords in Skryabin's music has made sonata form anachronistic. A conflict of keys is impossible unless tonality is at first clearly defined; in this music the prevalence of *Parsifal*-like augumented chords—along with the complexity of the counter-rhythms—gives the music a flushed and fevered atmosphere that leads on to the first of Skryabin's explicitly revolutionary works, the Sixth Sonata (1911).

Key signatures are here abandoned; and instead of the organizing force of tonality, Skryabin seeks to derive all his material from a basic chord formation. He is thus doing deliberately what Wagner in *Parsifal* was beginning to do without conscious awareness. Skryabin usually derives his 'mystic' chords from the harmonic series, treating sevenths, ninths, and thirteenths as concords, splitting them up to obtain linear motives that can be imbued, in his mind at least, with transcendental significance. The chord structures he chooses tend to be built on fourths rather than on thirds—the ground chord in the Sixth Sonata is G, C sharp, F, B, E, A flat, and D; and the function of the chord is in some ways comparable with that of the twelve-note row,* in that it is supposed to give coherence to every aspect of the composition. But whereas the row is an entirely linear means of organizing a composition, one could not hope to find a more complete example of the subservience of line to harmony than is represented by Skryabin's late works.

It is obvious that such a conception of harmony is essentially static, and therefore more suitable to short than to long compositions. We shall see later that Skryabin's music has much in common with the music of Debussy's middle years; both use the higher chromatic discords and the piano's overtones in a way

* See pp. 990, et seq.

that is nervous rather than structural. But Debussy's artistic maturity enabled him to know what he was about: to perceive that his 'moments of reality' implied a new—and in some ways very old—criterion of form remote from the harmonic processes of the nineteenth century. Skryabin had no such self-knowledge. He even tried to write big 'sonata' movements by basing the music on two chord formations rather than on one. The two chord formations cannot possibly have the effect of the traditional tonic-dominant opposition, for they are both so complex that the harmonically derived themes cannot be recognized as such. All the chords are so neutral in their complexity, all the lines so flaccid in their rhythmic elaboration, that the music could hardly be more remote from the dynamism of the sonata principle; it is pertinent to note how frequently Skryabin's basses alternate between the two notes of the harmonically neutral tritone. The music becomes a titillation of the aural palate. It depends on the pedal effects of the modern grand piano, which dominates all Skryabin's musical thought, even that for the orchestra.

As musical sensation, these titillations are often very beautiful. The fluttering overtones of his *céleste volupté*, the tolling bells of his *appels mystérieux*, the ecstatic shimmer of sound in the *douce ivresse* of his prestissimo dance movements—these represent a genuine minor contribution to European music, in that there is nothing quite like them, for all their affinities with Wagner, Franck, and Debussy. The danger inherent in this rhapsodic utterance—in anything other than very tiny pieces—is monotony of mood; and while to Skryabin's early disciples the Ninth Sonata (the 'Black Mass') was a hellishly gloomy piece and the Tenth Sonata (the 'White Mass') a seraphically happy, to us at this date they sound much alike. Skryabin whipping himself into ecstasy is not so different from that other cosmopolitan Russian, Tchaikowsky, whipping himself into fury or despair: except that Skryabin's melodic vitality is so much lower.

Franck fascinates us as long as he is preoccupied with a fight between his eroticism and his inhibitions: or when, as in the Quartet, his eroticism develops into something not less passionate, but less subjective. He begins to bore us when, as in the Organ Chorales, he has nothing to offer us *except* his masochism and auto-eroticism; for the fact that these experiences are genuine and common does not make them less tedious for other people.

In reducing every element of music to the momentary harmonic thrill, Skryabin in his later work has gone much further than Franck to create a music which is simply (if not purely) masochism and auto-eroticism. We can respond to Franck's turmoils because we have probably experienced something similar ourselves: whereas the heat of Skryabin's narcissism now leaves us cold. We are suspicious of a composer who *tells* us he is celestially voluptuous. He knows when he is voluptuous, no doubt; but what about the other part? We have more respect for Debussy, who wrote celestially voluptuous music if ever any man did: "Vous avez été au ciel, M. Debussy?" "Oui, mais, j'en cause jamais avec les étrangers."*

Wagner heroically made a new religion out of his senses; Franck's disciples, in a smaller way, tried to do as much for him. Skryabin, in later years, would have regenerated the world with a cosmic theosophy derived from the oscillations of his nerves. The gigantic symphony of sounds, smells, and colours which he was planning when he died was to be a rite and a sacrifice, its creator the new Messiah. The Mystery was to be performed in a hemispherical temple in India, mirrored in a lake so as to create a circle, the perfect form; and the performance would produce in the participants a "supreme final ecstasy", wherein the physical plane of consciousness would dissolve away, and "a world cataclysm" begin. The only objection was that, even in his lifetime, the Messiah was lunatic. Wagner's egomania was 'abnormal'; but he was great enough to persuade his contemporaries to believe in it, and still more to convince us, a hundred years later, that his madness was, while it lasted, truth. Skryabin, on the other hand, seems to us a man of exquisite sensibility who went crazy: by turns silly, pathetic, horrifying, a portent of Europe's sickness. In Skyrabin's music the bubble of the inflated ego bursts; and the metaphor, though grotesque, is apt if we think of the limp flaccidity of his technique. Perhaps it is not fortuitous that the only later composer who, starting from an unambiguously Wagnerian aesthetic, can still move us deeply, came to learn a new humility. Delius's humility has nothing to do with Franck's religious conscience; in the long run, however, it is difficult to know what to call it, unless it be a pagan, pre-Christian religious awareness.

* "You have been to Heaven, M. Debussy?" "Yes: but I never chatter about it to strangers."

3

DELIUS, SIBELIUS, AND NATURE

Delius's hyper-romanticism is in part associated with the fact that he was born, in the nineteenth century [1862–1934], in Britain—not, moreover, in the pastoral gentleness of the English countryside, but in industrial Bradford. His childhood passions were for the music of Chopin and for Byron's *Childe Harold*; and the sensitive soul and solitary pilgrim could hardly have been more completely a misfit in a materialistic world. In adolescence he was put into the family business. Mercantile visits to Norway produced few contracts for Bradford wool, much admiration of Norwegian scenery and of the non-industrial melancholy of Norwegian folk-song. Business trips to Paris were hardly more productive. Here the young Delius, romantic, athletic, handsome, affluent, became the associate of artists, poets, and (to a lesser extent) musicians in the bohemian coteries of Montmartre.

Delius's father not unnaturally regarded his son as a liability rather than an asset to the business. An opportunity occurred to acquire for Frederick a grapefruit farm in Florida; Delius accepted such a career, largely because Florida was exotic, remote from Bradford. The grapefruit did not prosper. On the other hand, Frederick's artistic proclivities developed so vigorously that they finally overcame the business-man's distrust of art. His father agreed that he should study music; so he went, of course, to Germany, for there was in Britain no indigenous school of composition. Here he developed a wild enthusiasm for Wagner and a lesser fervour for Strauss; and composed quantities of music, all undistinctive in style, passively Teutonic with a mild infusion of the chromatic nostalgia of Grieg.

Then in 1899 he produced a mammoth symphonic poem, *Paris*, a Nocturne, the Song of a Great City. The orchestral texture and to some extent the structure are modelled on Strauss; yet *Paris* is a work of unmistakably original genius. "It came to me very slowly what I wanted to do", said Delius; "and when it came, it came all at once." In *Paris*, Straussian opulence and vitality have already become retrospective. The music has the brilliance and energy of Delius's youth; yet the piercing chromatic intensity of the slow section—the first quintessential Delian moment—tells us that he is already cut off from the gay abandon of his Parisian days. 'Paris in spring' has become a cinematic cliché. Yet it can stand as a symbol of the hopeful joys of our youth. Delius's *Paris* recreates the impetuous joy, while transmuting the hope to regret.

Despite its superficial resemblance to Strauss, *Paris* is much further from the classical tradition than are Strauss's symphonic poems. The continuity of flow which Delius achieves between the sections has more affinity with Wagner; and his relationship to Wagner's last works is, like that of Franck, not so much conscious imitation as an intuitive discipleship. Like Wagner, Delius believed that the only reality is one's own passions. "The chief thing is to develop your own personality to the uttermost." Never mind if you make mistakes, nor even if you hurt other people, so long as you keep your soul intact. Like Nietzsche, he was a Dionysiac genius who held that the decline of the Greeks came with the growth of intellect; who held that all ethical judgement (and hence Christianity) was bad because it inhibited spontaneity.* The human creature's one essential duty was to have "high courage and self-reliance": which necessarily involved contempt for God and Society. "Humanity is incredible; it will believe anything to escape reality"—to avoid relying on its own resources. Yet Delius did not see that his attitude was itself an unrealistic extension of the Wagnerian Dream: for it is literally impossible to be entirely self-sufficient, and difficult to ignore the world unless, like Delius, you are economically independent of it.

This Dionysiac rejection of thought—this belief in personal feeling as the only absolute—is reflected in Delius's approach to composition. "I don't believe in learning harmony and counterpoint. Learning kills instinct. Never believe the saying that one must hear music many times in order to understand it. It is utter nonsense, the last refuge of the incompetent. . . . For me music is very simple. It is the expression of a poetical and

---

* Delius's biggest work—though not his best—is a setting of Nietzsche. The title of *A Mass of Life* is itself anti-Christian.

emotional nature." Just as Delius could afford to talk so grandly of courage and self-reliance because he had no material problems, so he could afford to ignore technique only because he came at the end of a great creative period whose conventions he accepted ready-made. He could compose empirically because he did not have to think about first principles.

Within his Teutonic inheritance, his extravagantly personal mannerisms grew alongside an increasing hatred of other people's music. He preserved a lifelong admiration for Wagner and a minor enthusiasm for Chopin and Grieg. He dismissed Beethoven's opus 110 Sonata as rhetorical passage-work, could see nothing in Palestrina but mathematics, and tolerated little twentieth-century music except that which was dedicated to him. In his pathetic old age he spent hours listening to recordings of his own music, which alone seemed to measure up to his ideal of Fine Feeling. And for him Fine Feeling meant the flux of sensation through the creator: the apotheosis of the personal life in chromatic harmony. Other composers have written music which is momentarily as chromatic as Delius's. But in Weelkes, Bach, or Mozart the chromatic intensification or disintegration is conceived in relation to an accepted norm of tonality. In such a passage from Delius as the wonderful entry of the wordless chorus in *A Song of the High Hills* this norm is ceasing to exist; the graded tensions and relaxations of the chords are themselves becoming the form (Ex. 38):

Ex.38. Delius: A Song of the High Hills
(Chorus)

Now and again Delius's music hints at a classical procedure —a hypothetical recapitulation, or a section built on a dominant-tonic relationship. More normally, his criterion of consonance and dissonance has become personal and empirical, rather than the property of a tradition. Like Wagner, he feels (rather than thinks) improvisatorily at the keyboard; and this is a dangerous method of creation because the composer has to be 'inspired' to carry it off. A failure of inspiration is less obvious in a composer who can fall back on a traditional mould. Delius can rely on nothing external to himself; 'inspiration' has to create the form appropriate to each composition. We can see why the one positive comment he ever made about musical technique was that "a sense of flow" was the only thing that mattered. His strength lies in the fact that, like Wagner, he so frequently attains this flow: that whereas Skryabin's obsession with the harmonic moment disintegrates line and structure, Delius creates in very long harmonic and melodic periods. His norm of progression may be personal rather than traditional; but his music, no less than Wagner's, does imply growth and cumulation.*

In one particular, however, Delius goes beyond Wagner. In *Tristan*, Wagner reduces God and Civilization to projections of his own ego. Other people exist only as the objects of his love and hate. But this at least implies the existence of people to be loved and hated: whereas in Delius's most typical music there is no human population at all—only himself and solitude. *Paris*, the earliest of his mature works, is the only one that is about people living and loving, together; and even then the passion is partly retrospective. It is significant that Delius's early operas, which deal with real people in a more or less realistic setting, are failures dramatically and, as music, not even typical Delius. The finest of his smaller works, *In a Summer Garden*, conveys the passive reactions of his senses to the sounds, sights, and smells of a summer in which he is alone. Among his larger works, *A Song of the High Hills* embodies his own yearning in communion

* In this context we may refer to the music of another composer of romantic nostalgia, Arnold Bax [1883–1953]. His most successful works are those in which his lyricism is most ecstatic. In the wonderful *Ora Mater Filium* the sensuous choral sonorities are given vitality by the compulsive flow of the vocal lines: and to a lesser degree this is the case with the instrumental writing of the finer (more rhapsodic) symphonic poems, such as *The Garden of Fand*. The big three-movement symphonies, on the other hand, tend to be convincing only when they are rhapsodic and non-symphonic in style. Though constructed with great care, they are apt to sound illogically episodic, because the elaborately engineered correspondences and thematic transformations do not 'work'. Wagner was right to insist on "the art of transition"—which was also what Delius meant by "a sense of flow". For the relationships between the elements of a composition cannot in themselves create order; what matters is how one gets from one 'correspondence' to the next.

with the solitudes of Nature; and the human voices of the chorus
are impersonally wordless.

From this there is a significant technical development. The
essence of the music may be the flux of sensation—the sighing
of the Wagnerian appoggiaturas with which the work opens, the
fluctuating chromatic woof of the choral texture. None the less,
all the component lines which make up the harmony *sing* and
are, individually considered, vocal, often modal, in contour.
Still more in the works involving a solo voice or instrument along
with orchestra and chorus, the rhapsodic solo melody tends to
be pentatonic, like folk-song or medieval monody, as though it
were seeking a oneness beyond the sensory flux (Ex. 39):

Ex. 39. Delius: Violin Concerto

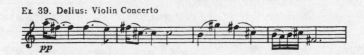

Again, the celebration of life in and for itself leads to the
desire to lose the self in the contemplation of Nature or in the
supposedly simpler satisfactions of a lost youth; for the passion
is too strong to be borne. Hatred of orthodox religiosity leads to
a pantheistic view of human experience. The theme of Delius's
first mature and representative opera is that, while passion is the
only reality, the sham that passes for reality renders passion
untenable. The ideal love of the Village Romeo and Juliet, like
that of Tristan and Parsifal, can find consummation only in
oblivion.

The desire for Nirvana as the only resolution of passion is
common to Wagner and Delius; the pantheistic ecstasy is
peculiar to Delius. Wagner never lost his belief in himself, even
when he found that his passions were synonymous with death.
Delius's hatred of God and Man was more radical, yet he found
something positive in his very isolation. His nature-mysticism
parallels that of Whitman and of Richard Jefferies. His music is
a Song of Myself and the Story of My Heart; and there are
obvious parallels between his empirical harmonic flow and the
free verse rhythm of Whitman, the surging prose of Jefferies.
His most perfect work—*Sea Drift*—is a setting of Whitman; and
it is music pervaded by regret for life once vivid and vital, from
which one is now separated. The technique whereby the solo

baritone line is woven within the orchestral and choral texture contrasts strikingly with the technique of Debussy's *La Mer*. Debussy's piece is a seascape which is also an epic of the strife of human existence. In Delius's work the all-encompassing sea is the eternal mystery from which emerges and into which dissolves the self—symbolized in the frail, lonely bird who sings of his separation from the beloved. Both Delius, who hated the crowd, and Whitman, who loudly proclaimed his identity with it, came to see—as had Wagner—that the relationship of lover and beloved is inevitably transient. The inescapable loss of innocence entails too the loss of love; it is significant that Delius's final evocation of past happiness (in E *major*) is even more heartbreaking than the immediate recognition of death.

Most people, when they think of Delius, remember not the magnetic, Byronic figure of his youth, but the blind, paralysed old man in his garden at Grez. This is not merely a popular misunderstanding; for there is a profound allegorical significance in the fact that Delius was crippled, that he became a spectator of his own imaginative life. His nostalgia—and his compensatory Nature-mysticism—is obviously 'limited'. It is also a perennial and universal human experience, in a way that Skryabin's auto-eroticism is not. This is why, though his weaker works sound faded, those works in which his inspiration flowered should remain impervious to changing fashion. He is not a fashionable composer at present; and the peculiar experience with which he was concerned may never again seem as important as it did when he was creating. On the other hand, it is unlikely, in any foreseeable future, to lose all meaning. Not even a Welfare State—nor anything short of the Kingdom of Heaven—will appease the ambiguous cravings of man, who will remain, as Delius came to see, at once "a proud, and yet a wretched thing".

Sibelius was born in 1865, three years later than Delius and, like him, in a country without a musical tradition. He too was in youth a fascinating personality who disliked big cities and loved solitude. But whereas Delius was driven by hatred for the world in which he was born, Sibelius was brought up, not in a vast mechanized society, but against the background of Nature —more or less the same lonely landscape that had so impressed the adolescent Delius.

Since Finland had never had a musical tradition, and England had forgotten hers, both Sibelius and Delius started to compose in what was then the accepted European idiom. The first works of both composers are Teutonic in style, and devoid of personality; both were well over thirty before they produced any music we could recognize as theirs. There is, however, a fundamental difference between them, associated with Delius's desire to escape from, and Sibelius's acceptance of, his environment. Delius was anti-traditional and anti-intellectual, and his musical god was Wagner. Sibelius was also an individualist, but one who still believed in civilization; his musical god was Beethoven, whom he admired as much for his character as for his musicianship. As an artist, Sibelius at least intended to be a reintegrative force.

From this point of view we may contrast Sibelius with his Danish contemporary Carl Nielsen [1865–1931], who is perhaps the only later symphonist to have worked consistently within the Beethovenian tradition. His First Symphony is obviously Brahmsian in temper; and while his later symphonies have grown increasingly personal in manner and thematically more distinguished, they remain 'conflict' symphonies based on the interplay of themes and rhythmic motives, and on a clash— and ultimate resolution—of tonalities. The range of key relationship is wider and more complex than Beethoven's, but the similarity of approach is unmistakable. Both Beethoven and Nielsen are preoccupied with the experience of 'Becoming'; Nielsen's themes change their identity through conflict just as Beethoven's do, and the victory his symphonies achieve is a triumph of humanism won, not in the interests of the self, but of civilization.

Perhaps Nielsen was able to attain this equilibrium between the ego and society because he lived in a highly developed civilization which was basically stable while being in touch with the violent upheavals Europe experienced during the early twentieth century. Both Tradition and Revolution had meaning for him, as for Beethoven. Yet his society did not, like Beethoven's, carry with it a rich musical tradition; and it is difficult to resist a suspicion that the revolutionary drama in his later work is sometimes too independent of the music. The Second and Third Symphonies are consistent and cogent musical arguments of a type related to Beethoven's symphonic principle.

The Fourth and Fifth Symphonies are certainly more interesting, more personal in their melodic invention; yet this invention seems less purposeful in its musical growth. The famous percussion improvisation in the Fifth Symphony—wherein the side-drum player attempts to destroy the music's evolution—is an externalized presentation of conflict which is exciting once or twice, but less exciting with repeated hearings. For Beethoven, Fate was not an external force which could be thus segregated from the battle of his inner life, which was his music.

It may be that it is no longer possible for a composer to maintain a Beethovenian view of the symphony. If we think that Sibelius's symphonies are in the long run more rewarding than Nielsen's, this may well be related to the fact that Sibelius's affinity with Beethoven is not what it seems, nor even what he thought it was. True, his First Symphony (and most of the Second) is broad, heroic music in the tradition of the nineteenth-century 'conflict' symphony. But in the first movement of the Second Symphony he explores a technique which was to have increasing importance in his later work. Whether or no the technique was suggested to him by the first movement of Borodin's E flat Symphony, he too starts with fragments of line, rhythmic motives, even the tone-colour of an instrument, which slowly interact and evolve until they coalesce in the main themes of the movement at what would normally be the recapitulation. The process is similar to that exemplified in Beethoven's sketch-books: only whereas in Beethoven's case the creation of the themes marks the beginning of the treatment of them—that is, of the composition—in Sibelius's case, as in Borodin's, the growth of the theme is the structure of the movement.

A similar technique is used, with more epigrammatic concision, in the last movement of the Third Symphony and the first movement of the Fifth. But if on the one hand Sibelius investigates the creation of themes from their constituents, on the other hand he winnows down the conventional symphonic structure to its bare bones. Both procedures are often used simultaneously: for instance, the first movement of No. 5 or the last movement of No. 3 may be regarded either as self-generative movements engaged in the creation of themes and of tonal order, or as elliptical telescopings of the customary sonata allegro and scherzo.

The climax of these complementary tendencies towards concentration is reached in the Fourth Symphony of 1911. However Germanic his origins may have been, Sibelius has by this date created an idiom as aggressively personal as that of Delius. The whole of this extraordinary work grows from various ramifications of the tritone—the interval which is most destructive of tonal stability. The first movement generates itself from a brief contorted figure involving a tritone (Ex. 40):

Ex. 40. Sibelius: Symphony No. 4 first movement

rises to a climax by way of a fluttering *moto perpetuo* on the strings; and subsides to its source. The scherzo reverses this process, beginning with a deceptively innocent pastoral theme on the oboe, which is gradually dissected and finally routed by vehement interjections of the tritone. Its stable tonality is also threatened; the tenuous whimper of a fragment of the melody at the end, in a remote key, is disturbingly jerked back to the tonic by the softest, most mysterious notes on the timpani (Ex. 41):

Ex. 41. Sibelius: Symphony No 4 Scherzo

The slow movement is a cross between thematic generation and a skeletonic sonata structure. In the last movement classical rondo style disintegrates into its components. The initial themes are fluid, even gay; but they soon split into their constituent elements of line and rhythm, and the work ends in desolation.

In his First Symphony Sibelius had used the dualistic conventions of the classical symphony in the normal way; in the slow movement of the Second Symphony he had exploited them in an exaggerated form. But it is obvious that his typical method of thematic growth is monistic: and that his winnowing down of the constituents of classical form likewise tends to destroy the dramatic implications of sonata development. So the taut concentration of his symphonies leads him to the one-movement structure of the Seventh, in which all four movements arise out of, and are telescoped into, a single rising diatonic scale and a perfect cadence. Every aspect of the music is a part of the thematic growth; in no music is it less possible to separate orchestration from line, since the tone colour is itself part of the structure—the means of imparting the appropriate stress to each strand.

In later years Sibelius has shown a considerable interest in the music of Palestrina, and it is not fanciful to see Palestrina's influence in the 'pure water' of the Sixth and Seventh Symphonies. Yet despite the hints of modality in the transparent texture of this music, Sibelius is not naturally a polyphonic composer; nor does he seek the late Beethoven's profound fusion of the contradictory principles of sonata and fugue. Indeed, the point at which he arrives in his later work turns out to be closer to Wagner and even to Delius than it is to composers—such as Palestrina and Beethoven—who may seem superficially to resemble him more; and this remains true despite his professed veneration for Beethoven and Palestrina, and his aversion to Wagner. In parts of *Tristan*, Wagner creates a continuous texture which grows from a seminal germ. It is true that the linear motives have less intrinsic importance than they have in Sibelius: that the effect of the music depends more on the flow of the harmonies which the motives generate. None the less, there is a deep affinity between Wagner's sultry and Sibelius's more Nordically austere harmony; and this affinity becomes more strongly marked in Sibelius's later work, especially the Seventh Symphony and *Tapiola*.

Wagner's 'monistic' generation of lines from harmony reduced the universe to his own passions. Sibelius was never thus egocentrically romantic. His preoccupation with formal problems testifies to an awareness of social issues which he inherited from the classical tradition; it was not for nothing that he said he regarded the Mozart allegro as the ideal symphonic movement. But neither is it surprising that Sibelius did not find the preservation of civilization as apparently simple as Mozart found it: that there should be, all through his work, another strain—a tendency towards separateness, a Delian desire to relinquish his personality in nature. Wind, light, space, solitude, all the qualities which he admits to finding in the Finnish land-scape, do not concern him because he wishes to create a musical picture postcard (he has never shown the slightest interest in the nationalist approach to folk-music); they fascinate him because they suggest an experience with which, as the years have gone by, he has grown increasingly obsessed.

Delius, in *A Song of the High Hills* or *Sea Drift*, strives to lose the burden of personality in the pentatonicism of his recurrent cadential formulae; but he cannot free himself from the pull and throb of the harmonic tensions. Sibelius, as he communes with Nature, goes further in self-obliteration, perhaps because his respect for civilization implies a measure of detachment. He goes furthest of all in *Tapiola*, his last-completed, large-scale work. This piece is the ultimate consummation of the trend we have observed, growing gradually stronger throughout his music. The search for oneness could hardly be carried further, for here the entire structure is monothematic, proliferating from a single seed. *Tapiola* is the *ne plus ultra* of Sibelian technique; and in it the human personality seems to dissolve away in Nature's infinities of time and space. It is possible to contend that the Fourth and Sixth Symphonies are more central achievements of European civilization. It is impossible to deny *Tapiola's* significance as a document of our time, or at least of our spiritual legacy from the immediate past. It is surely one of the most terrifying pieces of music ever written.

Sibelius once said: "Look at the great nations of Europe and what they have endured. No savage could have stood so much. I do believe in civilization." When we hear the final assertion of the tonic triad at the end of *Tapiola* we realize what moral strength was necessary to make that assertion, at the end of such a work. And when we look back from *Tapiola* we can see that something like this dissolution of the personality is implicit even beneath the civilization of the earlier symphonies. The spine-chilling *moto perpetuo* towards the end of *Tapiola* has its smaller counterpart in the *moto perpetuos* that occur from the Third Symphony onwards. The wild, inhuman howls of the long internal pedal points in *Tapiola* prove to be an extension of one of the most typical features of Sibelius's scoring. And we see that when all four movements of the Fourth Symphony, having grown from their seminal figures, fade away into their origins, their 'humanity' returns to the earth and air: to that which is not human. Perhaps this oneness in Nature is one of the few means whereby an artist may approach religious experience, in a non-religious and materialistic society. But it is not the oneness for which Beethoven fought so strenuously, nor that which Palestrina or the medieval monodist discovered in making a positive affirmation of faith. It is an escape from humanity. In *A Song of the High Hills* ecstatic strength is not joyful, but melancholy; in *Tapiola* ecstasy can hardly be distinguished from a frigid terror.

That Sibelius was aware of this is suggested by a remarkable letter which he wrote in 1911—the year of the Fourth Symphony: "Yesterday I heard Bruckner's B♭ major Symphony, and it moved me to tears. For a long time afterwards I was completely transported. What a strangely profound spirit, formed by a religious sense. And this profound religiousness we have abolished in our country as something no longer in harmony with our time." Sibelius, like Delius, had a religious sensibility without a faith; and it is possible that his music is a dead end, technically as well as spiritually. It is significant that in the thirty years that have elapsed since he wrote *Tapiola* he seems to have created no music of consequence; what, indeed, could come 'after' the hell of *Tapiola*? He has expressed an impasse in Europe's spiritual history and has brought home to us, with terrifying integrity, a predicament both social and philosophical. Perhaps we have to 'go through' *Tapiola* in order to live again.

4

DEBUSSY AND RAVEL

Delius is the composer of the twilight of a world; Debussy [1862–1918] is at once an end and a beginning. He carries the isolation of the sensory moment a stage further than Wagner or Delius; yet with him the cult of the ego became also a renewal of civilization. No less than Delius he was non-political, non-philosophical, non-religious, a sensual and instinctive atheist. No less than Wagner—and with more exquisite refinement—he was a hedonist and gourmet of the senses who adored cats, women, and silk. With Delius, he believed that learning kills instinct: that "there is more to be gained by watching the sun rise than by hearing the 'Pastoral' Symphony. To some people rules are of primary importance. But my desire is only to reproduce what I hear. Music was intended to receive the mysterious accord that exists between nature and the imagination."

In response to an outraged professor who asked him, during his student days, what 'rule' he followed, Debussy replied: "Mon plaisir." He accepted only "le règle de l'ouie", for "there are no more schools of music, and the main business of the musician to-day is to avoid any kind of outside influence". Living in the ivory tower of his senses, he always preferred " a subject where action is sacrificed to feeling". His ideal of the instinctive composer was Moussorgsky, whose empirical treatment of chords in some ways anticipated his own. He loathed Tchaikowsky because he attempted to stifle his spontaneity in academic convention. He loved Franck because, even in his weaknesses, he was spiritually innocent. He abominated d'Indy and Saint-Saëns because they were intellectually knowing—and also partially 'Teutonic'. He distrusted Beethoven's moral earnestness and, indeed, everything represented by the sonata principle. In apparent paradox, he loved Bach above all composers, even Moussorgsky; on the significance of this we shall have something to say later.

Again, he resembles Delius in that his early music is insignificant and unrepresentative. Naturally, he followed the French tradition in which he had been brought up, rather than the German; and he emulated not Saint-Saëns and the hated academics, but the unpretentious Massenet, who aimed always to charm the senses. None the less, his musical awakening came from Germany, though not from the symphonic tradition. The early symphonic poems of Strauss impressed him; while in Wagner's *Tristan* and *Parsifal* he saw the mingling of all the arts for which the Symbolists yearned. The relationship to Strauss was not, in the long run, important; his affinity with Wagner's last works was profound. Wagner, however, was heroic, Debussy intimate. Wagner wanted to become God, imposing his will on others. Debussy was content simply to be, to exist in his passive reaction to external stimuli. It is interesting that after the initial impact of Wagner Debussy was influenced, during the formative years 1890–1904, far more by impressionist painting and symbolist poetry, and by Nature herself, than by any aspect of European art-music. The music that did interest him was either exotic or primitive, or both—Spanish and Russian folk-music and, most of all, the Javanese music which he heard at the Paris Exhibition. Like Van Gogh, he saw in exotic art another world, valuable because it was remote. Just as Van Gogh found a new experience in the decorative colour of Oriental painting, so Debussy savoured exotic music—the clanging gongs of the Javanese Gamelang—as a new aural sensation.

This preoccupation with 'sound in itself' takes us to the core of the revolutionary element in Debussy's technique. We saw that although the logic of Delius's harmonic progressions is becoming more a matter of personal feeling than of traditional sanction, the idea of progression is still relevant to his music: from which point of view he is still intelligible in relation to the nineteenth-century tradition. For Debussy, however, a chord became an emotional experience in itself. As Wagner and Delius translated their feelings as directly as possible into the symbols of sound, so Debussy transformed into music the reactions of his nerves to the sounds, smells, and colours of Nature. We observe a paradox similar to that which we commented on in Delius: the absolute reliance on personal sensation leads, not to domination over things, but to subservience to them.

From the beginning there was, within Debussy's egoism, a strange humility.

Debussy's desire passively to exploit the aural effect of the overtone series is itself a kind of subservience to Nature. A chord becomes for him a complex of aural vibrations which are also nervous sensation, ranging from the absolute calm of the unison and octave, and the relative tranquillity of the fourth and fifth, to the higher chromatic relations of the harmonic series. One can say, if one likes, that such a passage as the opening of *La Cathédrale Engloutie* revives the technique of medieval organum* (Ex. 42):

Ex. 42 Debussy: La Cathedrale Engloutie

Yet Debussy's attitude to his material is different from that of the medieval composer. "The effect of fifths and fourths", he seems to be saying, "is very calm." The medieval composer also wanted his organum to sound calm, in so far as it was an act of praise, free from personal distress. But he did not think of it in terms of his own nervous system. He used the technique because it was an accepted convention; and it was an accepted convention because it was a natural way to write for voices. In this passage of Debussy's prelude the nerves remain relaxed, whereas they are subtly disturbed in the passages where he employs parallel ninths or elevenths (Ex. 43):

Ex. 43. Debussy: La Cathédrale Engloutie

or thickens out passing notes into passing chords, or fills in two

---

* ORGANUM: see Part I, pp. 41 et seq.

different positions of the same chord with chords of embellishment. But the method is identical in each case: the sense of progression from one point to another is almost entirely lost. Similarly with the many passages that employ added seconds without their resolution. These may sound wistful, nostalgic, and so on *because* they are unresolved; yet to Debussy the concept of resolution is hardly appropriate. These are simply titillations of the aural palate which, in their own right, create an atmosphere of nostalgia.

The most extreme instances of Debussy's tendency to isolate chords from the development of line and structure occur in those pieces which are sometimes described as being in the whole tone scale, though it would be more accurate to refer to them as experiments in the use of augmented fifths suggested by the whole tone scale. No chord is more devoid of tonal implications. *Voiles* presents it in varied 'registrations' and figurations, and the piece depends on the impression made by this single chord on the listener's nerves (Ex. 44):

Ex 44. Debussy· Voiles

The only passage in which any other aural concept occurs is a brief pentatonic section, in which we have melody as nearly as possible devoid of harmonic implications, to balance the cessation of harmonic movement throughout the piece. The music is thus static, has no growth and, in the conventional sense, no structure. Of such music the term 'impressionist' is almost justified. It approximates as closely as music can to painting, in that it destroys the temporal sense and, against music's nature, exists 'spatially' in the given moment.

The historical significance of this aspect of Debussy's music is immense. Because of, rather than in spite of, his preoccupation with chords in themselves, he deprived music of the sense of harmonic progression, broke down three centuries' dominance of harmonic tonality, and showed how the melodic conceptions of tonality typical of primitive folk-music and of medieval music might be relevant to the twentieth century. In a little piece like *Voiles* the musical significance lies in the delicacy of the melodic tendrils that undulate round one or two unmoving nodal points; in a comparatively large-scale piece like *La Cathédrale Engloutie* the modulations are never parts of a tonal argument, but shifts of perspective created, again, by melodic pattern. Even Debussy's most transitory 'moment of sensation' has thus a criterion of order, though it is not the harmonic criterion current during the eighteenth and nineteenth centuries. He wrote his greatest music when he was able to reconcile this profoundly revolutionary element in his work with an innate respect for classical tradition. Of this respect he was, as a young man, but dimly conscious. As he grew older he came to see that one part of his 'newness' was to experience afresh a comparatively distant past.

It is probably no accident that Debussy's relation to tradition and to the humane values of French civilization was manifest in his songs much earlier than in his piano music. The songs deal with his determination to preserve the purity of his sensuous perceptions, even in "ces lieux d'exil où il semble qu'être quelqu'un ne puisse aller sans cabotinage et où la musique manque d'infini". Only within "la vie intérieure" can the infinite still be found; and even in the Wagnerian eroticism of the Baudelaire songs of 1887 Debussy evokes a world of delicate artifice—the world of Pierrot, of the twilit balcony, of the paradisal park, of the Watteauesque dreamland which is more real than a reality seared by trade. The static, immobile harmony in the songs—even more than in the songs of Duparc, if not as completely as in the piano pieces to which we have referred—suggests precisely this withdrawal into the inner life of the senses. On the other hand, the supple vocal line safeguards the songs' humanity. For one thing, it is close to the inflexions of the speaking voice, so we cannot but be aware of the proximity of a human creature. For another thing, it already implies a relationship to the classical tradition. Lully and Rameau were later numbered among Debussy's enthusiasms. The Watteauesque world became not merely an ivory tower, but a once real world into which genius could breathe new life.

In the more mature songs, especially in the *Proses Lyriques*— settings of impressionist prose-poems by Debussy himself—the

vocal line humanizes the harmony, while the harmony divests
the line of drama. The songs thus combine intense human feeling
with a dream-like detachment; and it was precisely this subtle
ambivalence which Debussy brought to fruition in the work that
sums up the first phase of his career. The songs led him to opera:
to which form his attitude was characteristically equivocal. He
approved of opera because it was a mingling of all the arts; he
disapproved of it because it trammelled music's freedom—and
perhaps because the state of the French theatre in his day was
hardly encouraging to a man of delicate perceptions. In any
case, his opera, *Pelléas et Mélisande*, is Wagnerian in the fact that
most of the emotion is contained in the orchestra, while the
characters sing in a recitative no more lyrical than Moussorgsky's; it is anti-Wagnerian in its reticence and objectivity.
Tristan is the projection of Wagner's own life. The passions
in *Pelléas* are mundane and ferocious, and are certainly
emotions which Debussy, as an experienced amorist, had felt
deeply; yet he stands at a distance from them. The medieval
dream-setting suggests a plainsong-like declamation; plainsong
suggests a link with Renaissance monodists like Claude le Jeune;
and they link up with Lully, Rameau, and the classical tragedy
and opera. So, however instinctive Debussy's art may have been,
however intimate his early affiliation with Wagner, he is on the
way towards the classical objectivity of his last years. Though his
conception of tonality still has more in common with the melodic
'node' of plainsong than with Bach's compromise between
counterpoint and harmonic order, his reverence for Bach
already seems less odd than we might have thought.

The relationship between *Tristan* and *Pelléas* is closely
paralleled by that between Delius's *Song of the High Hills* and
Debussy's *Nuages* from the orchestral *Nocturnes*, begun in 1893.
Delius is interested mainly in himself in relation to solitude—
hence the Tristanesque fervour of his appoggiatura-laden
harmony, which 'points' the melodic phrases. Debussy shows a
characteristic humility before appearances. Instead of Delius's
emotionally-charged aspiration, the harmony of Debussy's
clouds is organum-like, without tension or sense of progression,
and such melodic contours as develop towards the end are
pentatonic. The human element is symbolized by a desolate,
fragmentary phrase, usually on the cor anglais, which wanders
in and out of the clouds' organum. There is no interaction

between the man (who is not specifically Debussy) and the clouds: none of Delius's yearning to resolve his harmonic passion in an endless, floating pentatonicism. The man is man, the clouds are clouds; each is irremediably distinct from the other. Delius's scoring is lustrously Wagnerian, to reinforce the passion of his harmonies and soaring lines. Debussy's orchestration, though sensuous, is transparent; the music disintegrates, at the end, into particles of light and air—into patches of 'sound-colour' which parallel his moments of harmonic sensation. In Sibelius's *Tapiola* the impersonal forces of Nature threaten to destroy the human personality. Debussy, in *Nuages*, accepts Nature's *otherness*. This is equally true of the second Nocturne, *Fêtes*, which is supposed to be gay; for the gaiety is someone else's, heard in solitude, from the dark hill. We are alone with Nature; but our exile is accepted, without conscious regret.

Though the lines are brief, the orchestral *Nocturnes* are more linear in conception than Debussy's piano works tend to be, and in this are closely related to his songs. In the orchestral sketches, *La Mer* (1903–5), this melodic strength shows a surprising development. Whereas the themes of the *Nocturnes*, though highly expressive, are incapable of growth, those of *La Mer* are unexpectedly grand in conception, and are treated in a manner not altogether remote from the classical symphonic tradition. Thus the first movement is a symphonic allegro with three clearly defined themes in D flat, B flat, and D flat; the second movement is a scherzo in free rondo form, beginning in C sharp minor and ending in the relative major; while the third movement, though the freest in form, also betrays the most striking capacity to develop the themes from within. The final metamorphosis of the rather Franckian theme on the brass is perhaps one of the most thrilling climaxes in the orchestral repertory. Yet although the traditional notion of progression and even of dramatic argument is again relevant to this music, Debussy preserves his detachment. The symphonic drama is epic rather than personal. The battle of the sea becomes the drama of mankind. The pictorial element is also an incarnation of moral qualities. The play of the waves involves grandeur, vivacity, tenderness, malice.

Even Debussy's *pointilliste* scoring serves, in *La Mer*, a structural purpose. Perhaps one might say that whereas in his earlier works Debussy exploits sonorities in much the same way as a painter like Monet exploits effects of light, in later works Debussy seeks a relationship between sonorities and structure which broadly parallels Cézanne's balance between colour and geometrical form. In *La Mer* Debussy's classical affiliation is with the symphonic tradition. When, in the next few years, he became consciously interested in the re-creation of the past, it was rather to baroque and still more to Renaissance and medieval music that he turned. This was not surprising; for, as we have seen, his technique, concentrating everything on the 'moment of reality' rather than on time-progression or rhetorical argument, had much in common with medieval and with Oriental music. This remains true however different, philosophically, his point of departure may have been.

So Debussy, the artist of Instinct, became the master of Artifice, admiring troubadour music, medieval polyphony, the Renaissance chanson, Couperin, and Rameau as much as, in later years, he hated Wagner. In songs like the *Promenoir des Amants*—settings of the mannered, seventeenth-century poet, Tristan l'Hermite—we can see how Debussy's interest in Renaissance declamation came to terms with his harmonic nervosity. In the *Chansons de Charles d'Orléans* we can see him adapting the technique of the chanson to his more harmonic ends. In the Villon songs and the wonderful *Martyre de St. Sébastien* we find him effecting an intimate, pagan re-creation of medieval organum and of Renaissance polyphony. The swaying parallel fourths and fifths of this work, and the static oscillations of the higher chromatic discords, can all be found in the earlier piano works: only whereas in the piano pieces they are isolated moments of sensation, here they become part of a sustained, ecstatic lyricism.

There is a comparable development in the late orchestral works: compare, for instance, *Gigues* from the orchestral *Images* with the earlier *Fêtes*. The music is more acutely melancholy in its gaiety, because the linear structure is more finely drawn—the harmonic tension more a part of the line. This is especially clear in the scoring. Debussy's scoring remained 'magical'; yet the spell now depends on the revelation of nuance within the instrumental phrasing. In *Images* he makes no attempt to approximate to the symphonic ideal; none the less, short, apparently self-contained melodic periods grow into structures of astonishing power. The dance rhythm of *Rondes de Printemps* gives the fragmentary, repeated phrases a cumulative vitality; elements of Renaissance tradition merge into Debussy's sensuousness, and that into the new traditionalism of his successors. If the *Rondes* look back to the past, they also look forward to Milhaud, Roussel, and Stravinsky.

The forward-looking implications of the late work of this apparently self-contained artist is most clearly revealed in the set of three sonatas, which were all he lived to write of a projected series of six. They are not sonatas in the classical sense—though the first movement of the Violin Sonata has something that might be a recapitulation. But they are works for solo instruments; and a piece for solo violin or solo 'cello with piano, or for flute and viola with harp, cannot rely on the sensory flux of harmony. It must be thought in melodic terms, however unconventional the melody may be. Thus, though the first movement of the 'Cello Sonata is short, the string line is so sustained, so spacious in its troubadour-like arabesques, that the music achieves an expansive grandeur. More habitually, Debussy's melodies in these sonatas move in short periods which surge up, with a slightly flushed intensity, to recurrent climaxes and then subside. Yet the fragmentary phrases now build up a cumulative line. Even Debussy's old habit of repeating his phrases in pairs, over an immobile harmony, is turned to structural purpose in the last movement of the Violin Sonata, when the broken sequential repetitions in ascending thirds provoke the thrilling liberation of the coda. The earlier works seldom move, harmonically, even when the tempo is fast. In these sonatas the harmony itself tends to be relatively simple; but it has unexpected momentum because it is always related to the melodic phrase. Consider the 'modal' juxtaposition of the unrelated triads at the opening of the Violin Sonata, where the E flat minor chord so poignantly underlines the tension in the melody (Ex. 45):

Ex. 45. Debussy: Violin Sonata first movement

consider the way in which, in the *Intermède*, the old processions of sevenths and ninths are no longer passively indulged in, but create a decorative background to the melody's piquancy.

The element of formal stylization in the harmony, in the structural devices, and in the melody itself, is perhaps the secret of this music's original force. The contours of the melody, for instance, are often exotic, and we have observed how important a part exoticisms played in Debussy's early music. Then, the exotic evoked the private dream—except perhaps in the thrilling *L'Ile Joyeuse*, where Watteau's 'Ile de Cythère' becomes vibrantly immediate in a profusion of Oriental arabesques. In the late works the exotic elements—the pentatonic roulades, the taut augmented intervals, and the Spanish rhythms—are no longer used for their glamorous associations. They rather produce a sense of deliberate stylization—as do the mannered sevenths and ninths in the lucidly spaced harmony.

In this respect it is interesting that each of the sonatas includes, by way of slow movement, a Harlequinade. Watteau and Couperin had seen in Pierrot a mythological creature who symbolized both man's dissatisfaction and his desire. The world of the *Fête Champêtre* was not real, but it was sufficiently like real life to be potential. In Debussy's early work Pierrot has become simply a figure of dream: the yearning for another world, intrinsically good because different from this. Now, at the end of his life, worn out by disease and by the attrition of the war, he begins to see that the Mask and the Phantom cannot be permanently satisfying. He looks back on his life, and sees it in the likeness of a puppet-show, himself moon-eyed, desiring but perpetually dissatisfied, in the mask of Harlequin; so regarded, his life seems at once a tragedy and an ironic comedy. He originally gave the first of the sonatas a sub-title— 'Pierrot fâché avec la lune'. He is fed-up with the moon. His newly-won self-knowledge is revealed in the lucidity of the works' technique. The Mask and the Phantom have failed him; and the failure is a new start.

This is why, although the sonatas are disillusioned music, they none the less convey an impression not of sickness, but of health. Without religious or social sanction, they take their place in a great tradition. Contemporary malaise achieves nobility, objectivity, wit, and tragic pathos. Debussy said of the last sonata: "C'est affreusement mélancolique, et je ne sais pas si on doit en rire ou en pleurer. Peut-être les deux. Rude et belle musique, jamais fausse pourtant. . . . Combien il faut d'abord trouver, puis supprimer, pour arriver jusqu'à la chair nue de l'émotion." Debussy never wrote anything more perfectly realized than the "chair nue" of these calmly complex sonatas. So although in one sense *opera ultima*, they are also pregnant with intimations of the future—their wry lucidity has, for instance, much in common with the music Stravinsky was to write shortly after he had dedicated his beautiful Wind Symphony to Debussy's memory. It is worth noting that the Harlequin-figure plays a significant part in Stravinsky's work also, as he does in the career of Picasso. This fact alone indicates how Debussy, who began as a composer of romantic twilight, ended as the herald of however pale a dawn.

Delius remained a composer of Instinct all his days. Debussy became a composer of Artifice as he learned to contemplate his experience ironically. Irony is no more conceivable in Delius's egoistic music than it is in Wagner's; in the music of Ravel [1875–1937], on the other hand, irony was implicit from the earliest years. As a youth, like Debussy, he hated academic authority and systematically shocked his teachers. The composers he admired were Weber (for his elegantly evoked fairyland), Chopin (for the richness of his harmonic sensibility), and Schumann (for his Pierrot-like nostalgia); yet he loved Mozart perhaps above all. Among his contemporaries he revered not only Debussy, but also Satie and Chabrier—and even the *grand seigneur*, Saint-Saëns. In 1897 he became a pupil of Fauré. Henceforth his affinities with the classical tradition were no less evident than his revolutionary sensuousness.

This traditional bias may have helped him to find himself relatively early. From the first, his music differs from Debussy's in three closely related ways, Firstly, he never attempts to sunder the bases of classical tonality, as Debussy does in some of the piano preludes, notably *Voiles*. While he is fascinated by the nervous titillation of the higher chromatic discords, he hardly ever seeks to isolate their effect from line and progression. Indeed, his harmonic experimentalism probably has more in common with Chabrier than with Debussy.

Secondly, his music is, even from the beginning, melodic in impetus. The *Habanera* of 1895 is a typical Ravel *tune*: it would hardly be excessive to say that there is no such thing as a typical

Debussy tune. The early piano piece, *Jeux d'Eaux*, may have anticipated Debussy's various experiments in water music; but it has more relation to Liszt's *Jeux d'Eaux à la Villa d'Este* than to Debussy's *Reflets dans l'eau*. Unlike Debussy's impressionistic 'reflexion', it is constructed like a sonata movement, with two well-defined themes that proliferate in pianistic figuration.

Thirdly, Ravel's music is always dominated by dance movement, whether exotic and Spanish, or with the courtly elegance of the eighteenth century. This preoccupation with physical movement may have had something to do with Ravel's Basque origin; Spanish virility was innate in him, rather than an exotic dream. Again, the lilt of the dance suggests an affinity with the robust vivacity of Chabrier, and complementarily with the refined grace of Couperin and Rameau.

Ravel's conception of tonality, line, and rhythm means that his music—even during the period of the String Quartet and of *Schéhérazade*, when he came directly under Debussy's sway—never disintegrates into moments of sensation. His most impressionistic work is the piano *Miroirs*, which are "mirrors of reality", in Debussy's phrase. Yet even these are highly organized pieces, in which piano figuration acquires melodic significance, and classical tonality is preserved throughout the experiments in multiple harmony. The climax of this phase of Ravel's work comes in the piano suite, *Gaspard de la Nuit* (1908). The first piece, *Ondine*, is a developing variation-set, with the figuration growing increasingly melodic until it explodes in a cadenza. In *Le Gibet* a dissonant internal pedal note and a series of unresolved appoggiaturas create a sinister impression of vacancy, while the separate planes of tonality remain clearly defined. In *Scarbo* dance rhythm and harmonic ellipsis combine with transcendent virtuosity to create black magic. There is nothing comparable with this in Debussy's piano music, not even *L'Ile Joyeuse*, where the excitement is incremental and incantatory, rather than structural. The music's demoniacal glitter finds a parallel only in some of the pieces from Albéniz's *Iberia*, which also exploit the percussive effect of unresolved appoggiaturas.

Ravel's ironic objectivity suggests that he was by nature a theatre composer, as Debussy was not. The *Histoires Naturelles* of 1906 were an exercise in declamatory technique, linked to French prose rhythm and to the declamation of Lully and

Rameau; and were a study for Ravel's first opera, *L'Heure Espagnole*, which is almost entirely a conversation piece. The orchestra has all the tunes and the dance structure, while the singers employ a recitative more civilized, but no less close to speech, than that of Moussorgsky's *The Marriage*. The scoring is exquisitely sensuous, yet sharp; the ironic detachment of the music matches that of the cruelly comic tale. Yet being essentially a melodist, Ravel could not remain satisfied with an opera in which the singers never achieve lyrical flesh and blood. The growth of his melody is the growth of his humanity; and the decisive work in which lyricism becomes the centre of the music was a theatre piece. *Daphnis et Chloé*, usually heard nowadays in its orchestral version, was originally written for Diaghilev's Ballet, and scored for orchestra and chorus, with solo instruments personifying the characters. Ravel said that he conceived the score, and imagined the *décor*, in the spirit of eighteenth-century French painting. Greece becomes for him a world of eighteenth-century enchantment; but the classical theme and the luxuriance of the theatre lead him to envisage his theme with unwonted grandeur. In the aubade a rich, supple song tune of enormous span grows out of a shimmering void. Ravel's instinctive vitality comes to flower in his desire to repeople a vanished world.

After this climax in his career, Ravel embarked on a phase of clarification both melodic and harmonic. Two works may be associated with this purgative process: *Ma Mère l'Oye* with the melodic clarification, the *Valses Nobles et Sentimentales* with the harmonic. We have seen that Ravel had always had a distinctive melodic gift; in the virtuoso figuration of *Gaspard* or the orchestral excitement of *Daphnis*, however, melody was only one contributory element. In the simple, piano-duet scoring of *Ma Mère l'Oye* melody becomes the music's essence. The typical Ravel tune is modal, frequently Dorian or Phrygian, sometimes pentatonic. Whether or no he owed his innate modalism to his Basque ancestry, its archaic flavour is far from being a romantic evasion. The 'antique' world which it evokes is that of the eighteenth-century *conte de fées*; but it is also an ideal of spiritual simplicity which, beneath his sophistication, Ravel associates with the mind of the child. It is significant that both the modal melodies and the harmony of this work strikingly resemble certain pieces of Satie, especially his *Gymnopédies* (Ex. 46):

Ex. 46. Ravel: La Belle et la Bête

Satie: Gymnopédie

In the strange, simple-sophisticated art of Satie,* childhood had become a symbol of a spiritual integrity which seemed alien to the adult world.

In the *Valses Nobles* for piano Ravel said that he aimed at a concentration of the harmonic processes explored in *Gaspard* and the *Miroirs*. He wanted to "condense the harmonies and bring out the contrasts", thereby "freeing the melody", in something the same way as Debussy had done in his sonatas. Many of his melodic mannerisms are here extended into the harmonic plane: for instance, his partiality for melodic processions of thirds leads to secondary seventh and ninth chords, formed on the modal tonics of D and E (Ex. 47):

Ex. 47. Ravel: Valses Nobles et Sentimentales

Again, Ravel develops the technique of the unresolved appog-

* In a small way Erik Leslie Satie [1866–1925] anticipated the 'cubist' re-ordering of the disintegrated materials of tradition such as we find in Stravinsky's work. In the first phase of his career he sought to organize apparently unrelated chords in reference to clear, usually modal, melodic patterns. In the second phase he related this linear pattern-making to an ironic distortion of popular music. In the third phase—notably in the *drame symphonique, Socrate*—he relinquished irony, but went as far as is humanly possible—perhaps a bit further—towards losing the personality in the 'pattern'. His art, like Stravinsky's, was closely associated with the formalization of ballet. *Parade*—the ballet he created in 1916, in collaboration with Cocteau and Picasso—was known as the cubist manifesto.

giatura melodically, so that he often writes bitonally, without destroying his tonal roots (Ex. 48):

Ex. 48. Ravel: Ibid

The music thus acquires its characteristic bite: the slightly acrid flavour which gives an ironic undertone to its sensuousness. It is worth noting that although Ravel is as fascinated by augmented fifths as was Debussy, he never uses them with whole-tone implications.

The fruits of this phase of clarification come in the great Piano Trio of 1915. Superbly written for this most difficult medium, the work has the luxuriance of *Gaspard* with the melodic and harmonic precision of *Ma Mère l'Oye* and the *Valses Nobles*. The long-drawn modal melodies lend themselves naturally to baroque structures such as the passacaglia; but the first and last movements are by no means deficient in sonata rhetoric. The music is both elaborately sophisticated and, in essence, simple: both passionate and chaste. Then, however, there is another change of front. A note of acerbity creeps in, as the Satiean and Chabrier-like irony which had tempered the sensuousness gains the upper hand. During the war years, Ravel creates a series of experimental works. The Duo Sonata for violin and 'cello explores a new linear virtuosity. The Mallarmé songs develop a style that is colouristic but at the same time severely linear, comparable with Schoenberg's *Pierrot Lunaire* and with some of the war-time works of Stravinsky. The black magic in all these works reaches a climax of frenzy in the extraordinary coda to the choreographic poem, *La Valse*; and perhaps a belated consummation in the sinister, exotically decorated Piano Concerto for the Left Hand. Here the passion is wild but disciplined, the scoring brilliant but taut—in a manner Debussy approached only in the *Images* and the strange ballet, *Jeux*.

This desperate exoticism is not, however, Ravel's last word. There is a second clarification; the white magic of the eighteenth-century *conte de fées*, the innocent eye of childhood, bring an ultimate serenity. Perhaps the first intimation of this is the exquisite slow movement of the (two-handed) Piano Concerto, in which rococo ornament becomes disembodied and Ravel writes the kind of music that his beloved Mozart might have written, had he really been 'childlike'. The Violin Sonata of 1923–7 resembles Debussy's in lucidity of texture, and likewise has for slow movement a Harlequinade—a blues which distils the mood of a generation into 'something rich and strange'. But in the first movement especially Ravel achieves continuity of line in place of Debussy's volcanic *fioriture*. This luminous serenity is still more evident in the vocal works of Ravel's last years—for instance, the "green paradise of childish loves" of the *Chansons Madécasses*.

In such music Ravel, like Satie, miraculously becomes the child's mind: whereas Schumann—or even Delius—is the adult who yearns for his lost childhood or youth. In Ravel's last testament—the opera, *L'Enfant et les Sortilèges*—Colette's touching libretto deals specifically with the theme that was nearest Ravel's heart: the war between instinct and sophistication and the child's discovery of his humanity. So we are not surprised to find that musically the score fuses the different economies of *Ma Mère l'Oye* and the *Valses Nobles*. "Here", said Ravel, "the vocal line should dominate"; and if we remember his first opera, *L'Heure Espagnole*, we shall understand how the triumph of vocal line is also the victory of humanity. In the first opera, toys and mechanical clocks were more interesting than men; in *L'Enfant et les Sortilèges* birds, beasts, insects, even inanimate objects, teach humanity to the child, who is man regenerate. In the second act we have a parable of redemption through the renewal of innocence. Throughout, the vocal writing has been richly supple, whether in the Fire's coloratura, the tranquil modality of the fairy-tale Princess, or even the love-song of the cats, a parody of Ravel's own *La Valse*, from which hysteria is purged, leaving only tenderness. But a new dimension comes into the music in the serene modality of the choral epilogue (Ex. 49). Birds, beasts, and trees sing a hymn of gratitude because the pity they have felt has found an echo in the corrupted heart of the child. He sings with them, until his song is stifled with a sob as he awakes—on the threshold of the house of man.

If Ravel seemed cold and aloof as a man, it must have been,

not because he felt too little, but because he felt too much. He feared, not without reason, that the unimaginative harshness of the adult world would kill love. Irony shielded the innocence of

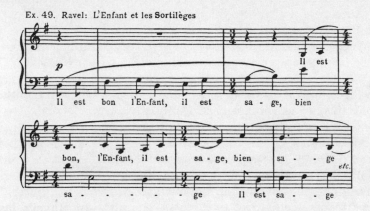

Ex. 49. Ravel: L'Enfant et les Sortilèges

a child, for the salvation of which, in a more than usually corrupt world, the artist lived.

5

TWO TRADITIONALISTS: FAURÉ AND STRAUSS

THE composers whom we have discussed in this section of the book, being individualists, are in many ways sharply distinguished from one another. Most of them, however, have one thing in common: they were misfits in the world into which they were born. Delius sought a refuge in Nature, Debussy in the creation of a private world of Art, Ravel in the evocation of an eighteenth-century fairyland which was also the spiritual integrity of the child. In our next two chapters we shall consider some composers who, though born into the mid-nineteenth century, accepted their world with dignity, even with enthusiasm. From this point of view, Fauré, Strauss, and Elgar form a natural sequence. France was the country whose cultural tradition had been least radically disturbed: so a composer of genius might still be a traditionalist and at the same time creatively original. Germany had seen the tremendous revolutionary phenomenon of Wagner, yet to counteract that had established, in the work of the Viennese classics, what had become Europe's dominant academic convention. England, at the further extreme, had forgotten her musical tradition ever since the seventeenth century and, at the height of her mercantile prosperity, was content to be musically parasitic.

For Fauré [1845–1924] academicism was an organic part of French life; he felt no urge to rebel against his masters, Gounod and Saint-Saëns, and the only hint of romantic protest in his early music is a suggestion of Schumann's poetic reverie in his treatment of the piano. The difference between his early songs and those of Debussy—or even Duparc—is striking. In Debussy the voice part tends to speech inflexion, while the piano's harmonies suggest, through their immobility, a withdrawal into the sensory inner life. The essence of Fauré's songs is in their melodies; and their form depends on a traditional balance between the tune and a freely moving bass. The poetic world of the songs is similar to that of Debussy's, for Fauré frequently set the same poets. But whereas for Debussy this world existed only in his inner dream, for Fauré it was an idealized version of a still living tradition. It would not have occurred to him that the world of his imagination was separate from the real world, except in so far as it was more lucid and more beautiful. Even his partiality for modal melodies (as in the exquisite *Lydia* or *Le Secret*) does not suggest an 'antique simplicity', as it does in Ravel. His modality is a part of his melodic thought, which merely proves the depth of his traditionalism. He did not, like Debussy or Ravel, rediscover the past. He was simply the natural successor to Gounod, Berlioz, Rameau, Couperin, Lully; and so, ultimately, to the Renaissance polyphonists and medieval monodists.

This becomes clear as soon as we turn to Fauré's instrumental music: for we see that his modality is inseparable from the fact that he is a linear composer. Fauré was born in 1845 and was composing up to 1920. It is extraordinary that, working during such a period, he could have remained apparently so impervious to the development of European music. He lived through the Wagnerian cataclysm, through Debussy's disintegration of harmony and orchestral sonority, through Stravinsky's disintegration of rhythm. Yet he showed virtually no interest in tone colour or the potentialities of the orchestra, being content to allow his pupils to orchestrate most of his larger works; while in rhythmic variety or pianistic figuration there is nothing in his music that would have alarmed Saint-Saëns or Schumann.

Yet his unhurried traditionalism is the root of his originality. Though in his chamber works he usually composes in the sonata form he inherited from Saint-Saëns, his approach is closer to Bach's than to Beethoven's. The core of his music, as of Bach's, is continuity of line and consistency of figuration; rhythmic variety is unnecessary where the form of the music is a spirally evolving melody that combines massiveness with grace. Of course, Fauré is not a Bach, and had not his social and religious advantages; he does not completely solve the problem of creating a large-scale melodically evolving movement which has the argumentative logic of a sonata. Climax, in such a structure, has to be created by the flow of melodies that move, mainly by step, through a continuous series of modulations, often enharmonic, often provoked by the modal behaviour of the lines;

Fauré, like such very different (but also modally-tending) composers as the Russian nationalists and Vaughan Williams, is especially prone to modulation between two keys a tone or semitone apart. It is true that his modulations tend to be more tightly packed in what corresponds to the development section; but he has hardly stamina enough to preserve the music's vitality over such immense melodic periods. The early chamreb works are more successful than the later ones because, allowing in more conventionally romantic style for harmonic climax and repose, they show more respect for the listeners' ears and nerves. None the less, the late chamber works are a remarkable achievement. The early First Violin Sonata is as strong as it is beautiful, with sustained *élan* in its melodies, vitality in its rhythms, sensuous refinement in its Schumannesque approach to the piano. But the late Second Violin Sonata has a profoundly Bachian quality in the calm and ordered strength of its relation between evolving melody and bass; and this implies a fundamental serenity such as we can find in virtually no other music of the first twenty years of this century. We must pay homage to such serenity, even though we may find it anachronistic and, in the long run, less satisfying than the music of Debussy and Ravel, who were more in tune with what seems to us, if not to Fauré, the spiritual essence of their time.

The basis of Fauré's technique, we have said, lies in a tension between melody and bass. How close his approach is to that of classical composers, such as Bach and Couperin, we may see by comparing the dialogue between melody and bass in the Libera Me of Fauré's *Requiem* with the opening of Couperin's noble chaconne, *La Favorite* (Ex. 50):

Ex. 50ª Fauré: Requiem (Libera Me)

Ex. 50ᵇ Couperin: La Favorite

In Fauré's music, however, this architectural solidity is modified by two features. The first is the incidental freedom of
his phrase-grouping within the conservative framework of the
metre. This may have been prompted by his sensitivity to the
inflexions of language and by his early interest in Gregorian
music; but while it is most obvious in his vocal music, it exerted
an influence over his instrumental thinking also. There is usually
a subtle balance between the metrical rhythm of the harmony
and the incidental rhythmic inflexions of the melodic parts.

This incidental subtlety of rhythm is complemented by an
incidental harmonic complexity. The harmony may be moulded
by a clear tonal scheme, expressed in the relationship between
melody and bass, as in Bach or Couperin; but the modal contours will create delicate modifications to the triadic harmony,
partly through their tendency to avoid leading notes, and partly
through a fondness for chromatic alteration which, as in the
work of some early seventeenth-century polyphonists, produces
a rapidly coruscating texture. In the song *Le Parfum Impérissable*
—an extreme instance—the firm progression of the bass, centred
on E, controls continuous enharmonic modulations which, being
melodically derived, have no connexion with the nineteenth-
century notion of modulation as a dramatic event (Ex. 51):

Ex. 51. Fauré: Le Parfum Impérissable

The strength of Fauré's music may thus be equated with its Bach-like characteristics: its long, serene melodies and basses, its unperturbed rhythms, its command of canonic devices, its spacious structure which has as much in common with baroque monistic 'continuity' as with the dualistic sonata. The charm of his music may be associated with his Mediterranean culture: his modalisms, his elliptical harmonies and enharmonic transitions, whereby his harmonic originality consists not in the chords he uses, but in the contexts in which they appear. Strength and charm come together in the creations of his maturity—the *Requiem*, the Verlaine song-cycle, *La Bonne Chanson*, and the operas *Pénélope* and *Prométhée*, significantly on Greek themes. So deep are the imaginative roots of Fauré's civilization that for him the Greek ideal can approximate to an order achieved in his own, superficially more tormented world. The only intimation that so joyous an order might no longer have an objective existence in the world outside is contained in the fact that, in the music of Fauré's last years, the radiance diminishes. The technique remains basically the same; but in the last chamber works, piano pieces, and song cycles the serenity has acquired an autumnal gloss. There is a descending mournfulness in the mirror-like stillness and undulating figuration of the song, *Danseuse*; in the gravely shaped dialogue between soprano and bass in the Tenth and Eleventh Nocturnes; in the glassy four-part writing of the final Nocturne and of the String Quartet (Ex. 52):

Ex. 52. Fauré: Nocturne No. 13

In the last Barcarolle there is even a suggestion of the phantasmagoric, for the softly fluttering harmonies suggest a scene viewed between sleeping and waking—a twilight phenomenon the more odd in a music that had habitually been as clear as day. It is as though in his last years Fauré became not only an incarnation of, but an elegy on, French civilization; and in this respect he resembles another conservative, Paul Valéry, whose poetic technique has certain features in common with Fauré's musical.

A Fauré could hardly have been born at a later date, as we can see if we consider his natural successor, Albert Roussel [1869–1937]. He was brought up under the aegis of Franck and the impressionist movement; yet as early as 1905 his *Poème de la Forêt* is not so much a Nature-impression as an evocation of the eighteenth-century *parc*; while the *Divertissement* for piano and wind instruments, written in the following year, is a bucolically sophisticated re-creation of tradition which has by-passed impressionism far more decisively than Ravel. If Fauré was still the representative of what seemed to him a living tradition, Roussel in his later work has more self-consciously to recover a tradition: which may explain the more strenuous quality of his (often polymodal)* melodic power, the more frantic quality in his rhythmic ostinatos. The fact that he composed four symphonies is evidence of the more vehement and dramatic quality of his imagination; yet his symphonies, like Fauré's chamber works, have some relationship to the melodically unified techniques of baroque music. Each movement tends to be dominated by a continuous figuration or rhythmic motive which to some extent negates the dramatic contrasts of sonata style. The symphonies are a (sometimes rather desperate) assertion of civilization, rather than a revolutionary challenge.

Fauré once said: "L'artiste doit aimer la vie et nous montrer qu'elle est belle. Sans lui, nous en douterions."† He would have wished for no greater satisfaction than to know that his best music falls not far short of his promise. Roussel, too, is one of the few twentieth-century composers whose music tells us that the artist loves life and finds it good. With him, however, we are more conscious of the ironic undertone in Fauré's last sentence.

Fauré—and perhaps even Roussel—had so deep an awareness of the traditional values of French civilization that one is hardly conscious, as one listens to their music, that they lived in

---

* POLYMODAL: a passage in which several melodic lines move independently in different modalities. This is a process different from, and more natural than, systematic polytonality, in which all the lines are in the same tonality while having different key centres.

† "The artist ought to love life and show us that it is good. Without him, we might have doubts about it."

a society dominated by trade. But Germany's industrial expansion in the second half of the nineteenth century was so rapid that no artist could have been indifferent to it. Thus though Strauss [1864–1949] was brought up in the wake of a great musical tradition, it never occurred to him that there was any disparity between these artistic values and the values of commerce. On the contrary, he not only accepted, but rejoiced in, his commercial world, and was by a long way the most materially successful composer of his time. He made a large fortune out of writing operas, and was a professional man of the theatre like Meyerbeer or Verdi. To have been able thus to accept the world in which he lived may have implied some deficiency in perceptiveness and spiritual refinement. It certainly involved a tremendous creative exuberance.

This is evident enough in Strauss's adolescent work. Nothing could be more striking than the contrast between his early career and that of Delius, Debussy, and even Wagner. They were all driven by hatred of the academic conventions of their day, which for them symbolized a moribund world. Strauss accepted those conventions not passively, but with enthusiasm. While Wagner and Delius were creating their own forms to replace the sonata which, in the minor works of Spohr and Mendelssohn, had become a shell rather than a living organism, Strauss breathed into the shell new life. This new life in, for instance, his Violin Sonata is quantitative rather than qualitative. Themes that in Mendelssohn are sweetly cantabile acquire in Strauss an energy that is soon exhausted; harmonies that in Mendelssohn are mildly cloying become in Strauss a chromatic orgy. At this date the music sounds no less faded than Mendelssohn's feebler works: perhaps more faded, for a period costume is more obtrusive when every flounce is exaggerated. Yet though its energy springs from a certain banality of mind, in the Century of the Common Man such energy is something to be reckoned with.

It is interesting that Strauss turned aside from academic convention and took up with the progressive composers of his youth largely at the instigation of Hans Richter.* Instinctively, he had no desire to be a revolutionary. But, living in a revolutionary era, he accepted Richter's suggestion that a fully

---

* Hans Richter [1843–1916], conductor closely associated with Wagner. He first conducted *The Ring* at Bayreuth in 1876.

professional composer ought to be aware of the most advanced developments of his art. So he studied the works of Liszt and Wagner and, with his superb traditional craftsmanship, soon became their acknowledged successor. Taking over the basic principle of the symphonic poem from Liszt, he combined it with techniques suggested by the late work of Wagner; but it is significant that his symphonic poems have more in common with classical tradition than have either Liszt or Wagner. *Don Juan* (1888) is a one-movement Wagnerian opera without voices, which tells a story and unfolds a dramatic situation in a flowing harmonic polyphony of more than Wagnerian opulence. But— though the Don was, of course, the kind of man Strauss admired and understood—it is operatic character-portrayal, in the traditional sense, rather than Wagnerian self-inflation. The structure sounds 'continuous' and closely related to the plot; it is also not very far from the classical rondo. *Tod und Verklärung* describes a dramatic situation in still greater detail; yet its continuous Wagnerian texture falls into three sections— a slow introduction, a middle section closely resembling sonata form, and a conclusion that recreates the introduction in the light of the sonata movement. In *Till Eulenspiegel* (1895) and *Don Quixote* (1897) Strauss unambiguously employs rondo and variation style for objective character-portrayal. Only in *Zarathustra* does he attempt Liszt's 'psychological' permutation of themes, and this work, though more ingenious, as well as more complicated, than anything of Liszt, is a triumph of craftsmanship rather than of art. Lisztian technique calls for something of the visionary temperament which Liszt developed during his later years. Strauss, with his feet firmly and prosperously on the earth, had little real sympathy for Liszt's ideals; and the excessively literal realism of his symphonic works is evidence of this.

Liszt's programme is always psychological; Strauss's realism, insignificant in itself, testifies to the dominance over him of the material world, which was all he knew and loved. He is at the opposite pole to Debussy. The latter always preferred feeling to action; Strauss is at his best when dealing with action. The tempestuous life and loves of Don Juan, Till Eulenspiegel, or Don Quixote provoke music of tremendous creative genius; even *Ein Heldenleben* is not so much a revelation of Strauss's inner life as a gigantic, externalized portrait of Strauss's ideal Man of Action. In *Tod und Verklärung* the fear of death may stimulate human activity: whereas transfiguration was for Strauss (as it was not for Liszt in the 'Faust' Symphony) an abstract idea. All his transfiguration music sounds, by now, cinematic.

Strauss began as an orchestral composer who related progressive techniques to classical precedent. The centre of his life's work, however, was in opera; and here again he re-created Wagnerian opera with a classical bias. Though he inherited Wagner's sensuousness he could not, in his worldly materialism, follow Wagner in identifying love—and the personal life—with death. *Salome* and *Elektra* sound Wagnerian in that they employ a luxuriously chromatic, massively scored harmonic polyphony, while the voices either declaim or double the instrumental melody. But the operas are immense symphonic poems constructed on broadly the same principles as Strauss's orchestral works; and the relationship between Strauss's chromaticism and Wagner's is superficial. *Tristan's* ecstatic dissolution of tonality implied a new formal technique and an experience that was an historical event. Strauss's music remains basically traditional; his dissonant techniques are applied to his diatonicism in order to build up a sensational effect. Thus side-stepping parallel seconds, sevenths and ninths obscure but do not—as they do in Debussy—destroy a traditional progression (Ex. 53):

Ex. 53. Strauss: *Elektra*

bitonal effects may be created, as in Elektra's notorious 'blood' chord, by thickening out a conventional movement of parts into triads; and the most abrupt modulations may be suggested by an extension of (say) the classical device of the Neapolitan cadence. Wagner's chromatic dissonance grows from within; Strauss's is applied from without: for *Salome* and *Elektra* are not a Wagnerian overflow of the ego, but an 'operatic' situation externalized. The brilliantly extrovert genius of Strauss deliberately presents sensation for sensation's sake; he is more interested in the effect of morbidity and hysteria on his audience than he is in the minds of his characters. This is a kind of artistic decadence, but it is not dishonesty. Strauss's melodrama would not be so devastatingly effective—and, at times, so beautiful—if it did not correspond to something dark that lurked beneath his buoyancy. Perhaps the wilfully manufactured horrors of *Salome* and *Elektra* delighted as they appalled his audience because there was an element of wilful sadism in the competitive spirit of an industrial community. The horrors of *Elektra* were to become life, instead of art, in two world wars; and modern war is likewise a prostitution of feeling, as well as of life.

Certainly though we cannot altogether believe in the manufactured horrors in these operas, we cannot ignore them: whereas the positive moral virtues of the 'good' characters seem to us, in a dismal way, funny. Strauss was aware of this, remarking that he was constitutionally unable to portray "a chaste Joseph". The genuine positive bases of his art consisted not in moral qualities, but in physical activity and in sensual enjoyment, as was already evident in the prancing themes and elaborate texture of his symphonic poems. In *Elektra* he had first entered into collaboration with Hugo von Hofmannsthal, an artist whose poetic sensitivity was deeper than his own. As well as providing Strauss with the most poetically distinguished opera libretti that any composer has had to deal with, Hofmannsthal revealed to Strauss the true nature of his genius. Henceforth his art becomes a tribute to humanity and a celebration of a social world.

We have seen that an inherent classicality of approach had modified the Lisztian and Wagnerian elements in Strauss's orchestral works. In the same way, Italian vocal *cantilena* always played a much more significant part in his operas than it did in Wagner's; and though he may have inherited this direct from Liszt, it also suggests a link with classical opera and with Mozart in particular. In later years Strauss seems to have felt intuitively that the moments of unexpected tenderness in *Elektra* were more significant than the melodrama, for he advised orchestras to play the score as though it were 'fairy music'—something by Mendelssohn. Superficially, the advice seems both unrealistic and perverse. What is the point of composing sensational music scored for an enormous orchestra unless you intend to play it as though you meant it? Yet if we think of *Elektra* in relation to the next Strauss-Hofmannsthal opera, *Der Rosenkavalier*,

Strauss's remark seems not altogether absurd. *Der Rosenkavalier* is also a symphonic opera scored for a very large orchestra. But the chromaticism of *Salome* and *Elektra* is discarded in favour of the chromaticized diatonicism which, in the orchestral works, had seemed to be Strauss's natural language; and the lyrical writing for the voice, especially the sopranos, acquires a Mozartian fluency. Mozartian and Schubertian pastiche is even introduced, and the Viennese waltz which pervades all Strauss's music assumes a particularly voluptuous and insidious form. The pastiche occurs because the opera is intentionally a period piece; it is justified because the period is one in which Strauss's imagination naturally lived. Of course, Mozart's world no longer existed, and Strauss was wrong in thinking he had written a Mozartian opera: the quicksands of his modulations may have much the same significance, in relation to Mozart, as the quicksands of Bruckner's modulations have in relation to Bach. But something approaching Mozart's Vienna at least existed within living memory; and the world of *Der Rosen-kavalier* is a periwigged, rouged reminiscence, which embodies Strauss's positive values as *Elektra* embodied the negative. In a sense, both are synthetic, and at the same time true to Strauss's experience. This is what Busoni meant by saying that Strauss was an industrialist, even in his art. He sees the delights of eighteenth-century aristocratic society through the eyes of a nineteenth-century business-man. Though aristocratic values are vulgarized, in being vulgarized they at least become relevant.

This being so, Hofmannsthal's next libretto was a no less acute perception than *Der Rosenkavalier*; he rewrites *Le Bourgeois Gentilhomme*, re-enacting a heroic opera, on the classical theme of Ariadne, in a bourgeois setting. The myth and the reality prove to be more excitingly related than the *bourgeois gentil-homme* had bargained for. Musically, the work shows its classical affiliations not so much in the fact that it includes transcription and pastiche of Lully's original music, as in the fact that it is scored for chamber orchestra and is a singers' opera. The music of the divertissement substitutes an inspired bourgeous banality for classical grace. The lyrical expertise of the vocal writing is as mellow as Mozart, without the edge of Mozartian wit; it floats over the self-indulgent suavity of the sensuously scored texture, which is a compromise between rococo lucidity and Wagnerian harmonic polyphony.

The sequence of operas that follows *Ariadne* returns to more normal operatic resources, but preserves the link with classical tradition. In writing *Capriccio*, a virtuoso opera about operas, and *Intermezzo*, a 'bourgeois comedy' based on an incident in his own domestic life and introducing his wife and himself as characters, Strauss seems to admit that, in an ever more democratic world, the classical idea of opera as a social act is no longer relevant. Yet if opera is becoming a game, this is perhaps only an extension of Strauss's habitual attitude. The 'classical' world of *Daphne* or the *Danae* remains the business-man's glamourized Vienna, in which Strauss plays the game of life with far more zestful humanity than the business-man—or than his namesake, Johann. After all, thirty years back Salome's Dance of the Seven Veils had turned out to be a bourgeois Viennese waltz which by now willy-nilly recalls the palm court. The evil of *Salome* and *Elektra* may be all the nastier for being only skin-deep. If the haunting beauty of the *cantilena* of the later operas is skin-deep also, we must none the less be grateful for so rich an expression of the delights of *l'homme moyen sensuel*. It is not fortuitous that some of Strauss's finest music should be contained in *Die Frau ohne Schatten*, a parable about man in relation to woman: nor that the last act, in which Hofmannsthal offers a mystical interpretation of fecundity, should be a relative failure.

So Strauss went on composing for thirty years, master of his craft, oblivious of changing fashion. The mirth, passion, and glamour in his music seem half-vicarious, an epitaph on a fashion that the old man would not allow to sleep, though it was long past nightfall. The liquid *cantilena* has, in the suave context of the Wagnerian harmony, a precious, manicured elegance. There is in the music an odd feeling, as of the gaiety of ghosts: "So round and round the ghosts of beauty glide And haunt the places where their honour died." The instrumental works of Strauss's old age, mostly scored for small combinations, have the same ghostly seductiveness. The Oboe Concerto, for instance, is an epitaph on rococo vivacity, with the solo oboe treated in much the same way as Strauss treats the soprano voice (Ex. 54).

One work, however—the *Metamorphosen* for twenty-three solo strings—suggests a different approach. For the first time in his long career Strauss approaches the 'inwardness' of *Tristan's*

harmonic polyphony. The themes of his youth had been a
development from the Beethovenian Heroic. Here he incorpor-
ates into the complex texture of the harmonic polyphony the

Ex. 54 Strauss   Oboe Concerto

theme of the Funeral March from the 'Eroica' Symphony; and
in the whirling virtuosity of the string writing and the extreme
fluency of the enharmonic modulations a world seems to be in
dissolution—as it is in some of the late music of Mahler and the
early work of Schoenberg.

The Oboe Concerto is a serio-comic epilogue to Strauss's
world. *Metamorphosen*—the title is accurate and significant—is
Strauss's ultimate farewell, in which he came to admit that his
world had literally destroyed itself. Schoenberg had admitted
this thirty years ago, without needing two wars to prove it. That
Strauss could have gone on living in the world of his youth, and
have written this music as late as 1945, is testimony both to the
strength of his convictions and to the deficiency of his imagination. The contrast with Fauré is revealing. The Frenchman
never wanted to be other than conservative, yet his style grew
with experience and became, in its reticent way, progressive.
Strauss made his reputation as an aggressive modernist and
relapsed into reaction. The composer of civilized refinement
turns out to look forward, while the composer who seemed
most vigorously in sympathy with an industrial, bourgeois
world remains arrested in the modernity of his youth. Perhaps
Strauss, who relished nineteenth-century prosperity, is not after
all so remote from Delius, who hated it from the depth of his
soul. The most beautiful music Strauss ever wrote is the
Countess's lament, in *Der Rosenkavalier*, for her lost youth;
and not even Delius's music is more nostalgic than the lyricism
of the trio with which the opera concludes. At the end, the
socially-minded Strauss and the most a-social composer who
ever lived both wrote from the consciousness of loss. In any
case, the warmth of this music suffices to prove that a 'reaction-
ary' is not necessarily inferior to a 'progressive' art. Everything
depends on the conviction behind the experience. We may

find Fauré's rarefied music congenial and some aspects of Strauss's music repulsive; we can hardly deny that Strauss has the greater vitality, the more significant power.

6

ELGAR AND VAUGHAN WILLIAMS

Wɪᴛʜ Fauré, an awareness of civilization proves stronger
than an industrial environment; with Strauss, a great musical
tradition and an industrial environment come to terms. England
in the latter part of the nineteenth century was, however, more
decisively dedicated to material prosperity than France, and
more oblivious of her musical heritage than Germany, largely
because the Industrial Revolution had here been longer en-
trenched, if not more violent in its effects. One result of this was
that the less 'poetic' forms of art, such as the novel, tended to
flourish at the expense of the more immediately creative forms.
There was plenty of room for imaginative and critical commentary on the human situation; but the burgeoning of the
human spirit in lyrical poetry, painting, or music was apt to be
stifled. If music suffered most disastrously, the reason may be
that music, by nature a relatively abstract art, needs to be
nourished by a continuous tradition; if the tradition is once
broken, the symbols cannot easily recover intelligibility. Our
musical tradition, largely owing to the effects of the Civil War,
had lapsed as long ago as the late seventeenth century. Since
then our music had been dominated by foreign models. It was
no longer a question of an intimate relationship between a
native and a European idiom, such as had existed in the time
of Dunstable, of Byrd, or of Purcell. As industrialism grew more
rampant, the local tradition withered. Our composers turned
out synthetic Handel, and later synthetic Mendelssohn, because
they had no inner conviction to suggest an alternative.

Into this materially prosperous, spiritually non-creative
world two men of tremendous creative energy were born.
Speaking of the position of the artist in an uncreative epoch,
W. B. Yeats once wrote:

> The rhetorician would deceive his neighbours,
> The sentimentalist himself; while art
> Is but a vision of reality.
> What portion in the world can the artist have
> Who has awakened from the common dream
> But dissipation and despair?

Perhaps we may say that, if Delius ran the risk of being the sentimentalist, Elgar [1857–1934] always felt the lure of rhetoric. At least, he is superfically as remote from Delius as is Strauss. He accepted Edwardian society as zestfully as Delius rejected it; and although both composers took over the idiom of German romanticism, Delius exploited it to express an egocentric isolation, Elgar to express a social conviction no less purposeful than that of Strauss. That Elgar could use this idiom with a technical expertise equal to Strauss's is a most remarkable achievement; he was able to assume the existence of a great symphonic tradition which, in this country, had never happened.

In order to do this he had to believe implicitly in his world, taking the bad (as we would think it) with the good. Before he discovered his genius, he wrote a quantity of second-hand, third-rate music in the Victorian oratorio convention stemming from Mendelssohn and Spohr; and throughout his life he composed 'functional' music expressly to celebrate Edwardian imperialism. He disliked, or affected to dislike, the company of artists and had bourgeois pretentions to High Society; *Swanee River* moved him (and George V) to tears. He was never ashamed to be the rhetorician, consciously addressing an audience and sharing with it tastes that may seem crude, even repulsive. In this, as in his technical mastery, he resembles Kipling.

Yet we cannot merely deplore this aspect of Elgar. We may not like his world; yet if he had not believed so powerfully in all its manifestations, he could never have revealed the soul of which it was but obscurely conscious. Elgar's jingoistic works, such as the 'Pomp and Circumstance' Marches, do not live in a different world from his symphonies and concertos. He believes in them no less: which is why they are, of their kind, so powerfully effective. Elgar's 'serious' works reveal the real nobility which was behind the strutting pomp, the *nobilmente* swagger. For all its tawdry materialism, Elgar's world had a greatness at which we can ill afford to sneer; but it took a genius to manifest in music the spirit that justified apparent banality, even brutality, of thought and feeling.

It is not surprising that Elgar, like Delius, took a long time to discover what he wanted to do. He was over forty when the 'Enigma' Variations, the first completely Elgarian work, appeared. In the Finale, we have Elgar the rhetorician, orchestrating with Straussian brilliance. But in 'Nimrod' we have the nobility that comes from within; while in 'Dorabella' and most of the quiet variations we find a sensitive melodic line, humanly intimate rather than rhetorical: a music of personal relationships, dedicated to Elgar's friends, rather than a social manifestation. Every element of the technique seems, on paper, German; yet one could not imagine a more individualistic or— we have come to think—more English style. The originality is perhaps more melodic than harmonic. Elgar's lyricism has the seething energy of Strauss's early symphonic poems, but the curves are more rounded. The surging-upward figures on the strings—usually beginning with a small interval which grows progressively larger—are balanced by a slow fall; and the persistent rise and fall of the sixth or seventh, with the upward leap often landing on an accented passing note, gives to his most exuberant phrases a relaxed amplitude (Ex. 55):

Ex. 55. Elgar: Violin Concerto (opening theme)

Harmonically, Elgar adds nothing to Wagner's vocabulary and is less enterprising than Strauss. None the less, the way in which he uses harmony and tonality is highly personal. Consider, for instance, his partiality for the Wagnerian sequence. With Wagner, the sequence is absorbed into the flow of the lines, so that one loses consciousness of the point at which the sequences begin and end. Elgar's sequences—which favour movement by thirds rather than by step—serve to build up climax; but we are usually aware of the cumulating planes of tonality. Wagner's sequences sweep us away on the harmonic swell. Elgar's sequences are rhetorical in no derogatory sense; our hearts uplift and our arms open. Again, the music has a spaciousness, an open quality, for all its ripeness. Possibly Elgar's familiarity with Handelian oratorio had some effect on his treatment of the sequence.

In later works this spaciousness becomes increasingly typical of Elgar's melodic and harmonic thought. While the sequences and the intermittent drooping sevenths and ninths do not disappear, the periods grow much larger. Most of the themes of the Introduction and Allegro for strings, the main theme of the first movement of the E flat Symphony, the first allegro theme of the 'Cello Concerto are all typical Elgarian melodies, undulating with apparent placidity, usually in step-wise movement, until they attain a peak from which they abruptly descend: only to start once more on their cumulative cycle. The length of the themes entails lengthy developments; far more than Strauss, Elgar approximates to the inward, evolutionary nature of Liszt's thematic metamorphoses—not merely in obvious instances like the translation of the A flat Symphony's scherzo theme into the theme of the slow movement. Yet Elgar manages to reconcile this with a subtle modification of the classical symphony. He starts off with tremendous dynamic impetus, and the development section seems at first to be a relaxation rather than an increase of tension. He meditates discursively on aspects of the themes, taking up now one, now another, gradually revealing the hidden affinities between them. The climax of the movement comes not in the development, but at the beginning of the recapitulation, when we discover the true identity of themes we had but partially understood. To some degree, of course, this is true of any vital sonata movement; no composer before Elgar, however, had made this feature the very core of sonata style. Regarded in this light, his symphonies are characterized not by excess, but by concision. If the rhetorician is still present in the impressive apotheosis of the A flat Symphony, the quiet conclusion of the E flat reveals the *spirit* of delight beneath the grand façade. Though it may come but rarely, it is worth waiting for.

The spiritual nobility behind Elgar's grandeur is related to his Roman Catholicism, though he is not a religious composer in the sense that Bruckner or Vaughan Williams is. It is both technically and philosophically interesting that the loveliest music Elgar ever wrote—the Prelude to Part II of *The Dream of Gerontius*—should deal with bliss attained, and should strikingly remind us of the modalism and diatonicism of Vaughan Williams. Yet on the whole Part II of *Gerontius* is less convincing than Part I, which deals with the search after faith. The work may be an implicit protest against the materialism of the age, but for Elgar—if not for Cardinal Newman—it is a drama rather than a liturgical affirmation. Elgar's fusion of the brilliant, stable operatic idiom of Handelian oratorio with the more subjective passion of Wagner's endless *melos* and enharmonic modulation, controlled by interrelated leitmotives, is beautifully appropriate to his purposes. The music becomes at once a social act and an intimate spiritual history; its ecstasy is remote from the religiosity of Victorian stained glass. Only when he tries to depict devils are we aware that Elgar's knowledge of supernatural beings was comically or pathetically subject to materialism. They are not much better than Franck's: with the difference that Elgar never really pretended to believe in them, whereas Franck would have believed in his if he could.

In his earlier works, Elgar, like most post-Handelian oratorio composers, had shown scant respect for English declamation. From the vocal writing of *Gerontius*, however, it would seem that the Englishness of Elgar's ostensibly Teutonic style may have had something to do with an intuitive, subconscious response to the language. For the sweep of the lines, even in recitative, is unmistakably Elgarian, while being related to the rhythm of speech. Certainly the Englishness of Elgar's melodies becomes more evident in his last works. He had long shown a fondness for the flat seventh in pastoral moods; the swinging tune with which the 'Cello Concerto opens even suggests the contours of English folk-song, in which Elgar betrayed no more conscious interest than he did in the revival of Tudor music, though he was acquainted with both. There may also be some connexion between his sensitivity to speech inflexion and the plastic nature of the phrasing in, say, the slow movement of the 'Cello Concerto. In music such as this the rhetorician is silenced; in the free rubato of the lyricism an intimate human voice speaks directly to you and to me, while an unexpected chord or modulation reveals the private heart beneath the public manner (Ex. 56):

Ex. 56. Elgar: Cello Concerto
Adagio

This flexibility is enhanced by Elgar's scoring, especially in the way in which he uses instrumental doubling not to make more noise, but to 'point' his phrases. Despite his debt to Wagner and Strauss, he scores much more 'melodically' than they do; in this respect his admiration for Meyerbeer is evident in all his scores, though he was going a little far when he said that he learned more about orchestration from Delibes than from Wagner! In any case, the most subtly constructed of Elgar's works is also the most subtly scored. *Falstaff* is a big symphonic poem which tells a story in Straussian terms, while being also a free sonata movement incorporating a scherzo and a slow movement. The construction is broadly and firmly planned; yet the plasticity of the melodic phrasing and harmonic detail reveals Falstaff as by turn manly, witty, malicious, robust, cowardly, tender, trivial—as was Shakespeare's Falstaff. Elgar's Falstaff is, however, not Shakespeare's, but his own: for he is in essence noble. He is Elgar's representative Englishman: perhaps even the kind of man Elgar wanted to be. Certainly he was a type of Englishman who was becoming rarer with the passing of the years.

It is interesting that although Elgar lived for twenty more years after composing *Falstaff* and the 'Cello Concerto, he wrote no more music of consequence. People no longer wanted his kind of music, he said: and he could create no other. In so far as the concert-going public was concerned, this seems manifestly untrue; yet in a deeper sense Elgar was right. He stopped composing (whereas Strauss went on), because his art belonged to a world that had had its day. Whether our day, though different, is any 'better' is extremely dubious; but better or worse we listen to his music in the same spirit as we listen to any other music of the past. In any vital art of the past there are some elements which speak to us, others which were meaningful once, but are so no longer. As we listen to *Falstaff* or the drooping chromatics of the closing pages of the E flat Symphony, we forget what seem to us pomposities, and admire a prodigious moral strength. Elgar had the power to make us believe, momentarily, that the Edwardian world was as grand as his music; while at the same time he subtly suggests that in his heart he knows, and knows that we know, that the grandeur is in his imaginative vision.

Elgar's music belonged to a past world, Delius's yearned for a vanished youth; both used a technique basically German. If there was to be a future for our music, it was likely to be associated with the recovery of a national consciousness: which was not, of course, a purely musical matter. The revival of English music during the early years of this century was connected with the rediscovery of English folk-song; but the folk-song movement in this country is not really comparable with the folk-song movement in nineteenth-century Russia. Though it implied, no doubt, a protest against an industrialized world, no one could have seriously believed that folk-song in our urban community could again be a living tradition, as it was in Russia. For our composers, the significance of the folk-song movement was more exclusively technical. After a century of German hegemony, it taught us once more what an English musical line, growing naturally out of the English language, was like. In middle life, Holst [1874–1934] referred to his early works as "good old Wagnerian bawling". To discover his real roots, the English composer had to start again from the beginning, to find himself in unaccompanied vocal monody. The essence of Holst's renewal of tradition is in his smallest works—the songs for voice and violin, in which he set medieval lyrics in lines that are vocally modal, and as free in rhythm, as closely related to the words, as folk-song or plainsong. Only a certain tonal precariousness tells us that Holst was not in fact a medieval cleric or peasant (Ex. 57):

Ex. 57. Holst: I sing of a Maiden

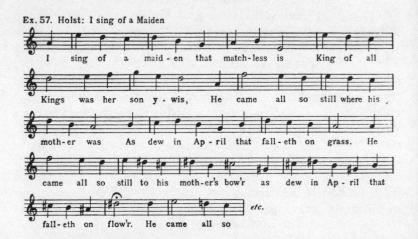

But the implications of unaccompanied monody are philosophically poles apart from a man of Holst's generation. Though he could find himself in a world irremediably remote, he could hardly be content to express himself exclusively in small lyrical songs, or through the prose declamation of a 'play in music'. In *Savitri*, for instance, the freely rhythmed, modal declamation of the early part is deeply moving. When, however, Holst feels a need to create a *musical* climax, he relapses into a Pucciniesque manner which, though admirable in itself, has no valid relationship with the modal declamation. Holst's difficulties become still greater when he tries to create choral and orchestral works on an extended scale, starting from a folk-like, medieval seeming modality. They are greatest of all in purely instrumental works, when he has neither a text nor stage action to provide continuity.

Now, all European music since the Renaissance had been based on the notion of harmony as alternating tension and relaxation, associated with a metrical time-sense. Even in his larger works, involving considerable orchestral and choral resources, Holst evades, as far as possible, this traditional conception of harmony. Thus, despite his admiration for sixteenth-century composers, there is little genuine polyphony in his music, of the kind which depends on tension between line and harmony. The texture of his music is influenced far more by the medieval organum principle; even a notorious harmonic audacity, like the clash of the triads of F sharp and G in *The Hymn of Jesus*, is created by an organum of 6:3 chords moving in contrary motion (Ex. 58):

Ex. 58. Holst: Hymn of Jesus

Chorus I

To you who grieve a lamp am I

Holst's fondness for bitonal effects has a similar basis; and although he developed an almost pathological horror of sensuous seventh and ninth chords and confined himself mainly to unexpected melodic relationships of diatonic concords, his harmonic thinking is, in principle, very similar to Debussy's. His harmony, too, tends to deprive his music of the sense of progression.

The self-contained nature of Holst's modal melodies, the lack of progression in his harmony, mean that he has to rely on rhythm, or rather on metre, to keep the music going if he wishes to compose in other than small forms. The most primitive of all methods of achieving continuity is the ostinato; and the dominance of the ostinato over British music dates from Holst. His ostinato patterns are often in irregular measures of five, seven, or eleven, so that they do not conflict too strongly with the prose-like flexibility of his melodies. Paradoxically, the effect of the ostinato is again to destroy the time sense. We are conscious of time when rhythm is associated with alternations of harmonic stress; divorced from harmonic tension, a repeated metrical pattern tends to induce hypnosis. All Holst's most characteristic music deals with experience to which the time sense is irrelevant: consider 'Saturn' and 'Neptune', the two most impressive movements of *The Planets*. In his finest, most representative work, *Egdon Heath*, he is alone with the emptiness of the heath, as Delius is alone with the high hills, or Sibelius with the vast forest. Perhaps Holst achieves what Delius passionately strives for: his personality is purged away in the bare organum-like harmony and transparent scoring. Yet if *Egdon Heath* is, in a strict sense, a metaphysical work it is without the consolation of faith. Only in the late Lyric Movement for viola and chamber orchestra is there a hint of lyrical warmth in the soloist's melody, of tenderness in the sonorous spacing of the harmony.

Holst greatly admired the music of Stravinsky. When we come to discuss Stravinsky we shall see that every element which in Holst's technique assumes a somewhat abortive form, reaches fruition in the work of the Russian. Apart from any difference in natural endowment, this is largely because modal figurations, organum effects, and ostinatos had a profound relationship to the experience of a Russian and cosmopolitan *émigré*: whereas their significance in the history of English music was mainly purgative and clinical. Vaughan Williams [1872–1958] from the start had a more positive relationship to the English tradition than had Holst. As a countryman, he experienced folk-song as his own inheritance, treating it dramatically, rather than with ruminative nostalgia. The 'tragedy' of Housman's 'Shropshire Lad' poems may be not so far removed from the synthetic emotionalism of the popular Press; but they made it possible for Vaughan Williams to respond to folk-song with vivid immediacy. In *Is My Team Ploughing*, from *On Wenlock Edge*, the lad's folk-tune is modally self-contained. The ghostly answers to his questions, on the other hand, employ sophisticated harmonies closely associated with opera. Similarly, the most beautiful song in the cycle—*Bredon Hill*—becomes a dramatic experience. Self-contained folk-melody is here accompanied by superimposed thirds and fourths used impressionistically and statically; a personal grief becomes universal because it is seen against the eternal joy or lamentation of the bells.

Not only folk-song, but still more Tudor polyphony was for Vaughan Williams a positive value, as it could not be for Holst. The work in which, perhaps, he first found himself—the *Tallis Fantasia*—and the later Mass for double chorus employ antiphonal choirs of strings or voices in almost exactly the same way as Tallis himself used them. But the difference from Holst's organum technique is crucial: for what most fascinates Vaughan Williams in Tudor polyphony is the device of false relation, and this is essentially an interaction of linear and harmonic thought, such as is alien to Holst's music. The *Tallis Fantasia* and the Mass may look like pastiche; but their large-scale structure convinces because Vaughan Williams's obsession with false relation is already implicitly dramatic. These works already intimate the harmonic style of later pieces, such as *Sancta Civitas* (Ex. 59):

Ex. 59. Vaughan Williams: Sancta Civitas

Vaughan Williams's preoccupation with this tonal ambiguity inherent in sixteenth-century style suggests that he was aware that even a man of religious temperament—as Vaughan Williams is and Holst was not—cannot merely go 'back' to the sixteenth century. The Renaissance may be closer to us than the Middle Ages; but the composer still has to face up to the fact that between vocal polyphony and his own time the tremendous phenomenon of the sonata had occurred. Holst evaded the problem, and never attempted to create a work which approximates to the Beethovenian symphony of 'Becoming'. The *Scherzo* which is all he completed of a projected symphony is one of his most remarkable works, but it is a denial of classical symphonic style in that the elements in conflict never attempt a reconciliation. It exists in a state of suspended animation, of deliberate irresolution.

Vaughan Williams, on the other hand, has been preoccupied with the symphony throughout his long life; one might say that the core of his work lies in his attempt to reconcile the dramatic conflict of the symphony with the vocal modality typical of his melodic language. The 'Sea' Symphony, his first effort, hardly comes to grips with the problem, for it is a cross between a German symphony and an English oratorio. Vaughan Williams gained a new insight into the English choral tradition—into Purcell as well as Handel—from the pioneer work of Germanically trained composers, such as Stanford [1852–1924] and Parry [1848–1918]. Even his earliest music has, however, a creative energy far richer than their art, which was a product as much of scholarly study as of life.

The Second, or 'London', Symphony was a more direct attempt to fuse modal thinking with the dramatic symphony; it was but partially successful. In the Third, the 'Pastoral', Symphony of 1922, Vaughan Williams seemed to be relinquishing the attempt to reconcile incompatibles; for even though one may recognize groups of themes which can be equated with the conventional first and second subjects, there is no hint of sonata conflict. The score grows melodically, from monophonic—usually pentatonic—principles, and ends with a wordless human voice, unaccompanied.

Such music seems comparable with works of Holst, like *Egdon Heath*, except that Vaughan Williams's dissolution of the personality achieves a poetic ecstasy, whereas Holst's vocal rhythm is that of prose. None the less, the 'Pastoral' Symphony is a work of symphonic scope. Though it is not an orthodox sonata conflict of keys and motives, its pentatonic lines generate tension through their very independence of one another. The melodies move on several modal planes simultaneously. There are 'false' relations not only within the triadic harmony, but also between the swaying lines of organum; and Vaughan Williams employs a large orchestra in this almost consistently quiet score precisely because he wants to delineate the melodic strands with the maximum clarity. There is drama beneath the unruffled surface; and this incipiently dramatic linear style finds a more extreme expression in *Flos Campi*, which starts with 'gapped'* arabesques which are specifically bitonal. The form of the work is the slow generation, from the fight between two melodic entities in themselves rhapsodically relaxed, of a spacious, lyrically modal 'theme'.

In *Job* this technique is given direct dramatic presentation; for the story inspired by Blake's reinterpretation of the Book of Job, is objectified in a 'masque for dancing'. In the introduction, describing Job blessing his children, pentatonic arabesques and organum movement suggest a 'state of Nature', while chromatic intrusions perhaps hint at an inner instability. Broad modal lyricism ('Saraband of the Sons of God') expresses the divine attributes of Job's spirit; tritonal progressions, fierce metrical patterns, immense leaps and fourth-founded, triad-disrupting harmony express the Satanic spirit of denial. All the themes are related, because they are all aspects of a single soul. The musical structure of the work is a conflict between forces of good and evil, resolved in the rebirth of pentatonic lyricism in Elihu's 'Dance of Youth and Beauty'. In the 'Galliard of the Sons of the Morning' the pentatonic 'state of Nature' theme becomes a noble modal tune related to the divine theme of the Sons of God. The epilogue restates the work's neutral opening, except that the final cadence replaces an ambiguously modal G minor with the affirmation of B flat. The chromatic instability is still present, however; for though a battle has been won, it is a battle that must be fought again and again in the soul.

Job is not only one of Vaughan's greatest works; it is also a crucial point in his spiritual evolution. Only after this dramatic presentation of conflict could he turn again to the symphonic problem without denying the bases of his art. The Fourth is the most obviously dramatic work Vaughan Williams ever wrote and, in its metrical ferocity and fourth-founded harmony, is

---

* GAPPED: pentatonic and other primitive modes are sometimes described as 'gapped' because some of the steps in a scalewise progression are missing.

closely related both to Satan's music from *Job* and to Holst's
fiercely unresolved *Scherzo*. It is a lesser work than *Job* because
the positive elements are here in abeyance; Satan's minor
ninths, tritones, assertive metres, and harsh instrumental colours
are more violent than they are in *Job*, but the tension is in the
long run less, for there is little effective opposition. Perhaps
Vaughan Williams had to let Satan have sway symphonically,
before he could achieve in symphonic terms the resolution which
he had achieved dramatically in *Job*. Certainly that resolution
occurs in the Fifth Symphony, a work which is, at last, both
modal and genuinely symphonic.

Though the Fifth Symphony is ostensibly in D, it opens with
a soft horn-call over an unresolved, modal flat seventh (Ex. 60):

Ex. 60. Vaughan Williams: Symphony No.5 in D

and all the themes are vocal in contour, far more lyrically
sustained than Holst's. Traditionally, first and second subjects
are associated with the central tonalities of tonic and dominant.
Vaughan Williams's modulations are not so much contrast as
evolution; the modal behaviour of the themes promotes side-
stepping modulations into keys a tone or a semitone apart.
Beethoven's modulations to the flat supertonic are dramatic
events; Vaughan Williams's are a shift of tonal perspective,
occurring as one theme grows into the next. The 'second subject'
is an extension of the opening horn call; and it is in E, arrived at
by way of E flat (with a hint of C minor).

Such an evolutionary conception of melody and tonality may
convince in the exposition; but what is to happen in the development? Vaughan Williams solves this problem—and it was, of
course, an instinctive, not a conscious intellectual solution—
by not developing the main themes at all. In a much more
extreme form, he does what Haydn does in some of his later
symphonies. In the codetta of the exposition he introduces a
tiny motive—a fall to the flattened second. This chromaticism,
usually in the penetrating tone-colour of oboe or cor anglais,

naturally generates harmonic tension, as opposed to the lyrical
modality of the main themes. The development is founded
entirely on this motive, while the modalism of the themes
becomes pentatonic arabesques, woven around the increasingly
restless modulations. This pentatonic figuration is comparable
with that which so frequently appears in the development sections
of Sibelius's symphonies; its effect, however, is much more
positive, since pentatonicism is a natural part of Vaughan
Williams's melodic thought. The ultimate climax, in B flat, is
hardly less powerful than that of a Beethoven symphony; but
whereas Beethoven's drama implies a conflict between the Will
and the forces that impede its fulfilment, in Vaughan Williams's
symphony the drama is inherent in the process of growth. The
climax of the development leads to a recapitulation, in which
the themes soar in liberated lyricism. But the flat seventh on the
horn is left suspended. The cycle of birth, growth, and decay is
perennial.

The scherzo is a more traditional symphonic movement; and
although it follows a key-sequence almost exactly parallel to
that of the first movement, the dramatic effect of tonal conflict
is much more in evidence. Thematically, the hollow fourths of
the F minor Symphony appear again, though they have now
become remote and spectral. The fight between Bunyan's
Pilgrim and the foul fiends, viewed retrospectively in this
diaphanously scored music, has none of the frightening
immediacy of the (technically comparable) devil music in *Job*.
The movement thus fits the context: for though the symphony
is about a battle of the soul, the battle is recollected in tranquillity.

This becomes evident in the last two movements. On the
original score of the romanza, Vaughan Williams wrote a
quotation from *The Pilgrim's Progress*: "Upon that place there
stood a cross and a little below a sepulchre. . . . Then he said:
'He hath given me rest by his sorrow and life by his death'."
The movement opens in liturgical diatonicism similar to that
of the *Tallis Fantasia*, with modally related concords of C, A,
and B flat. Against the string choir the cor anglais sings an
Aeolian melody, rising and falling very slowly, step by step.
This melody expands, in a distinctly operatic style, into woodwind arabesques. At first pentatonic, these grow increasingly
strenuous and chromaticized: until they are lulled to rest by the

liturgical music of the opening. The serene close prepares the way for the final passacaglia, which resolves the whole symphony into the unity of the seventeenth-century technique of divisions on a ground. Hints of the alleluias of the Easter hymn *Lasst uns erfreun* had been heard in the Romanza; now they become increasingly obtrusive. When the first theme of the first movement finally reappears, with its unresolved horn-call, we are aware that the melodic material of the whole symphony had been leading towards these consummatory alleluias. And in the Epilogue the alleluias create, at last, a harmonic resolution also. The flat seventh is sharpened. The final resolution of the cadence is the end of what had seemed to be an eternal cycle; so the alleluias of the Epilogue can only herald another life. "When the Day that he must go hence was come, many accompanied him to the River side, into which, as he went, he said Death, where is thy Sting? And as he went down deeper, he said, Grave, where is thy Victory? So he passed over, and the Trumpets sounded for him on the other side." Slowly, almost imperceptibly, entry upon entry, the strings spread out until the vision is fulfilled: it is as though one had found, unawares, that the sky is suddenly filled with angels. Despite the beautiful prologue to Part II of *Gerontius* which so resembles Vaughan Williams, Elgar stops short at the river-bank, as Vaughan Williams does not. Whereas Delius and Holst, in their search for a metaphysical ecstasy, disintegrate cadential resolution, Vaughan Williams discovers it. His greatness consists in his positive assurance.

In the Sixth Symphony modal serenity and the turbulence of sonata conflict are much more sharply opposed, and end in a metreless no-man's-land similar to that of Holst's *Egdon Heath*. In the last movement Vaughan Williams's obsession with false relation is divorced from melodic and harmonic growth, so that the music creates a tension which is paradoxically disembodied. Of all Vaughan Williams's works this is perhaps the most powerfully representative of our time. None the less, the religious assurance of the Fifth Symphony—and to a lesser degree of *Job* and of some choral works, such as *Sancta Civitas* and the *Magnificat*—is the quality that makes his art uniquely valuable; and it is no accident that this assurance should be closely associated with the figure of Bunyan. The Fifth Symphony is intimately related to Vaughan Williams's opera on *The Pilgrim's Progress*. Since he worked on the score for more than thirty years, it is not surprising that reflexions of this great 'liturgical opera' should appear at every period of his career. Bunyan had a profoundly religious, richly traditional mind; yet he was also a product of that Puritan consciousness which, turned sour, helped both to destroy our musical tradition and to create the chaos of the modern world. In Vaughan Williams's music Bunyan is, as it were, reborn in love and charity. The religious assurance of Vaughan Williams's greatest music may place it outside the experience of most of us; yet it is not altogether an eccentric phenomenon in the twentieth century. For Vaughan Williams recovers contact with our cultural tradition at precisely the point in the seventeenth century when it disintegrated. He shows us, not perhaps what we are or can be, but what we might have been. Though we cannot follow his path, we can, with his help, recover our self-respect.

After Vaughan Williams, the English composer may again become a European. His problems are those of his neighbours: those of any society cosmopolitan, eclectic, uprooted. Schoenberg, Hindemith, Stravinsky, and Bartok are probably the greatest composers of our time, as they are certainly the most influential. In discussing them, we shall come up against most of the issues involved in twentieth-century music. It is worth noting that they have all been deracinated, one of them twice.

7

SCHOENBERG AND HINDEMITH

We may perhaps usefully approach the four central figures in modern music by way of a composer who seems marginal: yet in whose career we find an allegory of the position of the twentieth-century artist. Busoni [1866–1924] was a man of prodigious personal force and intellectual distinction; yet the impact of his creative and intellectual power was less than it might have been, because he was culturally and spiritually divided. Born in Italy, he was educated in Germany; torn between two traditions, he belonged to neither. His rootlessness was emphasized by his career as a concert pianist. He was one of the greatest—and most creative—pianists of all time; and the familiar tug-of-war between career and creative ambition assumes, with him, a peculiarly poignant form. For his career involved creative activity of a kind, while frustrating in him another and more important creativity.

If we take the E minor Violin Sonata (1899) as representative of the first phase of his work, we can see how the basis of his style was the Teutonic tradition of Beethoven and Brahms; yet the sun-baked vitality of Verdian operatic lyricism was already in conflict with this northern introspection. The first phase of his work culminates in the mammoth Piano Concerto (1908): in which work we can observe how his hero Liszt was the catalyst who showed him how the Italian and German traditions might be fused. Yet what appealed especially to Busoni was the necromantic quality in Liszt's virtuosity: his ability to 'possess' and recreate other composers and other traditions. Busoni was always seeking a spiritual home, trying to accommodate his personal experience to that of other men and other traditions; this became increasingly difficult as he grew more deeply conscious of his isolation.

The Piano Concerto is thus the last of his works which attempts a relationship with the classical tradition: with the sonata principle as the musical synonym for 'Becoming'. The piano Elegies (1908–9) inaugurate a new phase in his work which may be related to the late piano pieces of Liszt. The Elegies are richer and more developed than Liszt's disintegrative epigrams, but they have the same pathological queerness: the Italian *cantilena* that breaks into stuttering recitative; the bitonal washes of piano 'colour' in the accompanying figurations; the persistent ambiguity between major and minor third; the abrupt distortion of tonal perspective that suggests a glimpse into another world. In the *Berceuse* the multi-plane figuration may be compared with that in Liszt's *La Lugubre Gondole*: it seems to carry us, in its lulling rhythm, away from the earth into space. But space is an airy void, rather than a heaven: for there is no lyrical fruition. In *Die Nächtlichen* a similar technique draws us into a murky night of the spirit. The first, traditional phase of Busoni's work was summed up in the Piano Concerto. This second phase is consummated not in a work associated with German sonata style, but in an opera, *Die Brautwahl* (1914). Significantly, Busoni's libretto deals, not with any of the traditional operatic themes, but with the artist as visionary.

Liszt was not, however, the only composer who had fused Italian and German traditions. German polyphony and Italian *cantilena* meet in the music of Bach, whose art represented an ideal spiritual resolution towards which Busoni aspired. The Elegies had included a chorale fantasia which became a starting point for the *Fantasia Contrappuntistica*, Busoni's completion of the unfinished 'problem' of Bach's *Art of Fugue*. Henceforth, Busoni's search for order becomes basically contrapuntal: though his counterpoint cannot in fact be the same as Bach's. In Bach the ultimate order and serenity of the counterpoint is inseparable from an inner turbulence contained in the complex harmonic texture; it is because Bach's serenity involves such profound suffering, as well as joy, that it means so much. In a passage from Busoni's counterpoint such as Ex. 61 the separation of the lines on, as it were, different planes of tonality creates an effect strangely disembodied, suggesting a deliberate withdrawal from experience. This phase of Busoni's work was again consummated in a large-scale work—the opera *Dr. Faustus* (1916–24), a highly personal reinterpretation of the Faust myth which emphasizes the isolated artist's visionary

significance far more than *Die Brautwahl*. The tenuous polyphony and polyphonically derived harmony and orchestration
of *Dr. Faustus* are a moving and disturbing experience, in which

Ex.61. Busoni: Fantasia Contrappuntistica

the almost continuous false relations suggest the enigmatic,
equivocal quality in this personal vision. Perhaps it is not
surprising that this music should have had so great an influence
on later composers who are likewise isolated, in quest of serenity:
and that at the same time the vision should remain in essence
incommunicable.

A modern composer cannot start from the same point as
Bach, as though everything represented by the sonata principle
had never happened. Busoni used to say that middle-period
Beethoven and Wagner between them brought ruin on music,
Beethoven through his rhetoric, Wagner through his lascivious-
ness. He hardly convinces us, however, that his purged world
of the spirit could satisfy most fallible mortals as richly as the
symphonic Beethoven or as Wagner; and there is no valid
connexion between his visionary serenity and that of Beethoven's
last quartets. Beethoven, as we saw, won through to his
'monistic' serenity through sonata conflict; Busoni—in the
'disembodied' polyphony of his late style—suggests that the
visionary moment is an *alternative* to the turmoil of world, flesh,
and devil.

Busoni's single-minded integrity is itself conditioned by his
art's limitations; the sense of solitude and the search after the
personal, visionary moment are manifest in the work and career

of all the great central figures in twentieth-century music, even in those who, like Schoenberg, were born into a long musical tradition. For, like Mahler, Schoenberg [1874–1951] was a Jew, and in that sense an isolated spirit. Whatever his ultimate stature may be, it is no longer possible to doubt his crucial position in European history. He was the heir to Wagner: who was the heir to Beethoven: who inherited the traditions of the classical sonata. Now both Beethoven and Wagner, we saw in Part III, had been preoccupied with the assertion of the ego. Beethoven, however, in his last works had appeased the fury of the Will by reconciling the sonata principle with its apparent opposite—the unity of fugue and of aria variation; in so doing he had created a new kind of religious art wherein we may understand, with Kant, how we may 'live in an invisible church', since 'god's kingdom is in ourselves'. Wagner, on the other hand, came to deify the ego itself in its most fundamental impulse, that of sex; had derived a whole cosmos from the surge of erotic feeling through his nerves and senses; and had ultimately come to admit the paradox inherent in such dedication to the self—the inescapable association of life-instinct with death-instinct, of love with guilt, of passion with renunciation. This being so, we can understand why one part of Wagner's legacy should have been a search for oblivion: such as we find in the music of Delius. But we can also understand why any composer, looking to the future from the heights or depths of the Wagnerian crisis, had to seek a renewal of life within the psyche itself. We can observe the beginnings of this in one of Schoenberg's earliest works, *Verklärte Nacht*, originally for string sextet.

This piece tells a story (based on a poem of Richard Dehmel) which is closely related to the theme of *Tristan*. A woman and her lover walk, through the night, in a wood. She bears within her the child of the husband she does not love; but the beauty of the moonlit night transfigures both sensuality and guilt, so that they do not, like Tristan and Isolde, die in the flesh. Their passion is spiritualized and they can accept the husband's baby as mankind's fulfilled sensuality and in that sense as the fruit of their own love. The metamorphosis of physical into mystical experience is directly reflected in the musical technique. For although the piece is of continuous, chromatic-harmonic, Tristanesque texture, the

lines attain an ever-increasing degree of independence. The
further they flow from the introverted harmonic tensions—the
more freely they leap and sing—the more ecstatically transfigured the night becomes. This is why the piece is in effect
so different from the Straussian symphonic poem that it superficially resembles. Despite the highly charged, harmonic nature
of Schoenberg's music the structure, even in this early work,
involves genuine polyphonic thinking: whereas Strauss's polyphony, which is not less elaborate, could be removed without
completely destroying the sense. As with Mahler, this development in texture is also a development in experience: a search
for a more spiritual, even mystical, resolution of the Wagnerian
crisis within the Self.*

This technical evolution is still more evident in those early
works which Schoenberg scored for an orchestra even more
gargantuan than that of Strauss. Strauss scores superbly, but as
a harmonist; and there are passages in the music of his middle
years in which the orchestral polyphony, in obscuring the harmonic structure, defeats its own ends. Mahler and Schoenberg
score with impeccable lucidity; however complex the texture,
the lines are aurally intelligible. Wagner and Strauss think polyphonically in the sense that their harmony is composed of a
number of interdependent strands; Mahler and Schoenberg
think polyphonically in the sense that polyphony becomes itself
a contributory means of order. The chromatic harmony is a
tonal disintegration; to compensate for this, the whirling lines
seek contrapuntal organization among themselves. The enormous scores of the *Gurrelieder* and of *Pelléas*—vast symphonic
operas without stage action—sound as rhapsodically sensuous
as Wagner. Yet the interweaving parts are full of contrapuntal
devices of a complexity and ingenuity rivalling that of the
unjustly maligned and misnamed 'Netherland' polyphonists.

It was well-nigh inevitable that, as his music grew increasingly chromatic, Schoenberg should turn from the mammoth
orchestra to chamber music. In the first two string quartets
and the First Chamber Symphony, the chromaticism has

* A comparable 'spiritualization' of Wagnerian harmonic polyphony occurs in
the music of Hans Pfitzner [1869–1949]; but with him erotic sensuality is modified
by deep respect for the social and religious values of the past. It is revealing that
his finest, most representative work should be an opera, *Palestrina*, concerned with
the life of a Renaissance humanist who, as composer, was also a man of the Church.
Perhaps one might say that the piece stands halfway between *Parsifal* and the ascetic
mysticism of Busoni's *Faustus*.

become inherent in the contours of the lines. Though the works all start from a tonal basis, there are passages in which the lines modulate so rapidly that they seem not to modulate at all. We lose consciousness of a tonal centre; and to offset this instability, Schoenberg emphasizes linear means of construction. Though the lines in these works are even freer than those in the big orchestral pieces, being characterized by enormous leaps and irregular rhythmic groupings similar to those in Mahler, they are subjected to elaborate contrapuntal treatment. Counterpoint is becoming more important, as an organizing principle, than the progression of tonal roots. It is significant that in the First Chamber Symphony Schoenberg strongly stresses the interval of the fourth, at the expense of the traditional triad.

At the time, Schoenberg probably did not appreciate the full implications of his preoccupation with counterpoint; he was more concerned with linear chromaticism than with the new principle of order it might entail. His next works, at least, appear to move in a contrary direction. He strives above all to make his disintegrative chromatic lines expressive in themselves, divorced from tonal implications or from any external organization. Wagner's last works and his own early music, he argued, had expanded tonality so far that it was possible to introduce into a given key any note foreign to that key. If a key can be expressed as well by other notes as by those proper to it, can it be said to exist? To talk of any notes as being foreign to the key is nonsensical, for harmony is simply a sounding together of tones. It is therefore time to create a music which accepts the twelve equal-tempered semitones as of equal significance, without reference to tonal concepts based on the triad.

Music composed thus empirically must either be confined to pieces of very short duration, or must serve as illustration to a literary text. In the *Buch der hängenden Gärten*, Schoenberg sets Stefan George's poems to a vocal line that is as much speech as song, while the piano offers a 'nervous' commentary on the text, without reference to traditional tonality, without relation to the vocal line, and even without repetitions of phrase. The fragmentary lines and harmonies are to be quintessentially expressive: feeling in itself, unmodified by traditional usage or even by the artist's conscious volition. Similarly, the third piano piece of opus 11 and the tiny pieces of opus 19 carry Debussy's 'seismographic' technique to an even more extreme point. The second-piece of opus 19, for instance, is a study in the aural effect of the interval of the third, in which the interval is even more disembodied, more remote from a tonal context, than it is in Debussy's *Les Tierces Alternées*. It is true that the pieces of opus 19 are not as surrealist in approach as the *Buch der hängenden Gärten*, for the quivering sonorities are full of discreet contrapuntal imitations. None the less, the fact that Schoenberg regarded the exquisite final piece as bell-music—a funeral bell tolling for Mahler's death—suggests that the music is apprehensible only as a moment of sensation, and is of its nature incapable of development (Ex. 62):

Ex. 62. Schoenberg: Opus 19

Debussy evaded this dilemma by a compromise with tonality and tradition. For Schoenberg, compromise was impossible. For him there were only two ways out. One was to ally music not merely with a literary text, but with the stage, so that coherence, development, climax could be provided by the dramatic element. This was only a stop-gap, for it left unsolved the problem of musical form. The other way out was to discover a new principle of order, to take the place of that which Wagner's and Schoenberg's chromaticism seemed to have discredited. At first, Schoenberg worked towards these two ends simultaneously. We can see this in his operatic monologue *Erwartung*, which deals with a story closely related both to *Tristan* and to *Verklärte Nacht*.

The libretto was written by Marie Pappenheim from the composer's own suggestions; and the piece is an operatic work that makes explicit the implications of *Tristan* and *The Ring* in that there is only one character, within whose mind the action takes place. Again a woman is wandering 'through the blind mazes of this tangled wood'. She is possessed by a sexual passion of Tristanesque violence. Waiting to meet her lover in the wood,

she seems at the same time to know that he will not come: that
he has deserted her for a ghostly white-armed other love (probably, psychoanalytically speaking, his mother). The climax
comes when she stumbles on his murdered body. It is not clear
who murdered him; she refers, confusedly, to the other woman
and to an indeterminate 'they'. But it is unclear because, of
course, the action has no real existence outside her mind. She
enters the dark wood of the unconscious; and the first stages of
her wandering are a mingling of her memories and inchoate
desires. Her discovery of the body is her recognition of loss:
and complementarily of guilt and renunciation. From this point
the unconscious takes over completely; text and music become
hallucinatory. Yet the pattern established by *Tristan* and *Verklärte
Nacht* is continued: for submission to the unconscious brings
release from terror; and the piece ends with a 'transfigured'
vision of her lover, wherein passion is fulfilled, hatred forgotten.

This fulfilment exists, of course, only in the music. The vocal
line carries Wagnerian song-speech into realms of the most
intense expressiveness, as it follows the vagaries of the half-
thinking, half-feeling mind. The orchestral texture—with its
high degree of dissonance, its lack of traditional tonal organization, its extraordinary polyphonic density and complexity—expresses the gradual disintegration of mind and senses. At the
same time, the resilience and power of the lines created out of
apparent dislocation, the radiant luminosity of the orchestral
fabric, convey a fundamental affirmation. Tenderness and
strength are inextricable in the passage in the second scene when
she thinks of her meeting with her lover in the walled garden;
ineffably moving is the cry of longing she utters at the end
when she imagines she sees her lover, and the sensory life of
the orchestral texture dissolves away in contrary motion chromatics. It is difficult to know what to call this if it is not, as
well as a moment of vision, an act of faith.

So although Schoenberg's disintegration of tonality is in one
sense a breakdown within the consciousness, it is also a step towards liberation and rebirth. It is not an accident that Schoenberg was born and worked in the same city as Freud. He starts
(like Wagner) from the primary human urge of sexuality; he
faces up to a hiatus in the flow of creative vitality that man's
dedication to Self has led him into; then he seeks a linear and
polyphonic integration of the chromatically splintered fragments

of mind and senses. It is not extravagant to say that there is a relationship between this search for integration and the Freudian reintegration of the dislocated facets of a personality; and both have affinities with what used to be called religious experience.

So Schoenberg's invention of the twelve-note or serial technique was at once a technical and a spiritual necessity. The technical need was simply that, since the traditional tonal basis of European music seemed, after Wagner, to be played out, a new principle of order was essential if composers were to construct works of reasonable dimensions. In the world of the equal-tempered semitone this principle cannot be harmonic. It must, therefore, be linear; so Schoenberg's early preoccupation with counterpoint answered to a deep need of his nature. In the later works of his 'expressionist' period, such as *Pierrot Lunaire*, we find that the declamation of a literary text is accompanied not by an empirical sound-commentary, but by a tenuously scored tissue of fragmentary motives, all related by the most elaborate canonic devices. The literary meaning of the poems concerns the Pierrot-figure as symbol of the sick, broken spirit of modern man; but the music—even more that that of *Erwartung*—achieves a radiant wholeness and compassion out of its apparently fragmentary complexity. The musical commentary seeks its own order in becoming a principle of perpetual variation. From his earliest years, Schoenberg had thus tended to think 'serially'; nor was the serial principle itself new. All that was new was the consistency with which the principle was to be applied. In twelve-note music every note in a composition is part of a variation, or rather a permutation, of a given series; every note is conditioned by linear, not harmonic, relationship.

The basis of a twelve-note composition is what came to be known as the 'row'—a specific arrangement of the twelve chromatic semitones. The row is not a theme, nor need it be aurally apprehensible. It is not a scale, though it serves some of the functions of a mode in that all the melodic material of the piece and to some extent the harmony is derived from the row and its permutations (the series inverted, or backwards, or backwards and inverted). Notes of the row cannot normally be repeated out of their order in the series, since concentration on one note might suggest a tonic. Consecutive members of the

series can be combined to form chords. The row may be trans-
posed to any pitch, and divided between the parts. Sometimes
the row may consist of two segments of six notes, or three
segments of four notes.

Schoenberg has said that the row is a linear means of organizing tones which concerns the composer rather than the
listener. Far from being an arbitrary sequence of notes, it is
the creative germ from which the composer derives themes and
harmonies. Its relation to what is commonly called 'inspiration'
is at least as intrinsic as the relation between inspiration and the
seminal motives which Beethoven jotted down in his sketch-
books; the composer's liberty of choice is neither more nor less
limited than in tonally organized music. At first the rows
selected would tend to be divorced from harmonic implications,
for, in creating a purely chromatic music, it was necessary to
avoid suggestions of diatonicism. Yet Berg, even after he adopted
the twelve-note technique, tended to use rows which included
major and minor triads, and therefore made possible some
compromise with traditional tonality. In the elegiac Violin
Concerto he can even introduce a Bach chorale, in Bach's
original harmonization, without committing a stylistic solecism
—and without entirely surrendering the row.

Schoenberg was probably right in thinking that this kind of
compromise, though appropriate to Berg's relatively regressive,
romantic temperament, was not intrinsically desirable; for the
more the row compromises with traditional tonality the less
need would there seem to be for any purely linear means of
organizing the semitone. None the less, Schoenberg increasingly
came to feel that even in music constructed serially the composer
had, from these linear relationships, to discover his own tonal
criteria. The lower members of the harmonic series may not
have the importance in our tonal thinking that they once had;
yet the harmonic series itself remains a scientific fact. There
must still be a relationship between the 'horizontal' and the
'vertical' aspects of music; and although a purely chromatic
tonality is still in process of evolution, the harmony in Schoenberg's 'purest' serial works is never fortuitous. Far less than
Debussy does Schoenberg, in most of his mature works, break
with traditional notions of harmonic progression. In the opening
of the Fourth Quartet the music acquires richness and intensity
because each harmony and accompanying figuration, being

serially derived, is related to the main melody. But the passage
is aurally intelligible because the main melody is immediately
recognizable as such, not so much because it has a D minorish
tinge as because it is sharply defined in rhythm: because the
'accompanying' parts also have a clearly defined rhythm and
proceed in ways related to the traditional treatment of leading
notes and appoggiaturas (Ex. 63):*

Ex. 63. Schoenberg: String Quartet No. 4
Allegro molto; energico ♩ = 152

The serially derived superimposed fifths at the end of the
wonderful Violin Concerto are a similar example: we do not
need to listen to this music with new ears—as we do with the
music of some of Schoenberg's successors—to perceive that its
harmonic logic parallels its serial integrity.

It is unfortunate that, for valid historical reasons, Schoenberg
has encouraged us to talk more about his system than about
his music. All musical techniques are artificial, artefacts that

* For a detailed analysis of this passage see the article by Oliver Neighbour
published in *The Score* for June 1956.

are man-made. If a twelve-note composer works within pre-conceived patterns, so does a pentatonic or a diatonic composer. It is true that the pentatonic scale is related to more funda-mental acoustical facts than the chromatic, and that there is a difference between Mozart's equal-tempered chromaticism and Schoenberg's. It is true that mental vocalization is the means whereby themes become memorable, and that not all our familiarity with equal-tempered scales can alter the fact that a purely chromatic music is difficult to memorize because it is difficult to sing. Yet it is also true that Schoenberg's music becomes tonally viable when we have listened to it enough; and that—as he pointed out—singers find his music comprehensible and performable when they have acquired a consciousness of the row, which indirectly conditions the music's tonal logic in directly conditioning its linear structure.

This is why an abstract work like the Violin Concerto can move us deeply, and in the same way as a piece such as *A Sur-vivor from Warsaw*, in which we have a speaker's verbal language and an urgently topical subject to help us. It is profoundly sig-nificant that in Schoenberg's later chamber works—such as the Third and Fourth Quartets and the String Trio—the Wagnerian resolution of his early works should come to terms with the 'religious' resolution of late Beethoven. They are the same *kind* of music as Beethoven's last quartets (which also use serial pro-cesses): though they do not enter Beethoven's paradise. They seek 'God's kingdom', which exists below the level of conscious-ness, along with nameless horrors and fears; and in this sense all Schoenberg's music is basically religious, and related to the unfinished opera, *Moses und Aron*, on which he worked for so many years. In this work Schoenberg associates himself—as Freud had done also—with Moses, the spirit's deliverer, as against Aron, the man of practical affairs. He creates music which is not only overwhelmingly dramatic, but also lyrical, and both technically and spiritually lucid. His Jewish fanatic-ism—which was also his 'modern' isolation—becomes the new world of the spirit at which Mahler's orchestral polyphony had hinted. And although Schoenberg could not complete the opera's vision of man regenerated, the integrity of his search remains truly heroic—from *Erwartung's* final cry of 'Ich suchte' to the tortured but undespairing polyphony of his last work: a *De Profundis*.

The new world that Schoenberg seeks, springing as it does from the decay of the past, gives him his central significance in the history of our time. We do not find this 'centrality' in the more readily accessible, but more elegiacally limited, music of his pupil, Alban Berg [1885–1935]. Romantically, Berg's music is half in love with the 'decadence' it reflects, and technically compromises between past and present as Schoenberg's music does not; none the less, Berg does renew decadence, if not with Schoenberg's religious intensity, at least with compassion. This we can see in his best-known and perhaps most representative work, the opera *Wozzeck*, which although not produced until 1925, after the appearance of Schoenberg's first twelve-note pieces, had been conceived, and partially composed, many years earlier. It is thus (significantly) an instance of the transitional phase between free atonality and the serial principle.

It is based on a play by George Büchner, a writer of precocious genius who was born in 1813 and died in his twenty-third year. Büchner lived through an era of appalling political oppression. He was typical of his time in the intensity of his response to suffering, not altogether typical in his unromantic acceptance of it. By the time of Schoenberg and Berg pessimism had become an accredited romantic attitude; but their pessimism was also a valid response to a sick world. Berg's *Wozzeck*, like Büchner's, is peopled by beings obsessed with neurotic terrors: the megalomaniac doctor who regards human beings merely as subjects for clinical dissertation and who, in Büchner's play, though not in Berg's opera, has the last word; the power-addict, the silly-sinister drum-major; and Wozzeck himself, the eternal scapegoat. The story, presented not in developing narrative but in a series of 'impressions', tells how the wretched Wozzeck is goaded by his 'superiors' into murdering his unfaithful mistress, who, slut though she may be, is his one hold on humanity. It is as gloom-crazed as any product of German expressionism; yet though Büchner's world is decadent, his play is not. Compassion, not hysteria, comes of the torment. Büchner was justified when he said: "I have always turned on suffering, downtrodden humanity more glances of compassion than I have expended bitter words on the cold hearts of those in authority."

No theme could have better suited Berg's nervously sensitive temperament. His music, like the play, is simultaneously

decadent and revolutionary. In some respects his method is
Wagnerian for—like Schoenberg in *Erwartung*—he gives a
minute musical illustration of the drama. Each character has
his motive, developed both as psychological commentary and
as part of the musical structure. Some recurrent phrases—such
as that which Wozzeck first sings to the words "Wir arme Leut"
—have a kind of ideological significance comparable with that
of Wagner's 'Ring' or 'Sword' motives. Like Wagner, Berg
concentrates the psychological drama in the elaborate orchestral part. The vocal lines have their origin in Wagnerian
declamation, but approximate much more closely to the
speaking voice, or at least to the voices of speakers who are
distraught. They range from passionate but brief lyrical out-
bursts to passages which, modelled on Schoenberg's 'free'
atonal works with speaker and instruments, are more spoken
than sung.

At the same time, however, as he pursues this psychological
realism, Berg strives to impose on the drama a purely musical
shape. Thus the opening scene is in the form of a classical suite
(prelude, pavane, gigue, and gavotte with two 'doubles');* the
scene in the doctor's study is a passacaglia; the opening of Act
II is described as being in sonata form; while Act III takes the
form of six inventions in different types of variation technique.
Some of these forms are perhaps valid only on paper. The
classical suite and sonata depend so much on a conception of
tonality which Schoenberg and Berg had repudiated that it is
doubtful if they can have aural meaning. They may suggest to
the composer phrase-groupings, effects of balance and repetition, even—in the case of the sonata—transpositions of motives
collateral to modulation; but the absence of a tonal centre and
the non-metrical nature of the rhythm mean that the form,
architecturally considered, is not normally perceptible to the
listener. Essentially the organization is linear, not architectural;
and is therefore not radically different from Berg's experiments
towards a completely thematic technique by way of variation,
passacaglia, and fugue. As early as this transitional work we can
see how appropriate are these linear forms to Berg's conception
of music drama: consider the association of the doctor's *idée fixe*
with the obsessive ostinato of the passacaglia.

What strikes one most forcibly about *Wozzeck*, as one looks

* DOUBLE: a repeat with ornamental modifications. See Part II, p. 535.

back at it after thirty years, is the flexibility of the technique. There are many sections, such as the scarifying scene in the copse, which now seem to belong to the ripely autumnal world of Strauss, though the highly charged emotion is expressed with an orchestral translucence more suggestive of Mahler or, quite often, Debussy. Yet *Wozzeck* achieves consistency of style. *Elektra*-like chromaticized diatonicism exists alongside extreme atonal passages without incongruity, just as the distorted, banal military music outside Marie's window is no more an anachronism in this fear-haunted world than is the almost diatonic lullaby she croons to her child. Once again, creativity renews decay. Though we do not know what will happen to him, the child at the close remains innocent in his play, as the water engulfs his father. Similarly, Berg's 'decadent' technique hints at a world of pure chromaticism that still awaited exploration in the mature music of Schoenberg and Webern.

While we may think that Schoenberg's response to chromatic disintegration faces up most squarely to the 'humanist crisis' of our time, it does not follow that all compromise with the past is 'decadent'. One of Schoenberg's senior pupils—born in the same year as Berg—provides a link between complete chromaticism and the re-created diatonicism of a composer such as Hindemith. As a young man in Vienna, Egon Wellesz [b. 1885] was associated with both Mahler and Schoenberg, but made his mark with theatrical works—ballets and operas on classical themes—that achieved an equilibrium between Schoenbergian chromaticism and conceptions of tonality suggested by Wellesz's researches into Byzantine monody and seventeenth-century opera. Both Byzantine music and heroic opera were ritualistic forms of art, one liturgical, the other secular; and whereas Mahler and Schoenberg were Jews whose religion was part of a Faustian struggle towards self-awareness, Wellesz is a Roman Catholic with a deep respect for religious and cultural tradition. It is significant that both the church music and the five symphonies which he has created comparatively late in life resemble Bruckner's in fusing sonata style's dualistic tonal conflict and kinetic motor rhythms with 'baroque' counterpoint and types of melodic organization derived from medieval cantillation. Perhaps the contradictory elements are juxtaposed rather than fused: on which fact depends the emotional and physical strenuousness of the composer's affirmation. One finds something similar in the music of Hindemith: for although his music does not share Wellesz's Catholic mysticism and Austrian lyricism, it attempts to subdue twentieth-century tensions to a concept of unity which is not, like Schoenberg's, discovered within the psyche, but is inherited from the past.

So although Hindemith [b. 1895] started, like Schoenberg, against the background of German romanticism, he was always more in sympathy with the classical tradition than with Wagner. Both Schoenberg and Hindemith had much in common with the elegiac gravity of Brahms; but whereas Schoenberg was interested in the revolutionary potentialities of Brahms's cross-rhythms and elliptical harmonies, Hindemith saw in Brahms the romantic heir to classical tradition. In so far as Wagnerian chromaticism affected him, it was by way of the pseudo-contrapuntal chromaticism of Reger [1873–1916].

The texture of Reger's music is no less complex than that of Strauss or early Schoenberg; but his chromatic elaboration did not follow Tristan into a transfigured night. He did not even attempt to romanticize the symphonic ideal; instead, he sought to control his chromaticism by a deliberate re-creation of pre-symphonic forms, relating his chromaticism, as Liszt had sometimes done, to that of Bach. In so doing, he created intermittently some moving and powerful music, while evading the central problem of form and tonality in his day. The subject of Bach's B minor Fugue from Book I of *The Forty-eight* includes every note of the chromatic scale, and the texture of the music looks superficially like that of a fugue by Reger. But Bach preserves continuity of line and tonal direction through all the chromatic vagaries; indeed, the form of his fugue is synonymous with the tension between the tonal progression and the apparent disintegration of the lines. Reger's fugues nearly always lack both tonal direction and linear continuity: so that, for all the growing elaboration of the parts and the piling up of *stretti*, they seem to be without climax. They have neither true contrapuntal form, nor Wagner's cumulative harmonic logic. One might even suggest that Reger is most impressive when he is least in awe of Bach: in large-scale works like the lovely Mozart or Hiller Variations in which, though avoiding the symphonic problem, he has a lilting cantabile lyricism to give buoyancy to the chromatic texture; or in works like the piano sonatinas, in which the modest proportions make the texture subtly sensitive rather than extravagantly rich.

In his most Bachian works Reger was attempting to put new wine into old bottles; and Hindemith soon became aware—emotionally if not intellectually—that if the composer today is to create a music convincingly contrapuntal in the same sense as Bach's music, it can only be within a tonal scheme as relevant to our world as Bach's was to his. Wagner may lead ultimately to a purely chromatic, serial technique; Bach never can, even though in his last chorale prelude he creates a completely thematic—and in that sense a serial—composition.

The first phase of Hindemith's discovery of Bach, which was also a discovery of himself, was perhaps mainly negative and corrective. Schoenberg found a new objectivity through accepting all the implications of his romantic individualism; Hindemith began by wilfully suppressing personal feeling. If the twentieth century wanted Utility music, he would provide it. Of course, his functional music did not really serve any function; he was a craftsman making solidly constructed chairs that no one would sit on, because they were not the commercially accepted shape. Moreover, a responsible artist cannot really believe that music is *merely* utilitarian, any more than he can discard his self-consciousness to become primitive and unreasoning. Yet Hindemith's utilitarian phase was of great significance in his development, and its importance was analogous to that of the primitive phase in the careers of Stravinsky and Bartók. In each case the primitive or utilitarian diverted attention from the self-regarding ego. Music became a creative act. In becoming ritualist or craftsman the composer encouraged forgetfulness of self; and this was a prelude to a fresh creative impulse.

Hindemith's utilitarian music has a direct bearing on the 'serious' music which he composed during the 1920s, for the preoccupation with sharp, hard sonorities and with continuous motor-rhythms which he learned from jazz became absorbed into neo-baroque techniques. Such sonorities and motor-rhythms gained a fresh vivacity when they served to discipline melodic lines of a nervous compulsive energy, or of unexpected tenderness. The tingling acidity of the *Konzertmusik* for piano and brass becomes an emotional rejuvenation; so in a different way does the lyrical *cantilena* for the solo instrument in the

Chamber Concerto for viola. A deliberately sharp, 'inexpressive' tone-colour, a deliberately stylized, quasi-baroque melodic pattern, a deliberately archaic structure usually veering to an ostinato or canonic device, become stimulating, even revolutionary in impact. The lines are aggressively diatonic, the rhythms metrically rigid; yet the mechanical patterns of the counterpoint create an acutely dissonant texture. If the music is only intermittently sensitive, it preserves a high degree of vitality.

In this music Hindemith creates a counterpoint which, while resembling the surface of Bach's texture, makes no attempt to achieve Bach's tension between line and harmony. On the contrary, the disturbing quality of the music depends on the apparently fortuitous way in which the parts bump into one another. The more Hindemith came to understand the spirit of Bach's art, however, the more he attempted to create lines which, like Bach's, imply their own harmony. First, he experimented with a number of works for solo stringed instruments; the difference between these pieces and Reger's suites for unaccompanied stringed instruments is interesting. The Reger works are simply pastiche of Bach; they add nothing to his technique and have not, of course, his genius. The Hindemith works emulate Bach's method; but the harmony their line implies expands the 'tonal universe' within which Bach worked, for Bach's world was still basically diatonic, whereas Hindemith wrote in the wake of Wagnerian chromaticism. When Hindemith began to combine several such lines polyphonically, in large-scale chamber or orchestral works or in operas, he produced a texture comparable with that of Busoni's later works. Hindemith's piano sonatas and Busoni's *Sonatina in Diem Nativitatis Christi*, for instance, are neither of them sonatas in the classical sense; and their transparent, luminous texture depends on an unusual degree of independence between the lines, which sometimes implies bitonality. But whereas in Busoni the 'separateness' of the lines grew sharper in his later music, in Hindemith the separate lines increasingly seek for harmonic relationships. These relationships are flexible and complex; but a new Bachian polyphony must inevitably entail a new concept of tonality, adequate to our time.

It was this that induced Hindemith to work out a theory of tonality which, being based on the harmonic series, was derived from scientific facts, but which offered a means of evaluating all possible combinations that could occur in music, whether modal, diatonic, or chromatic. If he is right, a composer will be able to employ any harmonic or melodic combination, while being able to assess its significance in relation to a criterion of tonality. He will know that some intervals, some melodic shapes, are more stable, more convincing, than others in a given context; and he will know why. The 'meanings' which the symbols of music have will be basically the same as those understood by Bach or any other composer. But it will be possible to relate to a criterion combinations and procedures of which Bach could not have been aware.

Hindemith has attempted to provide for the twentieth century a theoretical basis to composition similar to that which Rameau offered to the eighteenth century. It is a theory of tonality, not—like Schoenberg's serial technique—a method of composition; but, like Schoenberg's method, it was deduced from the composer's creative practice, and it certainly has a direct bearing on the way a composer works. Hindemith wrote *Ludus Tonalis*—a series of fugues and interludes for piano— to demonstrate his theory of tonality in much the same spirit as Bach wrote *The Forty-eight* to demonstrate equal temperament. It is a pedagogical work which is also fine music; nor is it fortuitous that Hindemith's most representative work—the opera *Mathis der Maler*—should be that which most clearly reveals that his technique is a chromatically expanded, logically disciplined, continuation of the German tradition of Bach, Schütz, and the sixteenth-century polyphonists. The theme of the opera is that the Artist, as the representative of truly creative Tradition, is indeed the 'unacknowledged legislator' of the world.

On the other hand, it seems possible that Hindemith, having evolved his theory, has in later years sometimes been tempted to write music to fit it. The more vocal, modal quality of his lines, the smoother harmony, the more fluent polyphony are not necessarily more convincing because they obey Hindemith's 'degree-progressions'. One may certainly question whether the revised version of the *Marienlieder* is an improvement on the original; and it is interesting to note that the finest song in the cycle, the deeply impressive passacaglia-like *Pieta*, is the only song that Hindemith left virtually untouched. Hindemith would like to think that his scheme of tonality represents a cosmos as universally applicable as that within which Bach worked: perhaps more so, because it is evolved with superior scientific knowledge. There is, however, little evidence that it is being universally adopted. It probably has fewer adherents than Schoenberg's pure chromaticism, which, according to Hindemith, is tonally arbitrary and, strictly speaking, non-sensical. That does not seem to be an adequate account of Schoenberg's music, though there are good and bad composers in any system. In the long run, the system does not matter. Such music of Schoenberg and Hindemith as may survive will probably prove that they have more in common than either would wish or suspect.

8

STRAVINSKY AND BARTÓK

Sснonberg and Hindemith both worked within the German —which was the main European—tradition. Stravinsky [b.1882], as a Russian, never came directly under the sway of the symphonic principle or of Wagnerian chromaticism. In his student days he was a pupil of Rimsky-Korsakov; and such tonal disintegration as occurs in his early work is associated, like Rimsky-Korsakov's, with the evocation of a Russian fairyland. The tritonal theme of King Kastchei in *The Firebird* is one example; the elaborate, but significantly more linear, chromaticism of the later fairy opera, *The Nightingale*, is another.

Even in his earliest music, however, we can observe a tendency to reintegrate traditional materials in untraditional ways. The horizontalization of chords, producing two or more harmonic streams that proceed independently of one another, is a typical method, which we have already noted in such composers as Holst and Vaughan Williams. As with Holst again, Stravinsky's partiality for bitonal effects is basically a linear, rather than a harmonic, habit; frequently—as in the notorious clash between the triads of C and F sharp in *Petrouchka*—the effect is neither linear nor harmonic, but percussive. The 'noise' is expanded into a long piano cadenza: much as Satie will construct a whole piece out of the alternation of two chords.

The influence of Rimsky-Korsakov on Stravinsky was no more than superficial. Soon he discovered that his Russian heritage had a deep relationship to the isolated sensibility of the twentieth century. We have remarked that the most distinctive feature of Russian history was that Russia had no Renaissance; to a Russian, therefore, the preoccupation with personal feeling, characteristic of most European art between the sixteenth and twentieth centuries, seemed comparatively extraneous. He was more prone to think of his art in terms of ritual and liturgy; and

Stravinsky gradually became imaginatively aware that such a ritualistic approach might be an answer to the disrupted self-consciousness of the modern world.

The first evidence of this is in the works directly inspired by primitive ritual. Even in *Petrouchka* a modern isolation is embodied not in a human being, but in a puppet, whose tragedy is enacted against the impersonal, ritual-like background of folk-incantation. By the time of *The Rite of Spring* and *The Wedding* the patterns the composer imposes on his material are almost exclusively metrical. In opposition to the chromatic flux, he insists on the validity of metre; for the wildest metrical eccentricity is conceivable only in relation to a norm. Thus all the elements of music are adapted to reinforce rhythm. Line is reduced to a series of insistently repeated modal patterns the effect of which is dynamic and incantatory; harmony becomes percussive; instrumentation is exploited for its physical and nervous impact. The long passages of parallel seconds, thirds, fourths, fifths, sixths, sevenths, ninths, and tritones, often moving simultaneously a semitone apart, are not harmony. They are thickened line; and since the line is deliberately without melodic interest, the effect is entirely rhythmic (Ex. 64):

Ex. 64. Stravinsky: The Rite of Spring

The music is orgiastic, like the primitive ritual it recreates. Positively, it represented a search for a new source of vitality in an emotionally hypertrophied world; negatively, it was an offshoot of the sadism latent in the war years. From either point of view it meant a regression from personal sensibility to the collective Unconscious: and was, in terms of musical technique, at once a reaction against chromaticism and a part of the same disruptive process. As Debussy in some of his middle-period piano pieces, and Schoenberg in his 'free' atonal period, reduced music to the vertical effect of simultaneously sounding notes, so Stravinsky reduced melody and harmony to rhythm. Harmony without melody and rhythm,

rhythm without melody and harmony, are static. Both the pandemonium of Stravinsky's *Rite of Spring* and the whisper of Debussy's *Voiles* deprive music of the sense of motion from one point to another. Though they started from diametrically opposed points, both composers mark a radical departure from the traditions of European music since the Renaissance; both are in some ways as much oriental as occidental.

Thus in *The Wedding* tonality is far more stringently restricted than it is in the Viennese classics: only it is a melodic kind of tonality, consisting of oscillations (usually pentatonic) around a nodal point. That the accompanying figurations are often a semitone apart from the melody does not affect this at all: for the figurations are percussive unresolved appoggiaturas which 'stand for' and sadistically intensify the note to which they should resolve. This technique enhances both the primitive barbarity and the 'modern' hysteria of the music; but it is significant that Stravinsky does not attempt to resolve the hysteria except when, at the end, the percussive dissonance ceases to accompany the vocal line. The male voice finally sings his pentatonic love song unaccompanied, his phrases being interspersed by gong-strokes and by pianos imitating gongs, in an immensely slow pulse which gradually swings to rest. This is the first of many such conclusions to Stravinsky's works, in which Time stops. This one, however, though impressive, hardly seems to have much relationship to Europe or the twentieth-century; it might be by an anonymous Balinese composer.

If Stravinsky had stopped at this point he would have been an historically interesting, but not great, figure in European music. But just as Debussy went on to relate the revolutionary technique of his middle years to a renewed tradition, so Stravinsky began to explore the relationship between his interest in primitive ritual and his position as a European composer, culturally uprooted. Now *The Rite of Spring* and *The Wedding* were both ballets. Stravinsky's primitive ritual could not, after all, be 'real', for he was not in fact primitive: so that in these works the two bifurcated strands of Russian culture meet. The primitive realism of peasant ritual (which had found its greatest representative in Moussorgsky) now finds expression through the sophisticated, westernized fairy-ritual of ballet. Obviously, Stravinsky's primitivism could be no more than a starting-point in the attempt to revive a ritualistic approach.

There was, however, a twentieth-century ritual that expressed itself in physical movement, and that had a direct and 'realistic' relationship to the stresses—and perhaps the evasions —of the modern world. Basically, the vitality in jazz came from a primitive (negro) source; and its technique was founded, like that of so much Russian music, on the ostinato and on incremental repetition. Consisting almost entirely of variations on a ground, it is music with no before and after. It is unconcerned with the process of Becoming and exists, not, like plainsong or Bach's last Chorale Prelude or Beethoven's last quartets in a metaphysical state of Being (!), but in the immediate physical moment. In its more extravagant flights it tends to encourage a state of trance; and in that sense may be said, like primitive orgiastic music, to carry one outside Time.

There was and is, however, a difference between the vigour of real primitive music and that of jazz: for the music the negro sang in slavery and in urban exile was very different from that which he sang in his native village. Jazz is the music of a dispossessed race; and it was precisely because its vitality was uprooted, dislocated, that it made so potent an appeal to sophisticated, urbanized western man. Stravinsky responded both to the vitality and to the sense of dislocation; and he valued jazz the more because it suggested to him how primitive ritualistic techniques might be reconciled with the sophisticated techniques of western Europe.

For the materials of jazz were in part European. The rhythmic drive came from primitive sources, the roots of the melody, with its flat sevenths and false relations, from pentatonic and modal folk incantation: as did the rhythm and melody of Stravinsky's own early music. But the harmony and texture of jazz came from Europe: from the white military band of the Civil War days, and from the Christian hymn. These in turn derived their material from nineteenth-century Italian opera and from the English oratorio (with German choral homophony behind that). Jazz showed Stravinsky how traditional European conventions—degraded perhaps to *cliché* —could be exploited in ways which divorced them from the idea of harmonic progression: and so liberated them from the European consciousness of Time.

Stravinsky's direct experiments in jazz style—the *Piano Rag-Music* and the *Ragtime* for 11 instruments—have worn extra-ordinarily well because they order into art the uncompromising harshness of texture, the dislocated rhythmic energy of the New Orleans blues player and band. How closely their immediacy is related to the 'realism' of one side of the Russian tradition is revealed in a work Stravinsky composed in 1918, the year following *The Wedding*. *The Soldier's Tale* is a morality based on a Russian legend which, like the text of *The Wedding*, is half pagan, half Christian. The story, telling of a soldier who sells his soul to the devil, is spoken by a narrator, while the action is mimed and danced—again in ritualistic style—to a septet of instruments which is more or less the New Orleans jazz band. The basis of the music's technique—rhythmic dislocation over seemingly interminable ostinatos—is identical with that of *The Wedding*; the difference lies in the nature of the material. Whereas the themes of *The Wedding* are mostly pentatonic, oscillating in a very narrow range around a nodal point, the fragmentary tunes in *The Soldier's Tale* are diatonic and related to *clichés* common to European art music. Thus the thematic material of the Royal March is comprised of snippets of early nineteenth-century Italian opera and corny Spanish figurations. These are employed, however, in exactly the same way as are the pentatonic phrases in *The Wedding*. They are not developed, and there is virtually no modulation; the music depends on the exciting effect of the tug-of-war between the patterns made out of the melodic *clichés* and a tonic-dominant ostinato in 7:8 which never coincides with the bar-lines.

Still more interesting is the opening Soldier's March. Here, there is an unceasing ostinato in the bass consisting of the note G followed by D and E sounded together, a ninth apart. This seems to suggest the key of G. But the fragmentary tootling tune, nearly always out of step with the ostinato, is un-ambiguously in D (with a few decorative bitonal flourishes on the cornet). This suggests that the D-E in the ostinato is really the tonic and dominant of D major elided together: and that the G of the ostinato represents the subdominant. Traditional harmony revolves between the poles of tonic, dominant and subdominant. In telescoping two or even all three of these chords Stravinsky places in space, as it were, chords that would normally progress into one another. Instead of a resolved argument, we have a tension clinched, suspended in time.

Thus although Stravinsky is now thinking in terms not merely of metrical rhythm, but of rhythm in relation to line and harmony, he still tends to avoid the notion of harmonic progression; patterns of line and harmony remain for him physical gestures existing at a point in time. Before his final dance in *The Soldier's Tale* the devil hymns his triumph in a Chorale. This looks like a parody of a Bach chorale: yet it is more disturbing than comic; and is so because it is an inversion of Bach's technique. A Bach chorale is an equation between melody and harmony. Each of the four parts is a singing line; yet its apparent independence helps to create the rich interplay of tension and relaxation which makes the music seem at once human and divine. In Stravinsky's chorale there are few chords that, considered as such, could not be found in Bach; their effect is, however, utterly remote from Bach. The major sevenths and minor ninths which in Bach resolve so poignantly occur in almost every chord in Stravinsky; since they remain unresolved their effect becomes, again, almost percussive. The recurrent cadences bear no tonal relationship to one another: they leave one suspended in a void. The only cadence that has any effect of resolution is the last; and it is significant that by this time the hymn melody has virtually disappeared, or at least has turned into a ritualistic incantation rocking through the interval of a fourth, and then by step around a nodal G.

Of course, it is dramatically appropriate that a Devil's Chorale should invert the technique of Bach. None the less, this Chorale is not a special effect in Stravinsky's music; rather does it suggest the technique he habitually uses when he turns to recreate the sophisticated materials of European tradition. In depriving Bach's style of those harmonic elements which we may refer to as humanistic, Stravinsky re-discovers a pre-Bachian ritualistic style. This is what he almost always does when he seems to be imitating the conventions of the baroque. Although the *clichés* of baroque music appealed to Stravinsky because baroque music was centred in opera, which was itself a sophisticated—as opposed to a primitive—ritual, he uses these *clichés* in a way that no baroque composer would have recognized. For instance, the last movement of the *Octet* for wind instruments opens with a bassoon tune that looks, in the cut of the phrases and the implied modulations to relative and dominant, like a typical baroque instrumental theme. But the contour of the theme is increasingly disguised by octave displacements and jazzy contractions and ellipses: while the tonal basis is neutralized by the fact that the tune is accompanied by an ostinato consisting of a rising and falling scale of C major. The clashes that occur between the tune and the ostinato have no relation to the dissonances in baroque music, which always implies an equilibrium between expressive melodic accent and tonal direction. As we shall see, however, they have some relationship to certain pre-Renaissance European techniques.

In Stravinsky's first neo-classic works the melodic patterns, the ostinatos, may have become more linear than they were in his 'primitive' works, but their purpose is the same. They establish rhythmic and modal 'cells' within which the music moves very slowly. Although all Stravinsky's music implies objectification in theatrical terms, it is a theatre to which the progression of Time is no longer relevant. This is why he favours ballet rather than opera. When, in *Oedipus Rex*, he adapted conventions from heroic opera he deliberately emphasized the ritualistic at the expense of the humanistic features, using a static chorus, a narrator, and a dead language, Latin.

"Composing for me," Stravinsky said, "is putting into an order a certain number of sounds according to certain intervallic relationships." The scale, he maintains, consists of seven diatonic notes with five intensifying chromatic notes. Not only is he always—until perhaps his most recent works—a tonal composer; he is also extremely cautious in his treatment of tonality. Whereas Schoenberg's early music is perpetual modulation, Stravinsky's modulates seldom. When, after the long sustained pentatonic ostinato in the beautiful G flat major section of *Persephone* the music at last modulates, the effect is as though a dancer moved from one almost sculpturesque posture to another. Even to the *Symphony in Three Movements* the notion of development is extraneous. Though the material of the successive sections is sharply contrasted, there is no suggestion of conflict between them. The elision of tonic, dominant and subdominant harmony which we referred to in

The Soldier's Tale may in that instance, as in Glinka's music, have been suggested by Russian peasant bands, as well as by jazz. But in his later music Stravinsky gives this peculiarity of Russian harmony a much deeper significance in relation to the European tradition. In this passage from *Persephone*, for instance, gradations of tension are immensely important; but each harmony tends to be telescoped into the next, to be heard in relation to the pattern of lines and rhythms rather than in a developing harmonic context (Ex. 65):

Ex. 65. Stravinsky: Persephone

With Stravinsky, time is what links a succession of harmonic 'postures'. He is less concerned, if at all, with the movements whereby the dancers proceed from one posture to the next. Though architecture may not be frozen music, it is not altogether inapt to describe Stravinsky's music as architecture or sculpture existing in time.

This balletistic effect is observable in Stravinsky's harmony whether he is using diatonic concords or chords, such as sevenths and ninths, which usually suggest a more romantic and personal expression. The transcendental alleluias at the end of the *Symphony of Psalms* are a supreme example of this dissociation of a chord from its normal emotional connotations. There is a similar 'dissociative' tendency in Stravinsky's linear thinking. Two or three ostinato patterns in different lines may establish independent modalities. This does not mean that the music is strictly polytonal, for, as Hindemith has proved, music cannot have two tonal roots at once. But it does mean that the parts emphasize their separateness from one another; and that Stravinsky's counterpoint has little in common with the traditional notion of polyphony as an interaction of line and harmony, involving alternations of tension and relaxation. For him, counterpoint is the link between his mosaic-like sections, his means of passing from one dance-posture to the next. The counterpoint precisely articulates the pattern of

rhythmic and harmonic gestures which is his music. The pattern
is the 'expression'.

It is obvious that while this conception of musical technique
differs radically from that current in Europe during the last
three centuries, it has much in common with medieval music.
The harmony in an organum of Pérotin, or even a motet of
Machaut, does not involve our sense of progression. Like
Stravinsky's, it is centred around the fundamental consonances
of octave, fourth, and fifth, while what happens in between the
points of concord is dictated more by linear and rhythmic than
by harmonic considerations. In medieval music, too, dance
patterns become a constructive principle independent of the
normal association of dance movement with time; the medieval
technique of isochronous rhythm—whereby a consistent
rhythmic pattern is maintained throughout a part, though
the interval relationships change—is similar to Stravinsky's
rhythmic and modal ostinatos. In the music of his middle
years, in which Stravinsky based his music largely on baroque
models, this medieval affiliation was probably unconscious.
The *Symphony of Psalms* superficially resembles a baroque
oratorio; the *Symphony in Three Movements* is related to the
principle of the concerto grosso; *Oedipus Rex* is based directly
on the seventeenth-century opera-oratorio. Yet these three
great works are all liturgical in spirit. In all of them the
technique is fundamentally closer to Machaut than it is to
Handel or Bach. Among Stravinsky's major works the only
exception to this is *The Rake's Progress*. Owing perhaps to the
nature of the theme, the technique is here less ritualistic, closer
to the 'humanistic' techniques of late eighteenth-century opera,
though it preserves the objectivity of a parable. Classical harmony is treated in a characteristically elliptical fashion; but it
is significant that the score contains relatively few ostinatos.
Even in *The Rake's Progress*, however, the ritualistic, ostinato-
dominated style is employed at the ultimate climax—the Dirge
sung over the dead Rake. This is logical enough: for his
'progress' is at an end. The dead, at least, are outside Time;
and the timeless 'Devil's Chorale' of *The Soldier's Tale* has after
all become an agent of the divine.

So in Stravinsky's apparently quixotic development we can
trace a coherent line. Primitive ritual gives way to the sophisticated ritual of the classical theatre; and that in turn leads into

the ritual of the liturgy. This becomes explicit in words like the Mass for chorus and wind instruments and the *Cantata*, in which Stravinsky consciously adapts techniques from Machaut and fourteenth-century polyphony. In his most recent works he has carried this linear conception of order to its logical conclusion, and has adopted a serial technique. He does not employ a completely chromatic series; but he uses diatonic and modal 'rows' in a way that amounts to a compromise between the isochronous patterns of medieval music, his own earlier use of ostinatos, and the serial technique of Schoenberg's pupil, Webern. In the sense that it is based not on a twelve-note, but on a five-note row, Stravinsky's *In Memoriam Dylan Thomas* is even more rigid than Webern (Ex. 66):

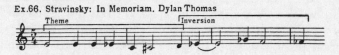

Ex.66. Stravinsky: In Memoriam. Dylan Thomas

Every note in this piece is derived from this series which, since it consists of only five notes, is more aurally intelligible and memorable than a twelve-note series, and can thus serve the function of a mode. Music could scarcely be more stringently disciplined nor, in the tenuous scoring for tenor voice with antiphonal strings and trombones, more stylized. Yet no music could be more strikingly individual in its ritual impersonality, more powerfully moving as it liberates us from self-regarding passion.

Stravinsky has composed music in a number of very different manners: think of the frightening grandeur of *Oedipus Rex*, the austere solemnity of the Mass, the tender limpidity of *Persephone*, the wit of *Dumbarton Oaks*. Yet all his mature works are linked by their ritualistic quality; and all have an intense seriousness, even when they are comic. In the music he wrote during the First World War there are many movements of parodistic, even cynical intention. Yet they are never merely parody. In *The Soldier's Tale*, as we have seen, Stravinsky employs techniques suggested by jazz in irreverent association with the liturgical chorale. Yet this work is also an order achieved out of new and startling sonorities; and this kind of scoring was one of the means whereby Stravinsky evolved the odd kind of counterpoint typical of his most 'serious' music.

He experiences afresh the sound stuff which is his material, inviting us to listen again to the noises instruments make. The composer's task is to integrate certain specified sounds. Every aspect of his art—tone-colour as much as melody, harmony, and rhythm—is a question of form, of the creation of an adequate 'objective correlative'. The new sound which is *The Soldier's Tale* is also a formal discovery: as is the scoring and spacing of the final chord of C major in the *Symphony of Psalms*.

One can thus draw no sharp division between Stravinsky's serious works and those which are apparently slighter and lighter. As with Mozart, the difference is one of degree, rather than of kind. The first movement of the Septet, for instance, comes close to the rococo aria form that Stravinsky had employed in many works, culminating in *The Rake's Progress*. In the coda, however, the music slows itself down like a pendulum coming to rest, by a process of rhythmic modification common throughout Stravinsky's work; and thus prepares us for the disembodied timelessness of the Passacaglia, Webern-like in its serial structure, and in the splitting up of the theme between various instrumental colours. Even the Gigue—in which each instrument has its own row, or rather an invented scale from which themes are derived—is the contemplative Essence of gaiety, rather than gay in itself. This piece—and still more a little piece like the *Tango* for piano—is entertainment music which is at the same time synonymous with ritual, and with Stravinsky's philosophy of art.

The same is true when Stravinsky borrows, in *Baiser de la Fée*, from such an apparently improbable composer as Tchaikowsky; for he sees in Tchaikowsky's ballet music the crystallization of emotion in gesture. Reference to Tchaikowsky also provides a precedent for Stravinsky's cosmopolitanism; for we saw that the Russian tradition had always been bifurcated between two cultures, one racial, the other rootlessly European. Stravinsky has merely made this rootlessness symbolic of the modern artist in general. He has salvaged what he can from Europe's past, and reintegrated it in ways that were possible, perhaps, only to a deracinated Russian. We can hardly deplore his cosmopolitanism, since all modern communities are cosmopolitan when they are not parochial.

Because he was Russian, Stravinsky's cosmopolitanism was

inherent in him. For Bartók, as a Hungarian, a national culture had a more positive significance; yet it was not long before his concern for a racial heritage began to merge into issues that were of much wider relevance. "Kodály and I", he said, "wanted to make a synthesis of East and West. Because of our race, and because of the geographical position of our country ... we felt this was a task we were well fitted to undertake. But it was Debussy, whose music had just begun to reach us, who showed us the path we must follow. . . . Debussy's great service to music was to reawaken among all musicians an awareness of harmony and its possibilities. In that, he was just as important as Beethoven, who revealed to us the meaning of progressive form, or as Bach, who showed us the transcendent significance of counterpoint. . . . Now, what I am always asking myself is this: is it possible to make a synthesis of these three great masters, a living synthesis that will be valid for our time?" The problem, as Bartók [1881–1945] presents it, is not specifically musical; it is hardly excessive to say that in these words he has summarized everything that makes his contribution to our battered century of central significance.

Like Schoenberg and Hindemith, he had started with a background of German romanticism. Brahms was his model, and later Strauss, with a superficial Hungarian garnishing from Liszt. His awakening to musical independence was inseparably associated with his fervent nationalism; and that was inseparable from his courage as a human being, his passion for liberty. "That man in his misery finds precious comfort in praying to an omnipotent Being is understandable. . . . But how unspeakably feeble! We should rejoice in life and be interested in everything that goes on in the world around us. . . . Were I to make the sign of the Cross I would say, 'In the name of Nature, of Art, and of Science.' " That is a positive confession of faith. It is also anti-clerical, for Bartók believed that Authority, both ecclesiastical and secular, had in his country proved to be against life and humanity. For this reason he hated all coteries, whether political or artistic, and said that he felt truly alive only among peasants. In Hungary a folk-tradition was still a living reality, as it could not be, in industrial Britain, for Holst and Vaughan Williams. Bartók did not collect folk-songs as a matter of antiquarian research. He did so to discover his own soul.

So folk-music was, for him both a spiritual and a musical

liberation. In particular, the oriental origins of Magyar song suggested to him modal types of melody and complexities of rhythm which were alien to the conventions of nineteenth-century Europe. Bartók said unambiguously that although he and Kodály [b. 1882] were interested in transcribing the songs for their own sake, in the simplest possible manner, that was only a start. In the long run, they valued the songs for their evocativeness, for their power to generate an 'imaginary folk-music'. Pentatonic and modal melodies, themes in Eastern scales with sharp fourth or sixth or oscillating in inflected scales around a nodal point, became as natural to his musical language as asymmetrical rhythms—measures of fives and sevens, and all the possible permutations of eight beats a bar. Especially interesting is Bartók's statement that folk-music was as fruitful in revealing new harmonic possibilities as it was in enriching conventional conceptions of melody and rhythm. To take a simple example, the free use of the chord of the seventh was naturally suggested by familiarity with pentatonic melodies. "We so often heard intervals of third, fifth and seventh as of equal value, that what was more natural than that we should try to make them sound of equal importance?"

But although Bartók achieved creative liberation through folk-music he was not, any more than Holst, a peasant. As a sophisticated European, he could use primitive material as a release from moribund convention; but he could not turn his back on Europe because some of it had died. This is why the music of Debussy had so crucial a significance for him. Debussy too had rebelled against academic convention. He had liberated the chord from harmonic argument; and had shown how such a static harmony could be combined with pentatonic and modal melodies that are not susceptible to classical principles of thematic growth. To Debussy, such melodies were exotic; to Kodály and Bartók they were their own racial heritage. So we find that throughout Kodály's career his music depends on an odd equilibrium between the 'communal' passion of folk-melody and the withdrawn sensibility of Debussyan harmony. Always a regional composer, he at once belonged to his community and was apart from it.

Bartók's first opera, *Bluebeard's Castle*, is a score of Debussy-like sensuous refinement, and a parable dealing with the cult of personal sensibility in opposition to a decaying world. There is a strongly Debussyan flavour about the harmony of so linear and modal a work as the Second String Quartet; and traces of Debussy's sensuousness are evident in the music of his last years. Yet Bartók's affinity with Debussy goes deeper than any incidental harmonic similarities; for we saw that the essence of Debussy's revolution lay not in its disintegrative character, but in its reconciliation of a melodic, modal tonality with the harmonic tonality of French classical music. Not being French, Bartók could not do precisely that; but he could absorb both his folk-culture and his nervous sensibility into a renewed respect for European tradition. In his early work, such as the piano *Bagatelles* of 1908, it is possible to 'explain' the dissonances as unresolved appoggiaturas, irregular passing notes, and so on; but it is not very profitable to do so. In effect, the dissonances are as static as the dissonances in Debussy's piano style and as nervously percussive as those in Stravinsky's 'primitive' works. As in Debussy and Stravinsky, the tonal order of the pieces is non-harmonic, consisting in the way in which the melodic lines oscillate around a nodal point. In his later work Bartók never entirely relinquished this folk-like, melodic criterion of tonality (cf. the slow movements of the Fourth and Fifth Quartets and of the Music for Strings, Celesta, and Percussion). But as he matured, and his powerful melodies became more complex, chromaticized, and sustained, he increasingly sought to reconcile this melodic tonality with the harmonic tonality of classical music. In so doing he established contact not only with Debussy, but also with Hindemith and Berg.

From this point of view, a key-work in his career is the Second Violin Sonata. In many passages of this work folk-like rhapsody in the violin line is organized melodically around nodal points, which the piano underlines with chords conceived statically and vertically. In other passages, however, Bartók returns to the classical conception of dissonance as harmonic *movement*, whereby the discordant passing note keeps the melodic parts flowing and adds emotional intensity. Although the resolution of the dissonance is often implicit rather than explicit, one is aware of a basic diatonic pattern; and dissonance, whether appearing vertically in the chord structures or in passing notes in the melody itself, serves to give direction—in the traditional classical manner—to this harmonic base.

This technique has interesting possibilities. For instance, an

unresolved passing dissonance on D sharp may accompany a
C major triad. The result is a major-minor ambiguity similar
to that explored in the later work of Busoni. Further, the
unresolved passing note suggests the unresolved passing chord,
and that in turn suggests the unresolved neighbouring tonality.
Two different tonalities may be suggested by the presence of
two fundamental fifths, yet though the effect is polytonal, the
relationship to a root is maintained; for the two lower notes are
unresolved appoggiaturas which are taken as identical with the
notes to which they should resolve. Thus Bartók can introduce
long passages in (say) G during which the tonality of G flat is
never relinquished, as in the piece from *Microcosmos*, *The Diary
of a Fly* (Ex. 67):

Ex. 67. Bartók: From the Diary of a Fly

In the quartets there are several passages in which the four
instruments enter within the space of a few bars, a semitone
apart. Again, he does not regard the parts as having separate
tonal roots. Bartók's music is always fundamentally tonal, even
when his ambiguous harmonic processes are complicated by his
partiality for modally inflected, non-diatonic scales.

Bartók seems to have associated his rediscovery of classical
principles of structure with the influence of Beethoven, likewise
a revolutionary composer who modified established precedents
under pressure of personal feeling. The core of Bartók's work is
in his six string quartets. Superficially speaking, the grounds
of comparison between Bartók's quartets and the late quartets
of Beethoven may seem far to seek—apart from the obvious
resemblance between the opening of Bartók's First and the
opening of Beethoven's C sharp minor. Yet there is a profound
sense in which the comparison is justified, for both composers
are seeking to reconcile the dynamism of sonata conflict with
the apparently contradictory, monistic principles of counterpoint. In so doing, both of them modify traditional notions of
tonal organization.

Consider, for instance, Bartók's Fifth Quartet, composed in

1934. The first movement is in dynamic sonata form. The first
subject is split into two groups: a reiterated percussive figure
in or around B flat, and a phrase syncopated across the bar-line,
involving a trill and a glissando suggestive of Magyar music.
The second subject, more flowing, sinuous and chromatic, also
has a Magyar flavour (Ex. 68):

Ex.68. Bartók   Quartet No.5

The development begins in—or rather on—E, a tritone apart
from the main key. As in Beethoven's quartets, the material is
itself transformed as it is developed in tonal conflict. In the
recapitulation all the material reappears, though not in the
same order, and in linear inversion and sometimes reversion.
Again there is a compromise between the tonal organization
of the Beethovenian sonata and the linear organization of
Bachian counterpoint. All the themes are gathered together and
telescoped in a coda in close stretto which ends unambiguously
on, if not in, B flat.

The second movement, adagio molto, opens with frail wisps
of sound which coalesce in a modally harmonized chorale,
reminiscent in mood of the Lydian adagio in Beethoven's opus
132. Over the chorale the first violin sings fragmentary lyrical
phrases which, since they contain unresolved appoggiaturas,
seem to be off key. These lyrical phrases are evocatively extended in a middle section. An elliptical recapitulation of the
chorale fades into the whispered trills and glissandi of the
opening. Both Beethoven and Bartók associate trills with the
relinquishment of Time's shackles; though Bartók's paradise, if
that is what it is, is certainly the more tenuous and tentative.
One could hardly say that his peace brings a Beethovenian joy.

The third movement is a scherzo and trio on classical lines.
It is in Bulgarian folk-rhythms, 4 plus 2 plus 3 quavers a bar in

the scherzo, 3 plus 2 plus 2 plus 3 quavers a bar in the trio.
The first theme, built on rising and falling thirds, has an almost
Debussyan pizzicato accompaniment; the second is more jaunty
and folk-like in character, with an obtrusive Lydian fourth.
The trio creates a magically sensuous sound while following
classical convention in being based on the bagpipe drone. Its
rusticity is disembodied, however, like the comparable musette
trio in the scherzo of Beethoven's opus 131. In the repeat of
the scherzo both themes are treated in their original form and
in inversion.

Then occurs the work's only departure from classical precedent: a second slow movement which balances, and is
thematically related to, the adagio second movement. In this
nocturnal music mysterious glissandi, pizzicati and swirling
chromatics accompany a canonic dialogue between violin and
'cello. In the coda the themes disintegrate on viola and 'cello,
while the two violins play a rarefied version of the adagio's
chorale.

The last movement is a rondo which, like Beethoven's
rondos, makes some compromise with sonata style and has also
a good deal of contrapuntal organization. The first theme is
stated twice, the second time in inversion and canon. Another
theme, marked leggierissimo, fulfils some of the functions of a
second subject. All the material is developed in close counterpoint, and the climax comes when a fugato passage reveals the
relationship between the first movement themes and those of
the last movement. After the climax there is a strange passage
in which the first theme appears in augmentation, in unam-
biguous A major. This moment of queerly comic relaxation is
swept away by the contrapuntal frenzy of the coda, which
ultimately lands us on the unison B flat of the opening of the
work.

This work has been discussed in some detail because it
includes every aspect of Bartók's creative relationship to
tradition. Of the four great, 'central' twentieth-century composers we have considered, he is the only one whose idiom
derives its force from the sonata principle: which may be why
he has gone further than the others towards establishing some
relationship to a public. Yet even with him, as we have seen,
counterpoint modifies his conception of the sonata; and the
highest point his music reached—the first movement of the

Music for Strings, Celesta, and Percussion—is a 'monistic' expression of the Bachian contrapuntal principle. The theme itself, narrow in compass, winding around a nodal point, seems to adhere to the melodic tonality of folk-song; but the structure of the piece as a whole is an expansion of the basic harmonic principle of classical music, for the fugal entries take place at successive fifths, beginning on A, in alternate ascending and descending cycles. When the two cycles meet on E flat—the tonality which stands at the ultimate distance from the initial A—there is a tremendous tritonal climax; the celesta enters for the first time (a vision of the bliss to be attained?); the theme is inverted and the cycle of fifths continues until it once more reaches A. There is a short coda, in which the theme and its inversion are stated simultaneously, ending on the unison A.

This is perhaps a fugal movement which, like that in Beethoven's 'Hammerklavier' Sonata, grindingly seeks the unity of paradise, rather than one in which paradise is attained. None the less, this climacteric point of Bartók's music is certainly monistic to the core; and we may recall that his melodic and rhythmic conception is in some ways as much Eastern as European. When we look back at the other central figures we have discussed, we remember that Hindemith too has tried to recreate the Bachian notion of fugal unity, and to establish a tonal order 'cosmically' related to the medieval view of music as science and ritual. Stravinsky's conception of music is still more specifically ritualistic. Whether in his primitive or his neo-baroque phase or in the serial works of recent years, his music implies a kind of unity as much medieval as modern, as much Eastern as European. And Schoenberg's twelve-note method is a technique of perpetual variation, an entirely monistic conception of form in which every note of a composition is a permutation of a single entity.

9

EUROPE TODAY

W<small>E</small> have seen that Debussy, Schoenberg, Stravinsky, Hindemith, and Bartók—the five central figures in twentieth-century music—have manifested, over the past fifty years, a partial but spontaneous turning-away from the humanism and time-obsession that are our European birthright. Nor is this tendency confined to these major figures, for we can observe something comparable in distinguished, but marginal, composers of the same generation, such as Karol Szymanowsky [1883–1937] and Ernest Bloch [1880–1959]. The Pole Szymanowsky began as one of the 'last romantics', creating in his opera, *King Roger*, a third act which is a single Tristanesque climax lasting some forty minutes—superbly luscious in its chromatic, polyphonic-harmonic texture and in its opulent orchestration. The nostalgic lyricism of this opera—significantly dealing with a conflict between Christianity and paganism—strikingly complements that of Delius's *A Village Romeo and Juliet*, just as the soaring cantilena of Szymanowsky's First Violin Concerto parallels that of Delius's concerto. The restless, fluctuating movement of the harmony is similar in both composers, producing an impression of inordinately slow tempo, even when the figuration is rapid. Both use the orchestra in the same way, though Szymanowsky is texturally much more sophisticated. Yet this elegiac composer of a world's twilight goes a stage further than Delius: the movement becomes so slow that it almost stops; and as this happens a new, linear element comes into Szymanowsky's music, suggested by the Eastern affiliations of Polish folk music and liturgical chant. The sensuousness is still present in his impressive *Stabat Mater*; but the music is now a ritualistic, rather than auto-erotic, experience. Ripely sonorous, harmonically conceived passages exist alongside sections that depend mainly on Asiatic-tending melodic arabesques in a sharply dissonant linear texture, with little harmonic movement.

This tendency is still more evident in the music of Ernest Bloch, the first Jewish composer whose music springs from his consciousness of alienated race. He is perhaps the most passionately ego-centred of all twentieth-century composers, and his rich scoring and thick texture have obvious affinities with Wagner and even Strauss. Yet the insidious power of a piece like his *Schelomo* for solo 'cello and orchestra depends on a dichotomy between the hysterical fervour of the orchestral climaxes and the improvisatory conception of the solo part: which assimilates into itself the age-old, basically pentatonic phrases of Jewish cantilation, and evolves by the Asiatic technique of melismatic decoration and 'division'; while the scoring often emulates the actual sounds of the Hebraic folk-band. Even when Bloch writes music closer to Western tradition, as in the first movement of his First String Quartet, the violent tonal and metrical tensions are combined with declamatory, prayer-like themes that also lend themselves to oriental melodic extension; and the anguish is not resolved in an orthodox recapitulation. Resolution—in this quartet as in the still finer Piano Quintet—ultimately comes in extended cantabile melody which is also an elegiac lament. The relationship of this singing lyricism to the liturgical manner—half Hebraic, half Renaissance European—of Bloch's *Sacred Service* indicates how Bloch's elegy—unlike Delius's—implies a tragic resignation to suffering. This quality, too, may affect us as Eastern rather than European.

While we cannot yet know what this general, cumulative trend away from the West means, it is at least feasible that we are living at the end of a cycle that began with the Renaissance: and that the values inherent in our music may come to reflect, in a vast international society, a changed conception of man's nature and destiny. Certainly there is evidence to support this in the evolution of serial music since Schoenberg: for while Schoenberg's music usually maintains a link with post-Renaissance ideas of progression, a serial technique need not necessarily do so, and some later developments of twelve-note music have attempted a far more radical departure from harmonic implications. The early music of Anton Webern [1883–1945], for instance, is sensory experience that titillates the nerves in the same way as does Debussy's music. In the tiny *Bagatelles* or the early pieces for string quartet the senses exist 'absolutely', apart from the Will: until they are so winnowed away that they dissolve into spirit. By the time this happens Webern's music has become completely serial in the organization of its pitch-relationships; and while it is possible that the dominance of a certain interval, or a relationship between a group of intervals, may sometimes serve as a nodal point which takes the place of tonality, there can be no doubt that Webern habitually selected rows which were as remote as possible from tonal implications. He especially favoured rows in which the parts were inter-related mathematically—for instance, in which the second half is a mirror reflexion of the first; often the two segments are linked by the neutral interval of the tritone. The texture is tenuous in the extreme, and the thematic line is often subdivided between a number of parts, each note having a different tone-colour.

Webern's instinct for sonority is of uncanny precision and the aural effect of his serial music is of the most exquisite sensuous beauty. Yet the effect is different from that of his early free atonal pieces, or from that of Debussy's impressionism, or from that of Schoenberg's early 'seismographic' works; and the differ-ence lies in the fact that the 'moments of sensation' are no longer fragmentary. Each single note in the wonderful slow movement of the *Concerto for Nine Instruments* seems part of a preordained order, a revelation of cosmic mathematical law, as are the notes of a medieval 'isochronous' motet.* It is not coincidental that Webern should have been an expert scholar in the field of mediaeval music. Though his style evolved out of Viennese chromaticism, with no conscious trace of mediaeval or oriental influence, there is a quality both mediaeval and oriental in the form of the *Piano Variations,* opus 27: for the piece describes the ultimate unity, the circle, in that the theme is accompanied by itself, backwards and inverted. The serpent eats its own tail. It is not surprising that in this work time seems to stop; and that the piano's bell-like noises should suggest, however remotely, the gongs of the Balinese gamelang. Nor, perhaps, is it entirely fanciful to sense a relationship between Webern's treatment of the human voice—far more 'unvocal' than Schoenberg's—and the deliberately unnatural vocal tech-niques used by mediaeval and oriental singers. The voice is

* Isochronous Motet: one in which the parts are organized in metrical series which remain constant though the pitch relationships do not. The metrical series sometimes have doctrinal significance (for instance, references to the Trinity). Cf. rhythmic pattern in mediaeval motets, Part I, pp. 57, 103, etc.

deliberately dehumanized because it must become supernatural law.

Almost all the poems Webern chose to set are, significantly, mystical and esoteric; yet although his music is much more remote than Schoenberg's from traditional European procedures it is still, in its precision, quintessentially expressive. We can see from the two beautiful cantatas how, in his maturest work, Webern as vocal composer still expressively 'interprets' his texts; and even so apparently abstract a work as the *Piano Variations* depends for its effect on the sensitive nuance of its melodic contours, as we know from the testimony of Peter Stadlen, who studied the work with Webern before giving the first performance. Thus we may suspect that while Webern would have appreciated the manner in which Stravinsky has used certain aspects of his technique as a ritualistic discipline (the latest of his many masks), he would be chary of acknowledging those who claim that he has inaugurated a new order in European music, above and beyond the concepts of 'expression' and 'communication'. Across the Austrian border, in Germany, Karlheinz Stockhausen [b. 1928], taking Webern as his point of departure, has developed a music that is serial not only in pitch relationships, but also in rhythmic pattern and dynamics. Sometimes it is so complicated that it can be performed only by electronic means. Such a revelation of mathematical law dispenses with the human intermediary of the performer and possibly with the audience as well. The composer is alone in his laboratory; recent experiments by Stockhausen in the direction of 'disciplined improvisation' would perhaps suggest that he is aware that the laboratory may be a new kind of plastic Ivory Tower.

But it is not only in the work of Webern and his disciples that a radical change of approach—and of philosophical implication—can be observed. Webern rarefies the senses into an exquisitely tense, hyper-subtle heaven-beyond-becoming: a hermetic paradise. Carl Orff [b. 1895], in Germany, seeks a comparable end by an opposite route: by reducing music to a lowest common denominator, divesting it of virtually all harmony and expressive melody, leaving only rhythm and the contrast of sonorities. During the years of the Second World War he has done again what Stravinsky did, in the *Rite of Spring* and *The Wedding*, during the years of the First World War: he has simultaneously expressed the violence and horror of breakdown and suggested that, if this is what our sophisticated consciousness has made of the world, it is time we returned to our primitive, pre-conscious roots. The difference is that whereas Stravinsky went on to relate the primitive, non-European elements explored in these works to a ritual, both secular and religious, relevant to Europe's past and present, Orff has, in later works, retreated still further from Europe. The oriental elements in his *Aphrodite*, for instance, extend to the investigation of elaborate melismatic melody which is far more interesting than his earlier obsession with incantatory rhythm. Orff is a minor, even a trivial, composer compared with Stravinsky; yet the success enjoyed by his music is symptomatic.* People were looking, unconsciously, for an escape from the dominance of Time and the Self. Orff offers such an escape: at a lower level than Webern or Stravinsky, but at a higher level than the jazz fanatic who expects his music to 'send' him beyond self-consciousness. Orff believes that the future, even our survival, depends on the existence of a popular religious art meaningful not to a few, but to the many. Whether the primitive and oriental features in his music can really fulfil the emotional needs of urban and industrial man is dubious indeed. But at least he is justified in thinking that an orgiastic act is religious in the sense that it puts us into direct communion with elemental forces: and to that degree with eternity.

A comparable concern with orgiastic experience and with Oriental ritual occurs in the music of a French composer of the same generation, Olivier Messiaen [b. 1908]. His orgiastic mysticism is, however, esoteric rather than popular: except in the sense that, being a zealous Roman Catholic, he presumably speaks, on behalf of his faith, to all who will listen. Whereas Webern refines away the senses, Messiaen expatiates on them, inducing a kind of auto-erotic ecstasy comparable with that found in some Catholic baroque art. The musical affinities of his early work are obviously with the sensory impressionism of Debussy: but still more, perhaps, with the obsessively 'introverted' harmony of Scryabin. Yet he carries the isolation of these

* It is relevant to note that another post-Nazi, post-war German composer, Boris Blacher [b. 1903] has created a music almost entirely reliant on rhythmic experiment. His art, however, being without Orff's deliberate primitivism, produces a curiously ascetic excitement: as though the mind were stimulating, perhaps even simulating, a vitality which the blood and heart do not possess. Perhaps it is not surprising that his music has been widely influential.

sensual moments from the idea of progression to a more extreme point than either Debussy or Scryabin. The more highly charged are the artist's sensations the more completely must they be released from the grip of the Will: so the movement of higher chromatic discords in Messiaen's earlier works is so slow as to be almost stationary, while the relationship between the chords is as disturbingly without harmonic direction as the comparable passages in the 'Rose-Croix' works of Erik Satie, which Messiaen much admires (Ex. 69). The later enormous piano

Ex. 69

Très modéré

Satie : Messe des Pauvres

work, *Vingt Régards sur l'Enfant Jésus* is literally a series of contemplative 'looks' in the sense that the movements are without movement. Each piece tends to be built on an alternation of two or three chords, an ostinato, a pedal note, a reiterated figuration. The burden of personality dissolves into timeless contemplation. The European time-sense is no longer relevant to music which evades the concept of beginning, middle, and end: which is why Messiaen's works tend to last, chronometrically speaking, so long, if not for ever. There is no reason why they should stop.

Even in Messiaen's early works the sumptuously sensuous harmony, being non-developing, tends to proliferate into melodic arabesques related not only to mediaeval cantilation, but also to the melismatic styles of Eastern music. In his later work oriental features have become both conscious and elaborate. The sensory harmonies tend to be increasingly percussive in effect, like gongs, and virtually without harmonic meaning in the Western sense. Complementarily, the organization of such works as the *Ile de Feu* becomes almost entirely linear and rhythmic: except that Messiaen's 'series' are not completely chromatic, but are closely related to the linear ragas and rhythmic talas* of Indian music. His chord complexes are also derived from raga formations, whether traditional or (like Skryabin's) invented; in either case the 'series' are given religious, or at any rate magical, as well as technical significance. In recent years Messiaen has added to his study of oriental melodic and rhythmic techniques an equally exhaustive enquiry into the cries of birds; and has stated that the rest of his composing life will be devoted to an immense series of works wherein his humanity will be reborn through the language of birds. Fascinating though some of the piano-sounds may be, we may think that this is carrying forgetfulness of the human will a bit far; there is something in the messianic self-dedication of this most appropriately named composer that seems, in the strict sense, eccentric from—even opposed to—the needs of most twentieth-century men and women.

Yet Messiaen has created a language: which very few composers succeed in doing; and that language has made a considerable impact upon twentieth-century music. There are even affinities between it and the rival French school of Pierre Boulez [b. 1925], for Boulez has combined a completely serial, post-Webern technique with serial processes derived directly from Eastern ragas and talas. The sonorities of a work like *Le Marteau sans Maitre*, with their high, ethereal resonance, are new, yet closer to Debussy and Messiaen than to Schoenberg or even Webern. They also recall the ritualistic music of Bali: with the

* RAGA: a linear pattern or series, usually with religious or magical as well as musical significance, used as the basis for improvisation in classical Indian music. TALA: a rhythmic pattern or series, similarly employed, in conjunction with the raga.

difference that the text the music sets (with a god-like exaggeration of human vocal resource!) is not a ritual celebration of the divine or the earthly, but a surrealistic poem that is, strictly speaking, nonsense. This is not a frivolous remark; for in a post-Freudian world we are, in exploring the depths below consciousness, seeking imaginative knowledge of reality. *Le Marteau* is concerned with an awareness of God, if not with an apprehension of him.

Webern and Stockhausen, Orff, Messiaen, and Boulez are, in their rejection of the West, saying something which Europe has at least partially to accept, if we are to live again. Their rejection may, however, easily become an evasion of our human responsibilities; certainly we feel more comfortable with those composers of Italy, Russia, and Britain who, while reacting against the exaggerated self-consciousness of Western civilisation, are not afraid to accept it in order to re-create it. It is interesting that in Italy—birthplace of Europe's Renaissance—some composers of both Messiaen's and of Boulez's generation have not carried the rejection of the West to anything like so extreme a point. Luigi Dallapiccola [b. 1904] has, particularly in his later works, made considerable use of serial techniques. Yet his music remains rooted in Renaissance polyphony and the unity of classical baroque texture. The forbears of his theatrical projection, his vocal lyricism, are the two great Green Men of Italian music, Monteverdi and Verdi.

While Dallapiccola is usually concerned, in his large-scale works, with religious issues, he starts not from a desire to obliterate the self in a mystical act, but from the necessity for compassion. His opera, *Il Prigioniero*, the choral *Canti di Prigionia*, stem from an awareness of the violence, suffering, and oppression which man has inflicted on man during the first half of this century. They are concerned with God because man seems impotent alone; but (like Schoenberg's music) they are in approach essentially humanistic, and it is not an accident that the central achievement of Dallapiccola's career should be a dramatization of the story of Job. This work reveals most impressively the way in which Dallapiccola's music belongs simultaneously to Italy's past, present, and future. In conception it is a *Sacra rappresentazione* in the seventeenth-century manner of Carissimi. The seventeenth-century Historicus sang in comparatively flat, emotionally uninvolved recitative. Dallapiccola's Storico speaks, but in rhythmically measured notation, his phrases being echoed by a speaking chorus, also rhythmically notated: as though a crowd of listeners (including you and me) were involving themselves in the story. This gives an extraordinary immediacy—a sense of present reality—to the setting.

The Storico recounts, impersonally. Job sings, lyrically and passionately, from within his being. Periodically the tension between the objective narration and Job's subjective passion crystallizes into operatic action; the characters in the story come alive and sing with Verdian incandescence. Various serial and contrapuntal devices are used, but in the interests of dramatic expression: for instance, the Comforters sing a double and then a triple canon, in which the processional rhythm and the contrapuntal unity suggest a girding of the loins. The climax comes in Job's desperate appeal to God, when human fortitude seems to be insufficient. The voice that replies 'out of the whirlwind' is represented by a *singing* chorus which, *largamente ma con violenza*, justifies the apparently arbitrary ways of God to man, while a brass choir blazes the Te Deum. The tortured and distraight polyphony grows gradually more sustained; but rises to a *furioso* climax as the voice from the whirlwind sings not only of man's dependence on God, but of God's dependence on man—a conclusion proudly in tune with the spirit of the Italian Renaissance and with what one takes to be Dallapiccola's attitude now. The music then fades into silence, eternity being symbolized by two flutes, one of which plays the other's part backwards. The silence seems the deeper because Dallapiccola has dared to set the profoundest imaginative statement about the nature of suffering except for Shakespeare's *King Lear*.

In Dallapiccola's music, as in Schoenberg's, the purely chromatic and serial elements seem not to deny but to extend the boundaries of the traditional elements; the exacerbated tension is never merely destructive. It is worth remarking, too, that the music of Luigi Nono [b. 1926], which is 'post-Webern' in being completely serial and extremely attenuated in sonority, also shows a quality of compassionate humanity. His works are concerned with an atom-threatened world; but the remote sighs and sobs of the dislocated choral and orchestral texture of his *Il Canto Sospeso* are intensely moving, not merely in their glimpse of a quiet beyond the harried present, but also in their response to the human suffering that must be borne in a broken, battered world.

In Dallapiccola and Nono there is, then, an embryonic religious sense combined with a social conscience.* The composers of Soviet Russia do not, of course, cultivate a religious sense, let alone the esoteric mysticism of a Webern or a Messiaen. None the less, their social conscience tends to direct attention away from a preoccupation with the self; and the official view that Soviet composers ought to study and make use of the folk traditions of the area they live in might be expected to encourage melodic and rhythmic techniques opposed to the traditions of western Europe, as it did in the case of Bartók and Szymanowsky. The paradox in the position of the Soviet composer lies, however, in the fact that he is building a new world in the interests not of a moribund peasantry, but of the proletariat: whose musical taste is still—as we saw when discussing Tchaikowsky and Rachmaninov—centred around composers of highly subjective neurosis, expressed through basically Western techniques! A Tchaikowsky 'cleaned up', rendered buoyantly extravert, seems a contradiction in terms. Yet the contradiction may have been a saving grace to Soviet composers: for it has meant that they have been able to create out of a tension between a sincere desire to affirm and an elegiac consciousness of personal frustration such as all human creatures are prone to in this state-before-Paradise (whether on earth or in Heaven). The numerous symphonies of Myaskovsky [1881–1951] are a fine example of this simultaneously optimistic and elegiac approach. The sustained melodies, the spacious proportions, the powerful rhythms lend dignity to the Tchaikowsky-like melancholy: while the melancholy reminds us of the fallible human heart.

Folk-music has no more influence on Myaskovsky's art than on Tchaikowsky's, and considerably less than it has on the work of the Big Five. He can reinvigorate nineteenth-century styles because he is, if not a great, a real composer, with something to say; and while it is true that, in Soviet Russia, much bad music has been poured into 'outdated' nineteenth-century moulds, it is equally true that a great deal of bad music has

* We should mention in this context a senior Catalan composer, Roberto Gerhard [b. 1896], who left his native country at the time of the Spanish Civil War and settled in England. His early works stemmed from impressionism and Spanish national tradition. The rhythmic energy and harmonic sensuousness of his music have survived since he has begun to explore complete serialization; and his fusion of a passionate humanism with an 'impersonal' mysticism makes his position in the European tradition more central and perhaps more important than his almost complete isolation, in his adopted country, would lead one to expect.

been created, in the West, by wilful attempts to avoid conformity. There will always be more bad music than good. Any composer starts from conditions as he knows them; what he makes of them depends on his integrity and vitality. This we can see in the work of the first two Soviet composers who have made —unlike Myaskovsky—an impact on the world outside Russia.

The fundaments of Prokofiev's art, as of Myaskovsky's, were closely related to Tchaikowsky, and still more to Rachmaninov: consider the big tune at the end of his Third Piano Concerto. In his Parisian youth, however, Sergey Prokofiev [1891–1953] learned, as an exile, to disguise the passionate heart beneath a veneer of sophistication. After the First World War it was natural enough that Paris should have fostered a deliberate cult of irresponsibility. Jean Cocteau, as mentor of the new artists, encouraged hatred of pretentiousness, love of everything supposedly simple and free of complication. Hence the cult of childhood, of Negro art, of music-hall and circus, of low life generally. Francis Poulenc [b. 1899] is the only composer of the group known as Les Six who has remained faithful to the ideals charmingly expressed in the works of his teens,* such as the *Bestiare* songs and the *Mouvements Perpétuels* for piano. These pieces are all of tiny dimensions, with aggressively diatonic themes, like nursery tunes or café songs, in regular rhythms. These banalities, however, are consciously pepped up by

---

* Of the other members of the group, two stopped composing and one devoted almost all his attention to film music. Of the remaining two members, Arthur Honegger [b. 1892] became a dramatic composer, dealing with large—often religious—themes on a large scale, in a re-created baroque style that is noble and ceremonial, though often sharply dissonant. Both his gravity and his 'public manner' are remote from the sophisticated banality of Les Six, but have much in common with the work of other Swiss composers such as Othmar Schoeck [1886–1957], Frank Martin [b. 1890], and Willy Burkhard [b. 1900]. It is interesting that the Swiss composers, whether their roots are German or French, seem to preserve a lucid neutrality. Comparatively uninvolved in the humanist crisis supremely represented by Wagner, they can use apparently archaic—medieval, Renaissance, and baroque—conventions with spontaneity and power. Their music is always civilized: and for that very reason, perhaps, seems rather remote from the issues that concern us most deeply.

The other member of Les Six, Darius Milhaud [b. 1892], has nothing in common with Swiss austerity. He is a composer whose uninhibited prodigality springs from his Jewish passion, his Latin (Provencal) vitality, and his prolonged sojourn in South America. From so many violent and contradictory impulses he has not achieved a coherent idiom; but in the *Concertino de Printemps* for violin and chamber orchestra, he created the most tinglingly vivacious of all pieces in the French pastoral vein, while *La Création du Monde*, though inferior to the real thing, is one of the few convincing, sophisticated evocations of Negro jazz. The value of his large-scale works—such as the immense operas on Latin-American subjects—is problematical.

sophistication: by the 'wrong' note or altered harmony; by the simultaneous (polytonal) sounding of several simple tonalities; by cheekily raucous scoring (with a prevalence of brass and woodwind). The feeling in this music is quite different from that in the music of the two composers—Chabrier and Satie—whom Les Six acknowledged as their masters. For Chabrier was a *positive* comic genius whose ironic wit was inseparable from his animal high spirits; while Satie did not play at being childish, but recovered the innocence of the child through the lucidity of his technique. In the music of Chabrier and Satie there is neither sentimentality nor nostalgia. Poulenc, on the other hand, is all sentimentality and nostalgia—for the presumed irresponsibility of childhood, for low life, for the pretty elegancies of an eighteenth-century rococo world quite distinct from Ravel's profound re-creation of the classical fairy tales. These 'regressive' qualities are Poulenc's genuine attributes, which have grown stronger with the years, as we can see from his Gounodesque church music, his Massenet-like opera, *Les Carmélites*, and his numerous, and most touching, later songs which reconcile Massenet with the malaise of the café-concert. (*Montparnasse* is perhaps the quintessential Poulenc song.)

When Prokofiev settled in Paris in the 'twenties he welcomed the debunking wit which he found in the music of Les Six, especially Poulenc; and the affecting, as well as amusing, quality of the music he wrote in this vein comes from the fact that he too loves what he laughs at. There was, moreover, a particular reason why he, as a Russian exile, should respond to the nostalgia incipient even in Poulenc's early music; in small works like the *Grandmother's Tales* for piano he gives a Russian reinterpretation of Poulenc's use of the nursery ditty. Prokofiev's themes too are short, with hypnotic repetitions; but, like so many of the modal song themes of Tchaikowsky, they invoke no urban environment, but the eternal-seeming melancholy of the Russian peasant. At the same time the haunting themes are now distanced by the disturbing relationships of the simple diatonic harmonies and the precise rhythmic patterns that accompany them. In acquiring a tender irony, their melancholy ceases to oppress.

This suggests why Prokofiev, on returning to the Soviet Union, was able to use his Parisian experience to such good effect. The sophisticated high-jinks become an element of mordant satire that can safeguard his romantic passion from hysteria and that can, at times, grow into a positive ebullience—the pride in a new world that finds expression in the finales of his symphonies and in the moto-perpetuo-like movements in his piano sonatas. (Perhaps one could not believe in these pieces if they were not, as well as vigorous, also intelligent.) Beneath the extravert gaiety, however, the tender nostalgia of Prokofiev's Russian fairy tale is always present, if never obtrusive. This is why his most moving and characteristic music tends to be lyrical. In both the early and the late violin concertos, for instance, his gaiety and nostalgia are held in equilibrium; the merriment makes the sadness supportable, and the sadness make the merriment credible. Even in his emotionally more ambitious works, when he writes under the pressure of tense, often violent, experience, he is most convincing when the lyrical basis of his art is strongest. It is not fortuitous that perhaps the finest of all his works should be a sonata for violin and piano—the mature work in F minor: wherein the interpenetration of the linear and the percussive instrument creates a piano texture that has both metallic sharpness and sonorous depth, a violin line that is at once warm and pungent.

Shostakovitch [b. 1906] made his mark at a remarkably early age with a symphony that, like Prokofiev's early music, reconciled a heartfelt Tchaikowskyan sweetness with a self-protective wit, Parisian in origin, yet growing, in the last movement, into a kind of communal frenzy. The tenderness, the cheek, the excitement, all grow to maturity in the sequence of his symphonies; but in his case the relationship to Tchaikowsky and to Parisian sophistication is complemented by another, and deeper, affinity. If Mahler seems an unexpected musician to influence a Soviet composer, we must remember that Mahler's conception of the symphony as an all-inclusive world, embracing every aspect of life, is in an obvious sense democratic. Mahler may have been an elegiac composer singing the swan-song of a once-aristocratic world; but any truly creative composer of a new world has to admit into his self-confident awareness of present and future an awareness also of the old world's death, and of the human disappointments and hopes that followed in its wake.

It is certainly not an accident that the most talented composer the Soviet Union has yet produced—perhaps her only

composer of indubitable genius—should betray this affinity with
a composer who, we saw, already suggested a turning away
from Western traditions. And although Shostakovitch's musical
materials remain Western, even nineteenth-century, the manner
in which he uses them marks a radical departure from the
eighteenth- and nineteenth-century notion of a symphony.
Whereas for Beethoven a symphony is growth through conflict,
Shostakovitch opposes the states of contemplation and of action.
So although Shostakovitch described his Fifth Symphony, in
Beethovenian terms, as 'the making of a man', he also said that the
symphony was 'entirely lyrical'; the drama which it incarnates
is not, like that in Beethoven's symphonies, subjective, but
epic. Thus the work opens with an enormous melodic period
that suggests, through leaping sixths in dotted rhythm, a ques-
tioning aspiration (Ex. 70). But this theme does not generate

Ex. 70

a 'dualistic' tonal conflict; it evolves lyrically, growing cumulatively stronger, until it is transformed into a spacious cantabile
theme, with a pulsing accompaniment, wherein the individual
life seems to be fulfilled. Although these long, winding melodies
tend to return to a nodal point, they have no relation to Russian
folk-music and—like the cantabile themes of Tchaikowsky and
Mahler—eclectically assimilate European elements from Italy,
Austria, and France. Yet the brooding, timeless quality of this
music is profoundly Russian. Its melancholy is at once introverted and impersonal. Self-contemplation leads, as in Mahler,
to self-forgetfulness and liberation; in this case, because a subjective sorrow is absorbed into the vastness of the Steppes, the
epic sorrow of a people.

Only at this point, after this immense lyrical paragraph, are
the contradictions inherent in experience admitted. The contemplative theme is transformed, on low brass, into a sinister
lament which grows into a grisly march: the lyrical fulfilment
is denied, metamorphosed into horror, rather as it is in the first
movement of Mahler's Ninth. So when the contemplative theme
returns, it does so in a more frenzied version; and its ultimate
disintegration into sweetly dreamy whimpers on flute, violin,
celesta and muted trumpet leaves us feeling that the vast
emptiness of the Steppes can be no assuagement for our loneliness. So the movement ends with a wistful, unresolved
restatement of the apparently affirmative opening paragraph;
and the scherzo that follows, although funny, is also wry. Self-
forgetfulness here becomes self-mockery; the gaiety is aloof,
deliberately uninvolved, as though the composer were saying
that if man's aspiration is as unrewarding as the first movement suggests, there is no answer but a shrug of the shoulders.
The continual modulations, the occasional acid harmony, the
sharp orchestration are disturbing as well as witty.

The largo returns to the brooding contemplation of the first
movement, but the questing element inherent in the leaping
sixths has gone. The rhythm is level, the contours of the melody
smooth; again the eternal-seeming spaciousness is emphasized
by the Mahlerian, chamber-music-like nature of the scoring,
the hollowness of the texture. This time there is no contradiction. The sustained lyricism gradually assimilates the introspective passion of the first movement: so that the personal contemplation can lead into a public resolution. The last movement
is all kinetic energy, sometimes fierce, sometimes hilariously
comic in its transformations of popular material. Shostakovitch's
epic resolutions plumb less deep than Beethoven's, for their
public fulfilment is juxtaposed to, not the result of, the private
struggle. None the less, the personal and social aspects of Shostakovitch's music are inseparable: for although the release of
power and gaiety in the external world is not the consequence
of inner growth, it could not occur but for the contemplation,
wherein a personal loneliness or frustration is mastered in becoming epical. It is significant that the overwhelmingly triumphant coda to the finale of this symphony is preceded by a
remote reminiscence of the contemplative lyrical theme of the
first movement.

Perhaps we may say that the resolution in Shostakovitch's symphonies is not so much the release of inner tensions as an act of faith. This accords with his prevailingly lyrical approach to the symphony; and although he is not, of course, a religious composer in the normally accepted sense, his communism has affinities with religious belief in that it sees personal problems in the light of an absolute. So he too manifests a turning-away from post-Renaissance principles which is not the less significant for being less obvious than that of his contemporaries in Germany, Italy, and France. It is not fortuitous that he seldom employs, either in symphonies or chamber works, the classical, dualistic first-movement sonata form. Contemplatively, he works by slow lyrical extension; dramatically, by the sharpest contradictions that remain unresolved; kinetically, by the release of rhythmic energy that sweeps all before it. We should remark too that his major piano work is a series of twenty-four preludes and fugues in all the major and minor keys—on the analogy of Bach's supreme masterpiece of baroque unity.

The conservatism of English music in the twentieth century is a more complex matter than that of Russian music because —as we saw in the chapter on Vaughan Williams—we have had to recover a spiritual heritage that our triumphant industrialism had buried. To re-create the past as Vaughan Williams did called for a passionate religious sense such as is, inevitably, rare in an industrially dominated society: so that it is not surprising that, though Vaughan Williams has had innumerable imitators, he has had only one true successor. We may say of Edmund Rubbra [b. 1901], as of Vaughan Williams, that the core of his work consists in his symphonies and his choral music, the latter being ancillary to, and in a profound sense connected with, the symphonies. These works are still more remote from the dualistic classical sonata than the symphonies of Shostakovitch, since they are in essence lyrical, contemplative—and unequivocally religious, having none of the Russian's unresolved contradictions and metrical animation. As an English composer, with a deeply mystical mind and a vocal rather than instrumental heritage, Rubbra creates melodic lines which—though they have not the pentatonic pastoralism of the imitators of Vaughan Williams—spring from the step-wise movement, the rhythms and inflexions, of the human voice in the same way as do the melodies of Dowland. From such melodic lines he builds

works which are genuinely symphonic and at the same time
are not opposed to the principles of vocal polyphony. This is a
very different matter from writing vocal polyphony scored for
instruments: for if the symphony has to be rethought in lyrical
rather than dramatic terms, vocal polyphony has, in its turn,
to acquire a long-range harmonic and tonal architecture.

Thus the whole first movement of his Fifth Symphony grows
out of the phrase enunciated at the outset by solo oboe. The
line moves 'vocally' by step: but involves too a rising augmented
fourth, followed by a falling perfect fourth (Ex. 71). So the

Ex.71 Adagio

symphony begins, like a symphony of Bruckner, as an act of
praise, a 'monistic' lyrical hymn that grows spontaneously, like
a tree. But as the themes expand, the tension within the augmented fourth grows increasingly dominant, reminding us of
the human tensions out of which the symphonic principle had
originally sprung. That the tensions are present, beneath the
surface, is part of Rubbra's contemporaneity; and is the reason
why he (like Bruckner) has chosen to write symphonies, rather
than to express himself purely in liturgical music. In the scherzo
the subterranean tensions disappear, and the structure is monistic in the most fundamental sense, being consistently contrapuntal: a deceptively simple dance tune, alternating stepwise
movement with perfect fourths, glides without climax through
every major key of the chromatic scale. Only the restless modulation belies the tune's tranquil gaiety and the unity of fugue.
With the short slow movement the hymnic lyricism is reinstated,
the pulse slower than the first movement's, the contours more
spaciously serene: though it is significant that the movement
makes some compromise with the sonata notion of development and recapitulation. The recapitulatory passage repeats the
song-melody in a key a semitone below that of its first appearance: a transition, perhaps vocally derived, which crops up
repeatedly in Rubbra's music. This restatement leads without a
break into a bounding allegro in $\frac{6}{8}$, a rhythm typical of Rubbra's jubilant finales. Themes in cross-rhythm evolve from
the initial phrase. Gradually a relationship is revealed between
this phrase and the oboe theme with which the symphony had

opened. Thus the work ends at the point where it began. The phrase has fulfilled its life-circle, and returns to its source. We may note that, for all the freedom of the modulations, the tonal sense is rooted firmly in the harmonic series. The keys in which the four movements start together make up the notes of the diatonic triad.

Since Rubbra's symphonies are basically a religious affirmation, and his vocal music is rooted in the poetry of the seventeenth century, his work may not seem to have much direct relationship to the twentieth century. Yet his 'celebrative act' has a deeper relevance to our needs than has the music of the only composer of his generation to start from an acceptance of the immediate past. William Walton [b. 1902] is an authentic successor to Elgar, as Rubbra is the natural successor to Vaughan Williams. His first works—such as the overture, *Portsmouth Point* —attempted a fusion of the materialistic vigour of the nineteenth-century symphonic poem with elements derived from earlier English traditions (the extravert aspects of Purcellian and Handelian dance-music) and with the jazzy distortions of the twentieth century. He made his reputation, however, with the brilliant parodistic or sentimental genre pieces of *Façade*, composed as accompaniment to Edith Sitwell's (spoken) poems; and although these might seem to debunk Edwardian glamour, they would not be so touching as well as funny did they not spring from love of the object laughed at. It is not therefore surprising that Walton's first considerable work—the Viola Concerto of 1925—should be prevailingly nostalgic and closely related to Elgar's elegiac 'Cello Concerto. The witty Walton of the first works is here transformed into the acid self-mockery of the scherzo; while the last movement, with its spacious marching theme over a stalking bass, hints yearningly at Elgar's public manner. But the core of the music is in the yearning, not the nobility; and the bittersweet false relations of the lyrically rhapsodic first movement return in the cadenza and valedictory epilogue. The tang of the false relations—the only element in Walton's music that harks back to our crucial seventeenth century—lends strength to the poignancy; in his later concertos for singing stringed instruments (for violin and for 'cello) Walton repeats the formula of the Viola Concerto perhaps too passively, for the retrospective nostalgia seems almost self-indulgent.

In the three concertos Walton expresses a private nostalgia which most people can share, if not always sympathize with. In *Belshazzar's Feast* he, as a North-Countryman, takes over the public manner of English oratorio, which had come to its heyday with the rise of our material prosperity. The rhythmic exuberance, the sonorous spacing, the physical excitement of the scoring have obvious affinities with the extravert animation of Handel's choral style, in its socially ceremonial vein. But the animation has turned to animus, revealing Edwardian pomp and circumstance in their true, luridly cruel colours. It is significant that this work—which is probably the last 'Handelian' oratorio—should be completely irreligious, and that the triumphant Christians should sing the same kind of music as the heathens. Now they are top dogs, they will clearly behave in exactly the same way; and this peculiarly savage irony is a logical conclusion to Walton's earlier satirical bent. *Belshazzar* 'exposes' material prosperity, the cult of power, while yearning for its personal satisfactions. The positive values in this piece are contained in the almost Delian chromaticism of the waters of Babylon episode: a heart-breaking music of elegiac lament, comparable with that of the Viola Concerto. Only once in his career has Walton attempted to create something positive from the acceptance of the violence inherent in a materialistic world. That is in the impressive (and Beethovenian) first movement of his Symphony; but it is significant that he found the work so difficult to finish, and that the last movement is a rhetorical gesture rather than a resolution.

Rubbra is essentially a religious composer, Walton an elegiacally sensuous composer; Michael Tippett [b. 1905], having both a religious sense and social awareness, perhaps touches the outside world at more points than either of them. He made his reputation with an oratorio to his own libretto, *A Child of Our Time*; and the difference between this piece and Walton's oratorio is crucial. Walton's oratorio is devastatingly negative and deliberately superficial in its public manifestations, while its positive experience is of personal lament. Tippett treats the public experience 'from within', expressing its relevance to all of us. Dramatizing a true story of the Nazi terror, the oratorio deals directly with war, oppression, persecution, and isolation. But the personal story becomes a twentieth-century myth: by relating the conception to Handel's *Messiah*, Tippett suggests some kinship with the oratorio-going British public; by substituting Negro spirituals for Bach's Lutheran chorales, he uses an oppressed people as a general symbol for the stifling of the human spirit—with the advantage that the idiom is related to the popular music with which his public is familiar. Tippett's acute awareness of the anguish inherent in experience, especially today, communicates itself to his technique which compared with Walton's assurance is in some ways strained and unfulfilled. Yet the inward immediacy and validity of the feeling conquer. Without offering any solution to our social evils, without castigating us for our wickedness, the oratorio grows into a lyrical affirmation of life. In the thrilling final chorus the polyphony swells, the solo vocal writing burgeons into ecstatic arabesque. What keeps us alive, the music tells us, is the human impulse to dance and sing, whatever man's bestiality to man.

The end of the oratorio effects 'the heart's assurance'—to quote the title of the song cycle that Tippett wrote to a series of poems about death by two young poets who were killed in the war. From this work, which deals in personal terms with the public issues involved in the oratorio, we can see how Tippett's affirmation of life entails a technical development also. Here the bounding, long-breathed melodies in their lilting 'sprung' rhythms flower into creative ornamentation (Ex. 72).

Ex. 72

O ne-ver ne-ver ne-ver ne - ver trust   your pride _____ of move-ment

Though the music is a new sound, its roots are in tradition—not so much in Renaissance music as in English music of the seventeenth century. Thus the compulsive rhythm is a more extravagant version of the Purcellian tension between vocal inflexion and physical dance movement; the polyphonically derived harmony intensifies the seventeenth-century partiality for modal variety and false relation; while the flowering of the lines into ever smaller note-values parallels the seventeenth-century technique of divisions on a ground. There is a baroque, sensuously exciting quality in the curling tendrils of Tippett's vocal line and piano texture; yet—as with such seventeenth-century masters as William Lawes and Purcell—the sustained lift of the melodies gives the music a spiritual buoyancy also. From this point of view, the contrast between Tippett's invigorating and Walton's elegiac false relations is striking.

The Heart's Assurance may have been a preludial study for Tippett's opera, *The Midsummer Marriage*: which differs from his oratorio in starting from, rather than ending with, the affirmation of life. The marriage is itself the mating of the senses' joy with the spirit's mystery; and in taking his operatic mythology from Jungian psychology Tippett has sought for imagery that will strike deep, to a twentieth-century audience, without need of intellectual explanation. Allegory is bound to be a tricky business, in a society that, believing itself to be rationalistic, has grown out of the habit of allegorical thinking. But Tippett's libretto is probably the only kind that he could have set; and its theme is closely related to the crisis in his own musical development. Technical limitations are always, perhaps, imaginative limitations; here Tippett sheds the inhibitions that partially frustrated fulfilment in earlier works. The *Ritual Dances*—if not the whole opera—are magical in the old, celebrative sense, offering not illusion, but a revelation of the deepest compulsions from which our lives draw sustenance. The difficulty of Tippett's music is evidence of the struggle most twentieth-century men must undergo in order to learn to celebrate. When once we are free, the act of celebration is itself simple. It is relevant to note that the features that make Tippett's idiom so distinctive—the sprung rhythms and lilting syncopations, the harmonic false relations, the technique of division—all have their counterparts not only in our seventeenth-century music, but also, in a cruder form, in the urban folk-music of our own day—jazz.

Both Rubbra and Tippett were slow starters. That Benjamin Britten [b. 1913] created a work of genius at the age of eighteen cannot be separated from the nature of his achievement. In so far as *A Boy was Born* was a choral work based on a traditional Christian theme, it was part of the heritage of Holst and Vaughan Williams. Where it differs from other attempts to evoke a relatively remote past is in the absence of either nostalgia or inhibition. The ripe chromaticism of Bax's or Peter Warlock's settings of mediaeval poems carries with it the knowledge that one is shut out from such single-mindedness; while Holst achieves it only by a denial of the lyrical warmth man needs to live by. The 'youthfulness' of Britten's music, on the other hand, seems to spring from a direct realization of what it felt like to live in a world dominated by faith. It is not (like a Rubbra symphony) a religious piece; it is simply about the growth of life in innocence. A boy is born indeed; and the affirmation is inseparable from the technical virtuosity which Britten (unlike Tippett) seemed to possess by natural endowment. This virtuosity is not merely a matter of contrapuntal skill. It also involves an element that one might call theatrical projection: the ability to discover, as did composers of the baroque era, a musical image that 'enacts' aurally, even physically, the visual and psychological images of the poem. (A marvellous example in this work is the simultaneously burning and freezing major and minor seconds that aurally realizes the 'bleak midwinter') (Ex. 73).

Ex. 73

It does not follow that Britten's *A Boy was Born* is a better piece of music than Bax's *Ora Mater Filium* or Holst's *Hymn of Jesus*; but it does follow that there was in Britten's work the germ of a future evolution. In his next significant work he began to develop instrumentally the element of theatrical projection present in the choral work—its cosmopolitan, unprovincial sense of style. The *Variations for String Orchestra* on a theme of Frank Bridge represent a deliberate break from English pastoralism and are intentionally eclectic. It is not an accident that the theme should be taken from Britten's teacher, Frank Bridge [1879–1941], for as composer Bridge had been relatively impervious to Holst's and Vaughan Williams's rediscovery of our past, and had tried out his hand in most fashionable Continental techniques, from Skryabinesque chromatics, to Stravinskian percussive dissonance, to Schoenbergian atonality.

The Continental composer who has, in this work, exerted a potently meaningful influence on Britten is, however, Mahler. No doubt the young Englishman was fascinated by Mahler's music for the same general reasons as was Shostakovitch; but there was also a particular reason for Britten's interest, in that one of the dominant themes in Mahler's work had been the search for a lost Eden, often identified with the innocence of the child. In *A Boy was Born* Britten, being still a boy himself, had expressed a childlike innocence with adult virtuosity. In the few years that had elapsed since that work he was growing up; so into the *Bridge Variations* comes an element of Mahlerian nostalgia for an innocence that is lost. The introduction, built on arpeggiated figurations in bitonal relationships, and the theme and first variation have a declamatory rhetoric and an intense pathos that recall Mahler; they have also a tender radiance that is the first unmistakable evidence of Britten's personality.

After the first variation, however, the work abruptly ceases to be a personal testament and becomes a series of genre pieces —March, Romance, Aria Italiana, Bourrée Classique, Wiener Waltz, and Moto Perpetuo—ranging from overt parody to a serious use of the 'mask' whereby the artist seeks to depersonal-ize his experience. The pathos, and the Mahlerian rhetoric, return with the Funeral March and Chant: until the accumu-lating tension is resolved in a brilliantly developed fugue. This combines the externalized vivacity of the genre pieces with the passion of the introduction: so the variations would seem to indicate, in purely musical terms, how one must lose the self in order to find it. It is as though Britten already knew that he was destined to be an operatic composer.

In the next stage of his career Britten began to explore the possibilities of operatic 'projection' by composing song cycles in the French and the Italian manner. Only when he had dis-covered how an English composer could exploit the heritage of European operatic style—as Purcell had exploited the Italian and French conventions of his own time—did Britten explore the possibilities of an aria and arioso relevant to the English language. The tenor *Serenade*, setting poems covering a wide range of English literature, resembles Purcell's music in being at once eclectic and almost aggressively personal. One can tabu-late the derivation of Britten's mannerisms—the melodies built on arpeggiated thirds, the expansive leaps, especially of sixth and seventh, the pentatonic undulations—while knowing that his melodies have become unique, if not inimitable.

The creation of an English operatic idiom was not, however,

a purely musical matter. Purcell's failure to create an English operatic tradition in the seventeenth century was not a personal failure, but the deficiency of a society. That had something to do with the division epitomized in the Civil War; and that had something to do with the 'disassociation of sensibility' that in England split mind and matter, spirit and senses, more rapidly and more radically than elsewhere. Perhaps that breach had to be healed, and the heart reborn in innocence, before an English opera could be achieved.

However this may be, the discovery of an operatic convention involves, too, the discovery of the necessary myth. Looking back, we can see that all Britten's operas deal with the same parable: the renewal of innocence as the condition of human creativity. *A Boy was Born*—almost literally a boy's work—could with dazzling innocence create innocence in our minds and senses. The operatic works of Britten's maturity, on the other hand, are concerned with the fight between the Fool's simple heart and the corruptions of the world. *Peter Grimes* turns on the ancient myth of the Savage Man who in Eden would be innate goodness: whom the depravity of humanity renders destructive. Deprived of Ellen's love, Grimes's innocence turns to cruelty and he destroys the Boy who is his own soul. Then the World (thrillingly represented by the chorus) rounds on him, harries him to his death.

Though Grimes may be an unheroic hero, his predicament is genuinely tragic; and the progression from innocence to exile, to persecution, is a theme as relevant to our own times as Nahum Tate's and Purcell's rehashing of Dido's story was to theirs. Arioso—the human singing voice become dramatic enactment—is the core of Britten's opera as it is of Purcell's; and the element of theatrical projection in Britten's work now becomes reality. No opera is more evocative, yet at the same time more precise, in its creation of time and place. The tang of the sea, the hues of Suffolk light, the bustle of anonymous human activity, are revealed through that baroque instinct for the appropriate musical image that first appeared in *A Boy was Born*. And this precise realization of the external world is inseparable from the music-drama's insight into the mind and heart. Britten's music, in association with Slater's adaptation of Crabbe, achieves its deepest insight through its operatic objectivity; and its Englishness is revealed through its eclecticism.

Albert Herring has the same theme as *Grimes*, treated comically instead of tragically. Herring is again the natural fool, a pathetic if not heroic figure: and though his exile and destruction by the World turn out to be only a charade, that does not deflate the almost-tragic potency of the threnody sung over him. These two operas most convincingly attain a balance between the private and the public aspects of Britten's habitual theme. In *The Rape of Lucretia* there is much heartfelt and exquisite music; but the Christian overtones of the end strike an uncomfortable, even synthetic, note. Perhaps something the same is true of *Billy Budd*. The profound humanity of Grimes comes from the fact that the light of innocence and the dark of depravity are both within him. In *Billy Budd* the separation of Billy's light from Claggart's darkness emphasizes the personal at the expense of the universal aspects of the theme, so there is something a little neurotic, even pretentious, about the dragging in of the Crucifixion. This may explain why *Billy Budd* has not become an accepted part of operatic repertory, in the way that *Peter Grimes* has, though there is a sense in which *Billy Budd* is the more consummately realized work.

Still more completely fulfilled, imaginatively and technically, is *The Turn of the Screw*. Perhaps it is not fortuitous that this piece tackles the basic theme most directly: for Henry James's horrifying *conte* enters the world of the child to explore the corruption of innocence. Britten's tightly organized score sees the innocence of the nursery ditty—which he had entered into in his own most touching children's operas—against the ghastly machinations of human spirits that have died in losing the innocence that they, presumably, once possessed. Britten's theatrical magic has never been more insidious; we submit whether we will or not. But the private claustrophobia of the piece means that it cannot challenge the human validity of *Grimes*.

There are signs in Britten's recent work, however, that the almost pathological horror of corruption is finding its resolution. The most beautiful of all Britten's song cycles with piano, written in between *Billy Budd* and *The Turn of the Screw*, is *Winter Words*, settings of lyrics and ballads by Thomas Hardy. Britten is a highly sophisticated composer, and Hardy a notoriously unsophisticated poet. Yet Britten has used Hardy superbly for his own purposes, setting a group of poems which all deal with innocence and experience, while finding in Hardy's calm acceptance a liberation from neurosis. The first song deals with the inevitability of Time's threat to the innocence of childhood. It is a lyric poem which becomes a musical image: the bitonal chords and dislocated rhythms of the piano part suggest the wind-blustered trees and the agitation within the heart, while the intermittent unison Ds suggest a firm acceptance of the inevitable. The telescoped harmonies and dislocated rhythms continue softly in the piano while the vocal line sings sweetly, in cooing sixths and sevenths, of childhood's innocence (Ex. 74):

Ex. 74

And the chil — dren____ who ram — ble through here____ con-ceive that there ne - - - ver has been a time when no____ trees____ no tall____ trees grew here

only to be swept away by the winds of Time. Then follow a series of ballads which are all operatic scenes in miniature, evoked again with astonishing economy: the little boy, with his ticket stuck in his hat, travelling through the night on the hooting train, vacant, knowing nothing of his destiny; or the other little boy, playing his fiddle in ironic simplicity to the convict in the railway waiting-room; or, comically, the wagtail that flies in panic from human contagion; or, pathetically, the angelically innocent modal music that evokes the choirmaster's ghostly visitation. Only in the last song does the lyric mode reappear. The poem deals, in philosophic terms, with the birth of consciousness which is also the death of innocence; but in asking when Nescience shall be reaffirmed it admits that Eden once lost can never be recovered. Britten's long, eternally flowing vocal line marvellously creates the simplicity of primal bliss and also the longing for its return: while the regular progression of the chords, thickly grouped in the low registers of the piano, accepts the inevitability of pain.

This acceptance of reality, within the vision of innocence, finds a still richer and deeper expression in the *Nocturne* for tenor strings and a series of obbligato instruments. This work, written after *The Turn of the Screw*, carries on at the point where its companion piece, the tenor *Serenade*, left off. The *Serenade* dealt in daytime experience, while ending with Keat's invocation to sleep. The *Nocturne* deals entirely in the world of night; but sees dreams as the source of the deepest reality known to us. Thus in the introductory song from Shelley's *Prometheus Unbound* the polytonal planes on which the intrinsically simple harmonies move create an extraordinary feeling of disassociation; out of the unconscious life of dream comes the creative imagination: 'forms *more* real than living man'.

But when the first obbligato instrument enters to introduce the first 'reality' that emerges from the subconscious the experience is frightening indeed. The poem, *The Kraken*, is one of Tennyson's juvenalia; yet one wonders if a more terrifyingly aware utterance ever came from the mouth of babe or suckling. The bassoon here becomes the creature's writhings and surgings, while the strings become percussive ploppings and sea-sizzlings. As the song fades into a recurrence of the lullaby music, the nightmare is succeeded by what seems to be a pleasant dream, in the remote radiance of A major, with the obbligato instrument, a harp, playing liquid arabesques over sustained string harmonies. The unchanging tonality, the pentatonic flavour, the slow waltz rhythm, give a hypnotic quality to

Coleridge's vision of the 'lovely boy' in the wilderness. But the innocent sweetness now hides a threat. Though he is a little child (in Britten's lilting thirds and fourths), he is 'plucking fruits'; and alone in the night, he has 'no friends'.

The succeeding songs grow from the tension between the dream and the nightmare, suggesting, in the settings of Wordsworth and Wilfred Owen, the half-conscious link between the terrors within the mind and their manifestation in the external world. The final song—a setting of Shakespeare's forty-third sonnet—'When most I wink, then do my eyes best see'—fulfils the cycle's theme: that the life of dream is the gateway to reality. Musically, too, the song is consummate, for the vocal line, over-slowly moving quavers, is more lyrically sustained than in any of the previous movements, and is rooted in C major-minor —the key that seems to exert a gravitational pull on the latent, neighbouring tonalities of the other songs. And perhaps, after all, Britten's quintessential experience turns out to be religious, in a personal, not ritualistic, sense. For when, after the wide-ranging octaves of the climax, we return to the lullaby's gentle rocking, in the serenity of C major—but with other-worldly, unresolved D flat major thirds on harp and string harmonics— Britten reveals the mystical depth beneath Shakespeare's conceit of the lover who sees his love 'bright in dark directed'. It is no longer the human beloved we are seeking in the darkness of the night; it is also the Beloved, the source of life that mysteriously renews the human spirit. 'There is in God, some say a deep but dazzling darkness.' It cannot be an accident that Britten's most recent opera is also a setting of Shakespeare—an adaptation of *A Midsummer Night's Dream*: that this piece should see the human and the spirit world as complementary: and that the magic music in the opera should be closely related to the music of the unconscious in the *Nocturne*. The opera is a ritual that is life-celebrating rather than death-stricken. And although there is nothing in Britten's work to suggest that he thinks a European should, or could, escape the 'pain of consciousness', it is significant that he (like all the composers discussed in this chapter, with the partial exception of Tippett and Prokofiev) has hardly ever written a movement in sonata form: and that his recent music, especially *A Midsummer Night's Dream*, relies more on melodic arabesque over relatively static ostinati and and pedal points than on harmonic movement.

10

MUSIC IN A NEW-FOUND LAND

T HIS book has been concerned with the history of music in
Europe. We have seen that, even in Europe, the composer's
approach to his art has been affected, over the past fifty or
more years, by the disintegration of tradition. The American
composer started from such disintegration, for he had no cultural tradition to lose. He had nothing but the old rags and
bones of European culture that, imported to a new environment, soon lost their savour. Then gradually, in the pulping
machine of a polyglot society, the rags and bones began to acquire a taste of their own. The process, however, took time;
and perhaps for this reason the earliest American compositions
to manifest a creative spark tended to be technically inexpert.
William Billings [1746-1800], in the late eighteenth century,
had little ambition except to produce devotional music in the
tradition of the Puritan hymn. His mistakes in text-book
harmony have, however, a whiff of creative genius: so that he is
an original who can still move us, while the professional competence of his European-trained contemporaries and successors
can move us no longer.

If the lack of a past means the loss of the wisdom that respect
for tradition brings, it also offers a supreme opportunity. Potentially, the artist becomes an 'unacknowledged legislator of the
world': so the first authentic American composer, Charles Ives
[1874-1954], held that music was a moral force, dismissing the
belief that it was primarily self-expression as 'the Byronic fal-
lacy'. He could not be content, like his contemporary, Edward
Macdowell [1861-1908], to write second-hand, if poetic, music
in the German tradition, even with a piquant spice of Grieg-like
chromatics. If he was to be an honest creator, he had to take his
materials from the world around him. Since he was born at
Danbury, Connecticut, this meant the provincial world of the
hard-bitten farmer, the small business-man and trader: which

in musical terms was the town band (which Ives's father directed), the corny theatre tune, the chapel hymn. The remoteness of this music from academic convention stimulated the aural imagination; and while Ives's father had given him a training in conventional harmony and counterpoint and a respect for the 'manly' classical composers, especially Beethoven, this was insignificant compared with the unpredictable sound-stuff offered to him by his environment. What excited Ives's imagination was the vast body of camp singers yelling slightly different versions of the same hymn; the horn-player who gets left behind his fellows in the town band; the four bands that, at celebration time, play different music simultaneously in the four corners of the town square; the chapel singing heard over water, mingled with the sound of wind and rustling leaves. Ives would have agreed with his father, who, when asked how he could stand hearing old John (the local stonemason) bellowing off-key at camp meetings, replied: "Old John is a supreme musician. Look into his face and hear the music of the ages. Don't pay too much attention to the sounds. If you do, you may miss the music."

Ives's empirical approach to technique relates him to Whitman; he shares the poet's all-inclusiveness, his ubiquitous love of every facet of the visible, audible, and tactile world. His gargantuan appetite 'absorbs and translates' experience as the original Leather-stocking pioneer attempted to subjugate the physical world; and techniques from conventional European music, from jazz improvisation, from chapel and bar parlour, and from the noises of Nature are to be used as experience dictates, often within the same work, and even simultaneously, since all experience is related and indivisible.

Paradoxically, these fusions of contrarieties sound purposeful, not chaotic. In *General Putnam's Camp*, from the orchestral *Three Places in New England*, a diversity of military songs and ragtime tunes are played together in different rhythms and tempi, and often in different keys, mixed up with the huzzaing of the crowd and various a-rhythmic, non-tonal sounds of Nature. The music evokes, with astonishing immediacy, the physical and nervous sensation of being present at such a vast outdoor celebration; yet the flux of life becomes one through the force of the imagination. Ives tells us that the piece derives from a recollection of childhood. It is difficult to think of any art that conveys more precisely the experience—common in childhood, rarer in later years—of being at once identified with the flux of appearances and detached from it, as watching eye, as listening ear. In this sense, the essence of Ives's art is discovery: a new-found land.

The third of the *Three Places in New England*—*The Housatonic at Stockbridge*—is another transient personal reminiscence that becomes a 'moment of reality'. The lovely, sinuous horn melody, with its almost Mahlerian orchestration, suggests both the chapel singing that Ives tells us he heard coming over the water, through the mist, and also the tranquil security of the love between himself and his wife (charmingly called Harmony). This melody is absorbed in a haze of floating strings that play, as from a distance, more or less independently of the rest of the orchestra. Gradually these sounds of Nature—of river, mist, and rustling leaves—grow stronger until they engulf the love-song: at which point the tumult abruptly ceases, and the song is left suspended, unresolved on a sigh. With great poignancy, the piece reveals both the centrality of human love and also its impermanence in the non-human context of the natural world.

For while Ives resembled Whitman in his appetite for experience, the obverse side of the American myth is present in his work, too: the Ego that would swallow all experience becomes progressively more aware of its isolation. The more immediate the artist's response to the external world, the more deeply he has to seek Reality beneath the flux. Ives accepted the world as it was, in all its chaos and contradiction, and for him there could be no division between the world of art and that of practical affairs. But he regarded his music and the insurance business in which he made his fortune as complementary activities. Both sought for a New World; in both the material and the spiritual were inseparable. He resembled the New England Transcendentalists in believing that he who would create a new world must first put his own house in order.

One of his most representative works—written, on and off, between 1908 and 1915—is in fact dedicated to the Transcendentalists—to those New England Heroes who lived in Concord between 1840 and 1860. The first movement of this Second Piano Sonata is a portrait of Emerson, hero of American strife; and this is a Beethovenian movement in so far as it dualistically opposes an 'epic' motive (the motto from Beethoven's Fifth) against a song-like lyric theme. But although Ives is a Beethovenian composer, he cannot share Beethoven's positives: so the opposed motives do not achieve reconciliation in tonal order. They interact; and change their identities as they are related in wildly opposed rhythms and on separate (polytonal) planes of harmony. Beethoven's transformations of themes are positively controlled by the Will; the form of the Fifth Symphony is the gradual revelation of the theme's destiny. Ives's transformations of themes are kaleidoscopic, protean like life itself, and the unity they seek becomes as much linear and serial as tonal: Ives even introduces Schoenbergian transpositions of the notes of the series to increasingly remote pitches (Ex. 75).

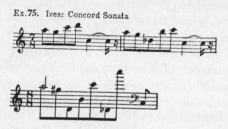

Ex. 75. Ives: Concord Sonata

But the permutations of the motives do not, at the end, coalesce into a sustained melody; the music gradually disintegrates over a slowly oscillating chromatic bass: for though Ives has immense courage, he has not—perhaps no one, living in a rootless world, could have—Beethoven's assurance.

In this Emerson movement the conflict between lyric and epic forces has been largely subjective. The fight goes on within the consciousness, and the Will attempts—with only partial success—to control destiny. The second movement, however, is quite un-Beethovenian, for it deals with the subconscious life: with dreams, nightmare, and the sensory impressions of childhood. Ives says that he has not stressed the most significant aspect of Hawthorne—his Puritan sense of guilt: though guilt is closely connected with the 'phantasmal realms' in which the movement deals. In this movement there is virtually no tonality, no metre, and, one might almost say, no rhythm, since every quaver is violently syncopated off a beat that is merely implicit. Into the amorphous hurly-burly fragments of both lyric and epic motive intrude. But they have no controlling force; they are flotsam, thrown up on the waves of the unconscious.

Occasionally they provoke confused, dream-like recollections of daytime experience (the circus band episode, the tipsy ragtime, the love song that dissolves in a pianissimo haze of note-clusters, played with a strip of board).

Emerson was the life of the mind and soul, Hawthorne the life of the subconscious. With the third movement, Ives turns to everyday reality: the Allcott's house, the 'witness of Concord's common virtue'. Here both lyric and epic motive appear in simple form, realistically, for Beethoven's Fifth is being played in the parlour. The opening hymn-like version of the epic motive is a tune now unambiguously in B flat, but harmonized with telescoped tonic, dominant, and subdominant chords of E flat, so that the harmonic progression seems almost immobile, compared with the turbulence of the previous movements. But although 'the richness of not having' may provide us with tranquillity of a kind, it does not release us from the burden of the Will or the mystery of the unconscious. That can come only with a mystical act: and in the last movement Thoreau sits in his sunny doorway at Walden—"He grew in those seasons like corn in the night. He realized what the Orientals meant by contemplation and forsaking of works." The music opens barless, almost rhythmless, with a fluttering of leaves: which involves too the fluttering of human nerves in response. Gradually, the fragmentary lines grow into a long, winding melody that fuses the lyric idea with the epic. Ives directs that this melody should be played on a flute, if you happen to have one handy. This is not merely quixotic: the other-worldly colour of the instrument would emphasize the effect of the melody as the goal of the whole sonata. As the melody sings over a swaying, unmoving ostinato built out of the thirds and fifths of the epic motive, the spirit is liberated from inner strife (the Emerson movement): from nightmare (the Hawthorne movement): even from everyday reality (the Allcotts movement). The lyric and epic contrarieties have become one, in a mystical communion with Nature. Yet the end of the work is characteristic. The epic motive sounds high up, this time neither rising nor falling. This seems to suggest a final resolution into D major. Yet the C natural G complex is still audible, reminding us of the point we started from: while into the last bar the leading note, C sharp, softly obtrudes (Ex. 76): seeming to suggest how for Ives each resolution into Being is only a stage in the eternal flux

Ex.76. Ives: Concord Sonata (last movement)

of Becoming. Experience is essentially incomplete, and never to be completed, except by death.

One might say that America has compressed its musical past, present, and potential future into the personality of Ives. The strife in his music is a still more violent development from European humanism (and the sonata principle); and its very violence leads him to a new, in part serial, search for order. That Ives anticipated by several decades the more experimental techniques of Schoenberg, Bartók, and Stravinsky (not to mention *musique concrète* and electronic music) is not in itself important; and his techniques are not always adequately realized, since he suffered—as any artist must—from working without a public. Yet in seeking order out of a polyphony not merely of lines, but also of freely evolving harmonies, rhythms, and tonalities, he may have more to suggest to the future of music than any of the European composers who are, in intrinsic achievement, greater. Nor is his significance merely 'historical'. His finest music—such as *The Housatonic at Stockbridge*—sounds now as ripely a part of the past as the Mahler and Berg whom it fortuitously resembles. If it has also something of the rawness of a new world, the rawness brings with it an authentic note of grandeur. It is a note that is becoming rarer; we should be grateful for it.

Carl Ruggles [b. 1876], is a man of the same generation as Ives; but whereas Ives is both gregarious democrat and solitary visionary, Ruggles is unequivocally the isolated spirit. (He is almost literally a hermit; and the walls of his study, in his Vermont house, are symbolically papered with the exquisite calligraphy of his own manuscripts.) Thus the texture of Ruggles's music has nothing like the multifarious complexity of Ives's, the rag-bag into which all experience is poured helter-skelter, to be re-created. Yet although Ruggles's music contains no direct reflection of the chaos of the American scene, he is still concerned with the New: for he is a solitary in New England, where so much that went to make America is rooted.

Though Ruggles has written only a handful of works, his music is singularly consistent. His is a dedicated art, affirming the freedom of the human spirit; and his affirmation runs parallel to Schoenberg's 'free' atonal period, in the Europe of the second decade of the century. As an American, indeed, with no past, Ruggles sought freedom—from tonal bondage, from the harmonic strait-jacket—even more remorselessly than Schoenberg. The sound of his music, with its preponderance of minor seconds, major sevenths, and minor ninths, is similar to Schoenberg's; but in place of Schoenberg's density, Ruggles cultivates a clear, 'open' resonance in his singing, winging polyphony. This spacious texture and resilient rhythm are perhaps Ruggles's representatively American qualities, which have their counterpart in the polyphonic textures of Ives in, say, the Emerson movement of the 'Concord' Sonata. But Ruggles differs from Ives in his desire to refine and concentrate. Ives accepts the Universe—the tawdry and trivial along with the sublime. Ruggles is concerned with his own soul—with the 'great things' that are done 'when Men and Mountains meet'. It is revealing to compare Ruggles's *Men and Mountains* with Delius's *A Song of the High Hills*. Delius starts from the burden of his own passionate heart—the appoggiatura-laden harmony that tries to drag down the singing lines. Ruggles's chromaticism is not, historically speaking, so far from Delius's. But for him, as for Schoenberg, singing polyphony overrides harmonic tension, seeking the One in the Many. Delius is a (belated and weary) humanist; Ruggles is a mystic in a non-religious society. Paradoxically, his mysticism is a part of his Americanism: for it is also his 'newness', his search for personal integrity.

Of the composers of the next generation—those born around the turn of the century—Roy Harris has something of the rugged, Whitmanesque character of Ives in his folk-hymnodic vein; and the essence of his music, as of Ruggles', is in the sustained flow of his melodies. The enormous opening theme of his Third Symphony (his best-known and perhaps best work) is vocal and modal in character, halfway between folksong and plainsong. Its primitive religious feeling, its pioneering aspiration, relate it to Puritan tradition; and the unbroken sections of the symphony are a germination from this single seed; a empirical process rather than a matter of conscious integration.

The American flavour of Harris's language centres in its 'vernacular' line and rhythm. If the opening suggests plainsong, that is not only because it is religious in feeling, but also because plainsong is close to speech. The racy vigour which the movement gradually acquires and the open texture—with a prevalence of fourths, minor sevenths, and major ninths—rejuvenate the continuous Wagnerian flow of the enharmony and the shimmer of the Sibelian moto perpetuo. So, imperceptibly, the moto perpetuo is transformed into the brusquely American fugued dance with which the work concludes. This exciting, if curious, mating of the Middle West dance-hall with the mediaeval *hoquet* is the most obviously 'contemporary' section of the score: and the closest in spirit and technique to the music of Harris's contemporary, Aaron Copland [b. 1900].

The pioneering, quasi-religious vein of Ruggles and Harris is remote from Copland's early music. In an arid machine civilization, he seems to have felt that he had to sacrifice the natural technique of lyrical growth. In the *Piano Variations* of 1930 he starts from skeletonic fragments: the ambiguous thirds, sixths, and sevenths of the Negro blues, and the declamatory leaps of Jewish synagogue music. It is significant that both Negro and Jew are dispossessed peoples who become, for Copland, symbolic of urban man's uprootedness. Since the dislocated fragments cannot grow spontaneously, they must be reintegrated in a personal vision. So the technique of the *Variations* is rigidly serial, based on a five-note figure (Ex. 77). The phrases

Ex.77 COPLAND

Variations

Grave ♩=48
(strike sharply)

f non legato, deliberamente

☀ *Press down silently*

never grow, though they are multifarious in mood—angry, fierce, protesting, naïve, warm, tender. Yet out of these dislocated fragments a whole is created by a kind of 'cubist' reintegration; and though the piano texture, derived from the 'blue' false relations of the 'series', has the metallic hardness and precision of a machine, the music achieves, out of its minimal material, an austere but humane nobility.

If Copland felt a need to humanize his music it was not because his early works were not born of the heart; it was simply because an artist—as Ives found—cannot long subsist without an audience. The simpler style of his ballets and film music does not deny the technique of his earlier work: though the music's deliberate lack of progression is less disturbing when allied to immediately recognizable, folk-like tunes, and to physical action or visual drama. Certainly the folky vein of Copland's ballets, especially *Appalachian Spring*, is not an evasion of the steel girders—within which Copland so miraculously discovers a human warmth—of the *Piano Variations*: for he sees the prairie as symbol of the irremediable loneliness of big cities, the hymn as symbol of the religious and domestic security that urban man has lost. It is interesting that although the ballets are naturally less static, harmonically and rhythmically, than the *Variations*, they show a Stravinskian partiality for the telescoping of tonic, dominant and subdominant chords.

The identity between Copland's urban and his rustic vein is revealed by comparing *Quiet City*—a sound-image of the empty city at night—with the elegy in *Billy the Kid*; it is also worth noting that his *Music for Radio* was composed in New York, as urban music for an industrial society; the sub-title *Saga of the Prairies* being added as a result of a competition for a descriptive tag. In any case, the ultimate maturing of his talent, in the works he has written since about 1940, involves a synthesis of the implacable isolation of the *Piano Variations* with the more outward-tending humanity of his 'functional' works. This is evident in the first movement of the *Piano Sonata*, which uses the technique of the *Variations* in a richer, more direct form. Again we have the brief figures, the 'blue' false relations, the splitting up of the phrases into their component parts. Again the buoyant, upward lift of fourths, fifths, and minor sevenths is pinned down by the immense slowness of the rhythmic and harmonic design. The energetic phrases seem, against this timeless background, curiously wistful, suggesting both urban man's ant-like energy and his ineluctable loneliness. This is even more remarkable in the nagging, wedge-shaped figure on which the scherzo is built: so it is not an accident that these two movements should

lead—by way of a strange bridge passage, like a sublimated
hill-billy stomp—into an andante which is a quintessential expression of immobility. The tender, cool melody, with its widely
spaced fifths and fourths, floats out of the material of the scherzo
and trio and comes to rest in empty harmonies that pulse as
unobtrusively as a heart-beat. The pendulum swings wider at
the climax, when the first movement's clanging thirds return;
but the regularity is never broken. The music runs down like
a clock, dissolving away into space and eternity, while the
grinding false relations of the opening movement echo from an
immense distance (Ex. 78). The music that here stills the heart's
agitation is closely related to the film score to Wilder's *Our
Town*, which involves images of vast space; its serenity is the
more impressive and (to most of us) moving because Copland

Ex.78 COPLAND
Sonata

is not a mystic like Ruggles or a primitive like Harris. It is
pertinent to note that one of his finest, most representative
works is a song cycle, setting verses of that supreme poet of
American isolation, Emily Dickinson.

The regional, Robert Frost-like aspects of Harris and Copland have had many imitators; yet most that is vital in American
music seems to derive from the tradition of solitariness, if the
paradoxical phrase be admitted. The music of Elliott Carter
[b. 1908], for instance, though more controlled and sophisticated
than either, has hints of both Ruggles and Ives in its sturdily
independent polyphony of line and rhythm; while the impressive slow movement of his First String Quartet reveals a much
more complicated form of Copland's dichotomy between the
energy of the component melodic lines and the tortoise-like pace
of the harmonic rhythm. Like Ives—but with a more Beethovenian awareness—Carter uses both 'dualistic' tonal techniques and 'monistic' serial methods in his attempts to create

order from chaos. Other composers, notably Roger Sessions [b. 1896], have gravitated from traditional tonality to acceptance of the serial principle. The Puritan austerity common to the composers we have mentioned thus far (with the partial exception of Ives) is characteristic of Sessions too, though his music has a sensuous rhetoric that suggests Mahler and Schoenberg, though his rhythms are more kinetic than those of the Viennese school. The whirring, whirling impetus of the movement, the kaleidoscopic texture, of the allegros of his Second and Third Symphonies have a—perhaps typically American—multifariousness and zest; and the serial unity which he seeks is, like the Reality of the poet Wallace Stevens, the truth of the imagination. The external world intrudes into his music scarcely at all; perhaps this amounts to an admission that a socially acceptable idiom is, for a 'serious' American composer, no longer a practical possibility. Certainly he and Carter have had far more influence on the younger generation of American composers than the regionalists.

It is understandable that though American music inevitably begins with an acceptance of the 'western' way of life in its most aggressive form, it also manifests, in all the composers we have discussed, a partial rejection of post-Renaissance humanism; a turning to the East comparable with, but more extreme than, that manifested in the European composers considered in the previous chapter. We shall not therefore be surprised to find that the most radically experimental tendencies we commented on in European music have their complement in American music: and that one American composer of the older generation was the pioneer of such developments on both sides of the Atlantic. Ives, in exploiting noise and non-European elements, had hinted at their abandonment. Edgar Varèse [b. 1885]—a French-American who lived and worked in Paris during the nineteen-twenties, but has now settled in the States—entirely discarded the conventional materials of melody and harmony, as well as rhythmic patterns related to harmonic tension. For him the post Beethovenian approach to music as psychological drama was irrelevant. He rather sought a musical complement to Action painting; music should be created, like the dance, as an act of the body itself, manipulating tangible and audible material 'concretely'. So he starts from the sound-characteristics of each instrument—what he calls its density, its timbre and quality independent of pitch relationships, let alone harmony. The instrument is a sound like any other relatively accidental noise; and Varèse's music is a polyphony of timbres, each instrument having its own typical linear figure and rhythmic pattern, both of which never develop. Construction, for Varèse, is an achievement of the sense of space. Harmonically conceived music achieves this through the development of themes, the movement to and away from a central key. Varèse achieves his 'opening of space' through the addition and contrast of rhythms and timbres.

Clearly such a conception of music is more ritualistic and magical than 'expressive': and has much in common with Oriental music and with the music of primitive societies. Varèse believes that this was necessary because the hyper-self-consciousness of modern man is one of the reasons for twentieth-century chaos; art's duty is to encourage forgetfulness of self, if not in mysticism (which is accessible only to dedicated spirits), then in magic. But he has always insisted that his ritualistic approach is modern as well as primitive, being related to a machine-dominated civilization. The percussive noises and patterns in his music have affinities with the sounds of city life that have become part of our everyday consciousness. The artist's task is to help us to perceive the patterns of order and beauty that lie beneath mechanistic chaos, if we have eyes to see and ears to hear. When we can all see and hear, the artist, presumably, will be unnecessary.

Some advanced composers have, indeed, already relinquished the notion of an audience. John Cage [b. 1912], in his early works, used 'prepared' pianos to create a melodically pentatonic and harmonically percussive music closer to Balinese music than to anything in Western tradition. In later works he first subjugated the ego to completely serial processes and then—in ultimate rejection of the will—to chance (for instance, the throw of dice). Though he begins with Varèse's preoccupation with sound as such, he has no use for Varèse's physical assault on the nerves. Music becomes therapeutic, an agent of Zen Buddhism: hardly discussable in the same terms as traditional Western music. It is perhaps interesting that his work appeals strongly to those concerned with the visual arts.

Such experimental extremism seems a far cry indeed from

Ives's attempt at an 'American' comprehensiveness: the dichotomy which he so profoundly distrusted would seem to be complete if we put on the one side the music of Cage and his associates, and on the other the world of common appetite, of mass-produced entertainment music. It is true that this is a situation that has developed only during the last hundred years: that up to Schubert's day (as we saw) there was a distinction in degree, but not in kind, between music written consciously to 'entertain' and music that was a testament of the human spirit: that even nineteenth-century composers such as Offenbach and Johann Strauss [1825–1899], whose art was basically social and functional, none the less entailed a sense of values consistent with the more 'serious' art of their time. But it is a tall order to convict the twentieth century of a kind of cultural schizophrenia. Though there may be two kinds of art today, one of which preserves the integrity of the human spirit while the other debases it, we must remember that the human mind has never shown much reluctance to being debased; the difference today is that machine techniques make the process easier and more efficient. Moreover, the nature of the debasement is not fortuitous. Commercial art prostitutes our feelings in the way that seems likely to yield the biggest financial return; but even commercial techniques assume the existence of proclivities that await exploitation. Though the Hollywood Dream may be shoddy compared with the myths in the light of which great civilizations have lived, we do not preserve our precious integrity by pretending it has nothing to do with *us*. It is even possible that commercial art is beginning to develop its own inner responsibilities. *The Desert Song* is pure (or rather impure) make-believe; but the glossy American musical is unconsciously evolving codes of behaviour, even of value, which are intimately related to an industrial society. Though we may not like them, their existence cannot be gainsaid: and should make us suspicious of glib distinctions between art and commerce.

In this connexion the work of George Gershwin [1898–1937] is of particular interest. He was an instinctive musician, nurtured on the restricted diet of Tin Pan Alley. His basic material was the thirty-two-bar tune, whether in 'common' or 'three-quarter' tempo: divided into a four-bar phrase answered by a four-bar phrase, both stated twice; followed by two four-bar or four two-bar phrases of 'contrast'; rounded off by a repetition of the first eight bars. The no less machine-made harmonic vocabulary came from fifty or sixty years back—from (say) Massenet and Grieg, with a garnishing of Ravel sauce. Yet the songs which Gershwin wrote within this convention revivify cliché: whereas all his attempts to extend his range proved —with one exception—disastrous. In the *Rhapsody in Blue* or the Piano Concerto the tunes themselves are often as good—as stimulating in melodic contour, in the unexpected ellipsis or contraction of rhythm—as the best of Gershwin's commercial numbers. But the tunes are complete in themselves, and are improved neither by the spurious 'development' nor by the bits of Lisztian tinsel with which they are flimsily tied together.

Significantly, Gershwin's only successful large-scale work is his opera, *Porgy and Bess*. Here the 'numbers', as in the commercial musical, can be held together by the story: so that it is comparatively unimportant that Gershwin's technique is not much less rudimentary in his opera than in his symphonic pieces. Habitually, he resorts to ostinato basses, rhythmic patterns, alternations of two chords and mechanical sequences to keep the music going; in moments of excitement he relapses into sliding chromatics. Yet *Porgy* is a moving, deeply impressive, work; and it is so because, for all its sophisticated facilities, Gershwin's tunes have never been more spontaneous or more fetching. These tunes cohere in a dramatic intensity, not because of Gershwin's 'external' attempts at thematic inter-relation, but because, working within commercial conventions, he has felt the drama deeply.

For all his urban glamour, he has created a folk-opera about a dispossessed people, with a hero who is both a Negro and a cripple. The idiom of Broadway may pollute the authenticity of his Negroid music; yet one can have no doubts as to the genuineness of the ecstatic nostalgia that pervades the score and even—in episodes such as the funeral oration in Act I—re-vitalizes the harmonic texture. Gershwin chose a libretto, by a white writer, DuBose Heyward, which dealt with corruption, oppression, isolation, and the inviolability of a radical innocence of spirit. He was not himself a Negro or a physical cripple; but he was a poor boy who made good: a Jew who knew all about spiritual isolation, and who had opportunity enough to learn about corruption. Perhaps he wrote such fresh and powerful, as opposed to cliché-ridden, music because even in the face of

temptation he preserved, like Porgy, a modicum of radical innocence. Gershwin has here created a twentieth-century myth
meaningful to himself: and meaningful to us, in so far as he was
representative of his and our generation.

Genius does not often flourish in the environment of Tin Pan
Alley. But it is not common anywhere; and Gershwin was in
no way frustrated by the commercialized conventions within
which he worked. When Ravel said he had nothing to teach
Gershwin, he meant precisely what he said: not that Gershwin
was endowed direct from heaven with a complete technical
equipment, nor that he was technically past praying for; but
that his technique was exactly adequate to what he had in him
to do. In this connexion we may compare him with Carlo
Menotti [b. 1911], who grew up a decade or so later, when the
techniques of commercial music had been sophisticated by years
of application to the cinema. Being intelligent and ingenious,
he adapted cinematic technique to solve one of the basic problems of opera in a democratic society. Taking his cue from
Hollywood and from Puccini, he has created an operatic stylization that seems almost as 'natural'—and therefore acceptable
to a popular democratic audience—as realistic drama. In no
discreditable sense he has also learned how to exploit subjects
that go home to his public. *The Consul* is a genuinely frightening
vision of the dehumanized world of officialdom, with the added
advantage that it can, if need be, be imbued with political
significance (on either side). *The Medium* exploits both our
pseudo-scientific desire to debunk the irrational and our vague
yearnings for supernatural excitement, if not satisfaction. Yet
Menotti, who seems to have liberated commercial cliché in
making it emotionally more malleable, is more a product of
industrialized inhumanity than Gershwin: because although
his musical-dramatic technique is much more complex, the
music itself is neither good nor bad, but so cinematically parasitic as to be without identity. A Gershwin tune exists in its own
right; Menotti's *parlando* lyricism has no existence apart from
his drama.

What counts, in any field, is the quality of the music.
Gershwin succeeded (and kept alive the human spirit) in his
theatre music while failing, on the whole, in his concert
music. Two other Jewish American composers, Marc Blitzstein
[b. 1905] and Leonard Bernstein [b. 1918], started as highly

sophisticated 'art' composers, but found fulfilment in a world at least allied to the commercial theatre. Blitzstein had a profound admiration for Kurt Weill [1900–1950], a German composer who wrote 'straight' music having affinities with Hindemith and Busoni, but who made his mark in such works as *Die Dreigroschenoper* (a modern version of *The Beggar's Opera*) and *Mahagonny*, wherein he expressed the malaise of the post-war years in a peculiarly haunting adaptation of the idiom of popular music. At the time of the Nazi persecution, Weill went to America and worked on Broadway and in Hollywood, where his music lost much of the evocative simplicity that had made it so memorable. But perhaps he could not be expected to 'feel' the American scene with the same authenticity as he had shown in invoking the urban Germany of his youth; certainly his example suggested to Blitzstein how the idioms of America's own popular music might be adapted to a comparably expressive purpose. His plays-in-music on social themes both refine and intensify popular idiom until it is first-hand, not mass-produced, feeling: but Blitzstein's American art is buoyant in its honesty, whereas Weill's had been pessimistic, if compassionate. The same energy is found in the work of Leonard Bernstein, who accepts the idiom of the commercial theatre more at its face value: so that his positive awareness of tenderness and compassion is perhaps suspect, when compared with Blitzstein's. Nonetheless, the musical and choreographic urgency of *West Side Story* is equated with the reality, as well as the topicality, of the human theme; and that is concerned specifically with both the herd instinct and the isolation of the individual soul.

This would seem to indicate that in American music the 'tradition of solitariness' and the social music of 'entertainment' are not as disparate as one might superficially suppose. From this point of view, the work of a minor composer, Virgil Thomson [b. 1896], has an interest more than commensurate with the intrinsic value of his compositions. He was a bright boy from Kansas whose musical legacy consisted of the kind of American bric-à-brac—hymns, parlour pieces, ragtime—that was also the background of Ives's experience. Intellectually precocious, he got himself to Harvard, and then to Paris, where, as American cosmopolitan but not expatriate, he became a member of the Gertrude Stein circle and wrote wildly experimental, often satirically debunking works as a protest against a world that had had its day. He might, given a more vigorous talent, have developed in any number of directions; yet in fact his sophistication, even his complexity, hid a peculiar naivety. His kinship with Satie is more illuminating than his association with Gertrude Stein; his bringing together of emotionally disparate elements—plainsong and café-tune, Bachian fugue and Middle West hymn—has Satie's childlike unsentimentality, while he too discovers a personal logic in unexpected relationships between triadic harmonies. Significantly, his innocence is also his most American quality. *Four Saints in Three Acts*, the Gertrude Stein opera that won him both fame and notoriety, is the first of his works to fuse the American-naïf with the Parisian-sophisticate. Although far too long for most of us, it reaches, beneath its *enfant terrible* elegance, the oddly poignant homespun humour which, on his return to the States, Thomson transplanted into his specifically American works, such as the second Stein opera, *The Mother of Us All*, and the beautiful elegiac piece for wind band, *A Solemn Music*. The vein of American feeling in these works is close to that of Blitzstein's plays in music; and it is not an accident that so much of Thomson's best music has been written for the cinema, to which medium the Satiean technique of musical *collage* admirably lends itself. The essence of Thomson is in his score to Flaherty's *Louisiana Story*: a film that, significantly enough, sees the clash between man and Nature through the eyes of a child. In the Chorale the serially related but harmonically unrelated triads that accompany the derrick's progress along the river are Satiean, yet have become at once original and indigenous. Thomson's American simplicity, which complements the American complexity of men such as Carter and Sessions—is most completely fulfilled in subservience to a function: which involves, too, a highly mechanized technique.

So if we view the amorphous, apparently chaotic American scene as a whole, it would seem that what matters most is the extremes. On the one hand stand the grand old 'progressives' —Ives, Ruggles, Varèse: with the more experimental Copland, Carter, and to a lesser degree Harris, Sessions, and some of the more recent experimentalists. On the other hand is the authentic element in jazz, as a communal, urban folk art; Gershwin when he is not writing symphonic works; Blitzstein and the Bernstein of *West Side Story*; the film music of Thomson.

Comparatively, the middle-of-the-path men, even such an excellent conservative musician as Samuel Barber [b. 1910] or such a clever theatre-man as Menotti, have little vitality and not much social or artistic justification. Perhaps there is a moral in this, for a new, if not for Europe's old, community. Certainly it suggests that the split between the esoteric and the popular is not merely to be deplored. In the long run the real split may prove to be between the creatively vigorous on the one hand and the emotionally and academically safe on the other. And that split has been with us since civilization began.

The 'western hemisphere' is not, of course, confined to the United States. There is also Latin America, which is rapidly becoming an important, creatively energetic part of the modern world. Its achievements in music are not as yet comparable with those of North America, but development will inevitably be sudden and spectacular. The problems of the Latin American composer depend on the fact that he lives neither in a New World nor an old. In the background he has a very ancient Indian civilization and a still vigorous primitive culture. In the foreground he has various European elements imported by the Spanish conquest (Spanish folk-music and urban popular music of the eighteenth and nineteenth centuries); a Negroid element growing out of the slave trade; and a new, stream-lined mechanistic civilization spreading from the United States. In the music of European composers, such as Janáček, Bartók, even Stravinsky, the primitive is involved in the traditions of civilization; in Latin America the various 'layers' of culture exist alongside one another, without apparent relationship.

Thus the music of Heitor Villa-Lobos [1881–1959]—the most representative Latin American composer—has obvious affinities with the Brazilian landscape, containing the musical equivalents of the jungle, the Lost City, the skyscraper and the road-house. In his jungle-like fecundity, his appetite for experience, for life in the raw, Villa-Lobos has points in common with Ives. But whereas Ives was conscious of creating a New World, both materially and spiritually, Villa-Lobos combines a Latin exuberance with a Latin passivity. He accepts the chaos of the contemporary scene; his energy, though intermittently purposeful, is directionless. This is why he was apparently completely unself-critical: and why his music tends to be most impressive when most fortuitous.

From this point of view, it is significant that his most technically sophisticated works tend to be no more than mildly interesting. He does something with the Debussyan and Ravellian idiom he picked up in Paris in the second decade of the century; but the vein of piquant nostalgia which he distils from this style—the mood of the Latin American *saudades*—spreads thinly over so large a number of works. Almost all his memorable music is conceived in the convention of the *choros*; and this, interestingly enough, is an art-composer's adaptation of popular improvisation. Especially at Carnival time, the *choro* party is an integral part of Brazilian life: a Latin American jam-session at which any number of musicians, playing any instruments that happen to be handy, improvise empirically and episodically, with no more than a scheme of rhythmic relationships between each section to keep them going. Villa-Lobos's innumerable works called *Choros*, scored for anything from a single guitar to a mammoth symphony orchestra, are, of course, composed music, notated; but he seeks always an effect of the maximum density of detail with the maximum energy of movement. Superficially, the sharp, hard sonorities he draws from imitation of the *ad hoc choro-bands* resemble those which Stravinsky derived from popular music of the war years and the early-twenties. Whereas Stravinsky preserved, however, an almost geometric intellectual control over his unsophisticated sources, Villa-Lobos sought, and at best achieved, the white-hot immediacy of improvisation.

In the seventh *Choros*, scored for a miscellaneous instrumental ensemble, we begin, for instance, with a nostalgically impressionist prelude—the composer's own, relatively sophisticated consciousness. Out of this emerges, from the depths *below* consciousness, the primitive jungle: obsessive drum rhythms and short, screaming melodic phrases in incantatory patterns and exotic coloration. Then, with a scoop on the violin, we are in the world of nineteenth-century Spanish popular music: a waltz in which an urban nostalgia is interlaced with a savage vigour. Later, Indian incantatory elements turn Negroid, so we find ourselves in a world halfway between the jungle and the urban violence of Chicago-style jazz. At the end we return to the impressionist opening—to the composer's own sensibility that apprehends the chaotic vitality of the Brazilian scene. Yet the piece has no real structure and no development; the brief, quasi-improvisatory sections shift between the various levels of culture in a way that is exciting, but, in its rootlessness, also sad. Occasionally—as may happen in genuine jazz improvisation—the creative imagination takes complete control. Then, as in the marvellous *Nonetto* of 1923, the jungle and jazz, the primitive and the urban, become a new world of sound. That the music has no beginning, middle nor end becomes a positive quality: for the whole piece is a tremendous incremental climax that destroys consciousness, and with it the time-sense. When the chorus enters it represents not humanity but a terrifying animistic force. This is a twentieth-century primitivism that exposes the glibness of such a composer as Carl Orff.

While Villa-Lobos's most violent music is easily his most impressive, it is hardly surprising that, living in a world embryonically coming to birth, he should have been impelled too by a complementary yearning for 'civilization'. The most curious example of this is the sequence of works which he called *Bachianas Brasileiras*. To attempt to fuse the empirical, episodic *choros* technique with the unity and continuity of Bach's idiom would seem a forlorn hope indeed. Yet the remarkable work for eight cellos does achieve, at least in the slow movement, a sustained line and an extraordinary depth and richness of harmony. The richness has not, of course, Bach's tense serenity; it is not a faith accepted or achieved. But in this *modinhya*—a sentimental urban song derived from eighteenth- and nineteenth-century Spanish elements—nostalgia becomes almost a positive virtue; one can understand how the miraculous new cities may rise in the midst of the jungle. Villa-Lobos felt the need for order if he could not himself create it.

The nature of the 'new order' is revealed in a Mexican composer of the next generation, Carlos Chavez [b. 1899]. The thematic and rhythmic patterns in his music are again brief, incantatory, ritualistic, related to primitive sources; the instrumental colours are hard and fierce. But he has none of Villa-Lobos's chaotic prodigality; the linear texture of his music is sharp, dry, consistent, and continuous in figuration as a baroque toccata. The unity is achieved at a cost; the linear patterns are closer to the more arid manifestations of Stravinsky's 'white note' music than to the lyrical pliancy and harmonic density of Bach—or even of the *Bachianas Brasileiras*! Yet there is a positive side to the aridity also: for this music grows from the hard light and sunbaked plain of the Mexican scene, while at the same time having affinities with the metallic urban world of the earlier works of Copland. Copland's music is discontinuous, Chavez's continuous; but while Copland's 'dislocation' is probably deeper and certainly closer to us, it is the driving motor rhythm in Chavez that builds new cities in the mountains or the jungle. There is a valid relationship between the texture and spirit of Chavez's music and the remarkable achievements of twentieth-century Mexican architecture.

Today, Latin American music seems to be trying to preserve the geometric lucidity of Chavez without sacrificing the copious sensuality of Villa-Lobos. We can observe this in the music of the Argentinian, Alberto Ginastera [b. 1916]: for while his music has a clarity of linear contour and a rhythmic excitement characteristic of Chavez, it has also a lyrical tenderness and harmonic evocativeness more suggestive of Villa-Lobos, if we can imagine the Brazilian without the strain of banality that is part of his vigour. There is a pathos in the hollow texture of the slow movement of Ginastera's beautiful String Quartet, a plaintiveness in the bird-noises of the slow movement of his Piano Concerto, that complements the driving energy of his quick movements. There is nothing comparable with this in the hieratic, hymnic, dissonant diatonicism that Chavez exploits in his (usually brief) slow movements; and if Ginastera's melancholy embraces Villa-Lobos's nostalgia, it pierces deeper, being a sign of growing maturity.

This is in part, of course, a regional difference. An Argentinian composer—or still more a Chilean composer of the older generation, such as Domingo Santa Cruz [b. 1899]—is further removed from primitive and Indian sources than a Brazilian or Mexican composer, and so may turn spontaneously to the more 'adult' traditions of Europe. But the difference is not merely regional, for all over Latin America composers are becoming less aggressively concerned with indigenous values. As their new civilization comes to birth they remain conscious of their birthright, yet aware of their place in a community of nations. Cultural barriers, at least, are no longer unbridgeable, whatever may be true of political barriers; and a Peruvian serialist is no longer an anachronism.

INDEX OF MUSIC EXAMPLES
VOLUME IV (from 1800)

VOLUME IV

GENERAL INDEX